Comedia Series ● No – 27

THE YEARS
OF THE WEEK

Patricia Cockburn
Introduction by Richard Ingrams
Original introduction by Claud Cockburn

Comedia Publishing Group
9 Poland Street, London W1V 3DG   Tel: 01-439 2059

Comedia Publishing Group was set up to investigate and monitor the media in Britain and abroad. The aim of the project is to provide basic information, investigate problem areas, and to share the experience of those working in the field, while encouraging debate about the future development of the media. The opinions expressed in the books in the Comedia series are those of the authors, and do not necessarily reflect the views of Comedia. For a list of other Comedia titles see page 288.

First published in Great Britain in 1968

© Patricia Cockburn, 1968

Extracts from *The Week* © the estate of Claud Cockburn

This edition published in 1985 by Comedia

ISBN 0 906 890 845

British Library Cataloguing in Publication Data
Cockburn, Patricia
The years of "The Week"
1. Cockburn, Claud, Week, The
I. Title
   827'.912'09   PN5130.C6

Cover design by Amanda Heath

Typeset by Photosetting, 6 Foundry House, Yeovil, Somerset BA20 1NL
Printed in Great Britain by
Unwin Brothers Ltd., The Gresham Press, Old Woking, Surrey.

Trade distribution by Comedia
Distributed in USA by Marion Boyars and the Scribner Book Companies
Distributed in Canada by DEC Book Distribution, 229 College Street, Toronto, Ontario, M5T 1R4.
Distributed in Australia by Second Back Row, 50 Govett Street, Katoomba, N.S.W. 2780.

Contents

CLAUD COCKBURN: A MEMOIR

INTRODUCTION BY RICHARD INGRAMS

I FIRST heard the name of Claud Cockburn in 1959 when I was working in the Oxford Summer Vacation as a part-time tutor to Felix, son of Sefton Delmer. Delmer, who lived in a beautiful isolated farmhouse in a hidden Suffolk valley, had been recently fired by Lord Beaverbrook after thirty years of loyal service as the *Daily Express*'s foreign correspondent. Now he was writing his memoirs and in the evening would read out to me and his wife Peggy what he had written during the day. Like most university students I was disrespectful and said at one point that good journalists couldn't be expected to write good books. To show me that I was wrong, Delmer gave me a book to read called *In Time of Trouble* by Claud Cockburn. I was forced to agree with him. Not only is the book beautifully written and extremely funny, it is a definitive guide to what journalism is all about and should be read, along with *The Years with Ross*, by James Thurber, by any young, aspiring hack.

What appealed to me especially at that time was Cockburn's account of how he started *The Week*, the story of which is told here by his wife Patricia. I have never seen a copy of the paper and don't especially want to. I expect I would be disappointed by it, as I would be by Ross's *New Yorker*. It was the idea that was exciting – one man writing and printing his own paper in a garret; a paper that is pored over by all the Top People with amazement and disquiet. It seemed to me the ideal career.

When, two years later, I was involved with a group of friends in starting *Private Eye*, I myself had Cockburn's example very much in mind. So I was delighted when I had the opportunity to meet him while on my honeymoon in Ireland with my wife, Mary. The introduction came from Donald Maclachlan, then editor of the *Sunday Telegraph*, who warned me in advance that Youghal, where Claud lived in a dilapidated Georgian mansion, was subject to climatic extremes and that I should go prepared for awful weather. (Later I discovered how this idea had got into Maclachlan's head. Claud was then writing a column for the *Sunday Telegraph* and every week Maclachlan would ring him up to discuss possible topics. "Have you seen the story in this week's *New Statesman?*" Maclachlan would ask. Not wanting to seem out of touch, Claud would reply, "Terrible floods here, Donald" – or snow, or gales – "No papers getting through." In the end, Claud became bored with making these excuses and resorted to saying in a very authoritative and dismissive tone, when Maclachlan raised some article, "Yes, I saw that, Donald. Absolute balls!"

The first thing that struck me about Claud was his total lack of "side". He had no airs, and certainly no air of the Grand Old Man. He remained until his death "One of the Boys" – an apt expression, because he was always game for anything and always ready to have a go; not only that, but he never lost a certain schoolboyish approach to life which was very infectious and very charming. So although he was much older than all of us, he fitted quite naturally into the *Private Eye* circle when, the following year (1963) he first came over from Ireland to be guest editor for an issue. It was on that occasion, when they were short of something to put in the paper, that he said to Willie Rushton, "Is there anyone who nobody has got a bad word to say about?" After some thought, Rushton nominated Albert Schweitzer. "Right," said Claud, "We'll attack Schweitzer."

That may sound as if he was totally unprincipled, prepared to savage anyone for the sake of creating a sensation. But it was rather an example of his brilliant journalistic instinct to go against any consensus. If everyone – especially all the papers – were united on a particular issue, Claud's view was that the opposite was almost bound to be the case. When Sir Alec Douglas Home was appointed Tory leader later that year, all the political commentators like Peregrine Worsthorne agreed that whatever might be Home's failings as an economist, etc., he was a frightfully *nice* man. But Claud would have none of it. "Everyone says – Home – awfully nice chap. Not a bit of it! Stoat! Weasel! Rat!"

I see that I have already told two or three stories about Claud. But then he was very much a story man. Not only were stories told about him, but he himself had a wonderful collection. Mostly they were about journalists. There was one, I remember, about a reporter who had been sent to cover Queen Victoria's funeral. Returning to his paper he shut himself up in a room to write his piece. As the deadline approached and he failed to emerge, his colleagues became more and more frantic. Finally they broke into the room, where they found the man slumped on the table, an empty whisky bottle at his side. On the floor were lots of crumpled sheets of paper on which were written the opening words of his story – "Not since the days of Jesus Christ..."

Claud's best stories were about his own exploits in journalism. Some of them are in his books, like the one about the *Times* man who spent a whole day in the British Museum trying to discover the correct way to spell Kuala Lumpur. But to appreciate Claud's stories you had to hear him tell them in person. He had a deep bass voice and spoke a bit like Mr Jingle in *Pickwick Papers*, in staccato bursts rather than complete sentences. He said once about a well-known publisher, "You go into his office – knee high carpets – eight telephones on the desk – you or I assume at once – the man is *bankrupt!*" When I think of Claud I think of him at the *Private Eye* table in the Coach and Horses, Greek Street, with his thick dark blue overcoat and his battered hat, *and* the rest of us trying to get him to tell stories. Some of them were set pieces which got embellished over the years. The longest and funniest was about Claud and his great friend Maurice Richardson when they were hired to start a new magazine by Lady Hulton some time in the fifties. A kind person had warned Lady Hulton that she was employing two notorious ex-Communists so, in order to impress on her their essential respectability, they decided to organise a dinner party at Maurice's home in Hampstead to which would be invited a number of their upper-class friends. Each promised the other not to touch a drop of drink during the day; but, just as Claud, who claimed to have kept his side of the bargain, arrived at the house, a taxi drew up and Maurice, clutching two bottles of champagne – in Claud's words – "fell out!" He then staggered into the house and went straight upstairs to bed, leaving Claud to entertain the guests – Mrs Richardson having gone on strike and provided only a token dinner of cold ham and lettuce. The climax came when later in the evening Maurice suddenly re-appeared and, by way of livening up the proceedings, cried,

"Shall I do my chimpanzee?" Without waiting for an answer he vigorously pummelled his chest and leaped into Lady Hulton's lap. The magazine never got off the ground.

As a journalist Claud was unusual – partly because he was a highly intelligent and well-educated man who could have earned his living in all kinds of other ways. He went into Fleet Street not only because it was fun, but because, unlike many colleagues, he did really mind about what went on in politics and the effect it had on ordinary people. The fact that he was, or had been, a Communist was difficult for someone of my generation to understand, especially as he was so fond of America and never expressed the slightest urge to go to Russia. But part of the explanation lay in the fact that during the thirties the Communists seemed to him the only people who were prepared actually to do something about standing up to Hitler and helping the unemployed. Although he gave up his C.P. membership during the war, he never completely lost his adherence to the Party Line and would sometimes complain to me if he thought an article in the *Eye* smacked of revisionism.

Introducing Claud's memoirs when they were re-published in 1981, his great friend Graham Greene said that Claud Cockburn and G. K. Chesterton were the two greatest journalists of the 20th Century. I mentioned this to Claud at the time and he said, "Pity he had to bring Chesterton into it." He died later that year after many years of ill health, which he endured with great courage and good humour.

Aldworth, 1985

Dedication and Acknowledgment

To Claud

I would like to dedicate this book with affection and gratitude to my husband Claud Cockburn for his help and encouragement at all times, and also for his permission to draw freely from the published issues of *The Week*.

Writers are not notably charitable, especially when their copyright is involved. Had Claud not been exceptional in this particular as he is in many others, *The Years of the Week* could never have been written.

P.C.

INTRODUCTION

IN the Chinese fable the beetle walked all day from east to west, exhausted but proud of pulling the sun along with it. If the beetle stopped, the sun would stop too. Darkness would cover all creation.

Every good editor feels the way the beetle felt. If he stops the light will go out.

Ridiculous, obviously. But better than the sort of false modesty which suggests that the man dared not suppose that what he was doing amounted to anything.

It is naturally difficult for me to write anything about the place of *The Week* in its period, or its impact upon that period, without seeming to over-estimate its role.

Refusing this dangerous task, I pass the buck to Mr Philip Toynbee, literary critic of *The Observer*. In a review of a book of mine he referred to me, alarmingly enough, as "the patron saint of the Thirties".

He went on to quote me. I had said of *The Week*:

"This small monstrosity was one of the half-dozen British publications most often quoted in the press of the entire world. It included among its subscribers the Foreign Ministers of eleven nations, all the embassies and legations in London, all diplomatic correspondents of the principal newspapers in three continents, the foreign correspondents of all the leading newspapers stationed in London, the leading banking and brokerage houses in London, Paris, Amsterdam and New York, a dozen members of the United States Senate, twenty or thirty members of the House of Representatives, about fifty Members of the House of Commons, and a hundred or so in the House of Lords, King Edward VIII, the secretaries of the leading Trade Unions, Charlie Chaplin and the Nizam of Hyderabad.

"Blum read it and Goebbels read it, and a mysterious war lord in China read it. Senator Borah quoted it repeatedly in the American Senate, and Herr von Ribbentrop, Hitler's Ambassador in London, on two separate occasions demanded its suppression on the ground that it was the source of all anti-Nazi evil."

About that claim Philip Toynbee had this to say:

"This sounds like the raving of a paranoiac. But Mr Cockburn has always been sane enough and everything that he says here is certainly true. This little cyclostyled sheet, which made public all the news and rumours of news which the official press fought shy of, was a squib which exploded effectively in many strange places. It was produced by Mr Cockburn and a few part-time helpers in a dusty, one-room office in Victoria Street, and most of its business was conducted in the Café Royal. I would have supposed in hushed voices, if I did not know Mr Cockburn and know that his voice is unhushable."

Friends and enemies are in agreement on at least one fact. It is that *The Week* exercised an influence and commanded an attention grossly, almost absurdly out of proportion to its own resources.

I say this is important because it is a demonstration of how much you can do with little. People who try to measure influence quantitatively, as for instance in terms of money or circulation, are wrong in their premises and will be wrong in their conclusions.

The report that God is on the side of the Big Battalions is propaganda put out by the Big Battalion commanders. They hope thereby to spread alarm and despondency among the smaller forces.

CLAUD COCKBURN

Youghal, Co. Cork,
    December 1967

1 Man in a Hurry

CLAUD COCKBURN once described *The Week* as "unquestionably the nastiest-looking bit of work that ever dropped onto a breakfast table".

He was referring to its physical appearance, the general effect of that dark brown ink, rather smudgily transferred to the six sides of three buff-coloured foolscap sheets.

Throughout its career there was always a high percentage of its subscribers who sincerely felt and loudly proclaimed that it was not only the nastiest "looking" bit of work they ever saw; it was the nastiest bit of work, period. Its content, and style, matched its looks. They said they only went on subscribing to it because it was essential for them to know what villainy it was going to be up to this week. Or they said that they had to read it because misguided friends kept quoting it at parties.

I was living in Tahiti when *The Week* started. Tahiti in 1933 was a great deal farther from London than it is now. Far more important events than the birth of a modest little news-sheet failed to reach us there. And I was busy preparing for a journey to Thailand. I was going there on behalf of Sir William Goodenough, President of the Royal Geographical Society, to study the nomadic tribes in the hinterland of the country.

While *The Week* was growing up and becoming famous or infamous according to one's viewpoint, I was in the Northern Congo. Again on behalf of the Royal Geographical Society, I was seeking to make a language map of the Northern Congo and parts of French Equatorial Africa as it then was. As everyone knows, many scores of languages are spoken in that enormous territory.

By the time I returned to London, Claud's sheet had already reached middle age, though not by any means respectability. In London I began to hear a great deal about it. *The Week* was required reading, I found, for those who wanted to be considered insiders, or wanted to be able to refute what the insiders were talking about.

I remember that I first took out a subscription to *The Week* after a Foreign Office official had sternly dismissed some information I'd offered him about Ruthenia, where I had been the previous two months. He said, "I suppose you got hold of those lies from *The Week*."

I met, and later married, the owner-editor. I became one of his assistants and at one time, when he was in America, was acting editor of the paper.

I remember clearly my first visit to the office. There was a dangerous-looking cage supposed to be doing duty as a lift, but it wasn't working. I had to walk up flight after flight of dark stairs, which ended in a flight that was more like a ladder. The dingy gloom of the stairs gave the place a suitably conspiratorial air.

The office was low-ceilinged and grubby in a comfortable sort of way. It was filled with cheerful assistants (mostly unpaid, I discovered) who were struggling to make the ancient Gestetner duplicating machine work. This machine, which had the appearance of an "Emmet" steam-engine about to explode, apparently always put on this show of temperament on press days. Just when everyone had become frantic at the idea of missing the vital posts—*The Week* was distributed entirely by mail—and had started to ring up mechanics all over S.W.1, it began to work perfectly.

Claud wasn't there, though he should have been. He had been urgently expected for the past two hours.

I soon learnt that Claud's helpers regarded him rather in the way that our prehistoric ancestors must have regarded one of their tribal gods—as demanding, unpredictable, unreasonable, and absolutely indispensable. They were devoted to Claud and found him intolerable.

Then came a hurried clumping of feet on the stairs. A heavily-built man seemed to be pounding up them at speed, and then throwing himself against the door as though he expected it was locked and he had to burst it open. But Claud, now rushing in, turned out to be the reverse of burly. At first sight of him I was reminded rather of one of those rag-dolls with unnaturally elongated arms and legs dangling, though in this case the legs and arms were not dangling but in vigorous movement.

To Claud, everything was urgent. Everything was absolutely vital. Do this, do that. An important source of information from the City had already been waiting for him an hour. He must go. Snatching a handful of change from the petty cash, he went, pursued in vain by the wailing keeper of the books, who would now never get them straight.

I assumed that some sort of crisis had occurred. But the others assured me that this kind of thing was absolutely standard. *The Week* had been produced in this way from the beginning.

What that beginning was like has often been described to me since—by Claud, and also by other less excitable and prejudiced witnesses.

Claud, whose sense of self-preservation is stronger than sometimes appears, had left *The Times* after working for it for three years in America. He had then spent six months in Europe. Being, for sufficient reasons, fairly high on the Nazi black-list, he had got out of Germany two days before Hitler came to power. He had stayed in Prague, and then Paris, until his money was almost finished. He had returned to London with very little cash, and with an obsession.

Quite in the manner of the traditional Cheltenham colonel, Claud had gone about saying that the country was going to the dogs and that something had to be done about it. Being a journalist, he had naturally thought that the first thing to do something about was the state of journalism.

He would explain to friends that since, in his view, the big newspapers were all rotted with stupidity, or else actively wicked, the thing to do was to collect a few pounds and start a news-sheet that would "let some air in".

He had got the idea for a news-sheet of this kind from several sources. One was the admirable tradition of the English news-sheets of the eighteenth century. Another was the example of a man he had known in Washington who, it seemed, single-handed and armed only with a duplicating machine, had won an apparently hopeless battle against the huge power of the American Radio Trust.

A third was one which his friends, not unnaturally, found surprising. This was a duplicated weekly he had seen in Berlin. It was circulated by a General Schleicher, who was German Chancellor for a short time and was later murdered by the

Nazis. What Claud had found appealing about Schleicher's weekly was not its political line, of course, but the disparity between its tiny circulation and its very wide influence, especially in the Officer Corps and among the non-Nazi "gentry".

Whenever, in its early years, the fortunes of *The Week* were at a low ebb, someone would remark that the influence of Schleicher's sheet had not prevailed against the Nazis, and "look what had happened to the man himself." But Claud would dismiss the argument as defeatist.

Claud's chief inspiration for the idea of *The Week*, however, was his favourite weekly newspaper, the Parisian *Canard Enchaîné*. "*Le Canard*", he would assert, "is the best-informed publication in France. Or at least it publishes the most information. Much of it, thank God, is in what you people would call execrable taste, and here it would be hanged, drawn and quartered by the libel laws. Note, above all, that it carries no advertisements, receives no subsidies, and still breaks a little better than even."

Evelyn Waugh, who was a cousin of Claud's, once described his surprise on first meeting him at Oxford. Claud had struck Evelyn as a product of Budapest rather than of Berkhampstead School. (Though, when you come to think of it, a school that sent such a trio as Graham Greene, Peter Quennell, and Claud to Oxford in the same year, must have had something unusual about it.) Evelyn's impression was understandable. Claud had spent his school holidays for two years in Hungary, and was there during all of his Oxford vacations. After Oxford, first with a travelling fellowship from Queen's College, and then on the staff of *The Times*, he had lived in Europe or America for nearly seven years.

He was thus largely ignorant of facts, issues, and developments in Britain which were matters of common knowledge to his contemporaries. Some of them found his ignorance amusing. Others considered it shockingly impudent of the man to turn up like that and claim to be able to run a paper telling the British what was good for them.

To such critics, Claud used to quote an acting Foreign Editor of *The Times* who was assigning a correspondent to some capital the man was unwilling to go to. The man said,

"But I've never been there, and I don't speak the language. I know absolutely nothing about anything in that country." "So much the better," said the acting Foreign Editor, "you'll bring a fresh mind to the job."

At the outset there weren't many such critics, amused or otherwise, for the simple reason that Claud was then known to so few people. He had some old Oxford friends. Most of them were, of course, pretty much preoccupied with making their own careers. For a man with his particular objectives in mind, his situation looked an unpromisingly isolated one.

The few friends who were interested in Claud's idea for a news-sheet, and keen to do something about it if they could be shown anything at all sensible, even hopeful, to do, found it hard to think what that something might be.

Claud's main advantage, it turned out, was his resignation from *The Times*, though he himself at first mistook it for a liability. He thought that because he had quit *The Times* for political reasons, people on the Right would shun him as likely to be a Red, while those on the Left would view him with suspicion because, in spite of his resignation, his association with the paper had been a long and happy one. A few people on both sides did indeed behave as he expected. But in the main his prediction was wrong: and this was typical of his misunderstanding of things in Britain. In the atmosphere of that period, his behaviour was, as I say, a positive asset. It was at least believed, accurately I think, that he was the only man who had three times refused offers of a job with *The Times*, and accepted the fourth offer only when it gave him just what he wanted, which was the chance to get to New York. This in itself had, as the Irish say, "made talk". Then, after three years or so, and to unhappy cries of protest from *The Times*, he had resigned, expressing his love for the paper but explaining that his political principles prevented him working effectively for it any longer. That, naturally, made a lot more talk.

His friend Philip Jordan told me years later, when Philip had become sufficiently respectable to be chief public relations officer to Prime Minister Attlee, that these actions had the effect of someone loudly and unashamedly exploding a paper bag in the middle of a bishop's sermon or a company chairman's speech.

Claud was ignorant of the British scene. He saw his own behaviour as simple and obvious. He assumed it was the sort of thing energetic young men were doing all the time. So he was much taken aback by the interest aroused. He was astonished, though delighted, to learn the facts from friends. Various young City types, they said, wanted to meet him. Presumably these men were stifled by the Depression and what they considered the particular stuffiness and ineptitude of the government in relation to it. Officials, notably in the Foreign Office, who were disturbed and exasperated by the prospect of Europe tottering to war, asked him to lunch. And several leading American foreign correspondents got in touch with him.

He had known many such Americans in New York and Washington but supposed that they had all, with the exception of some genuine kindred spirits, cultivated him simply because he happened to be an energetic, hard-drinking, and influential correspondent of *The Times*. It never occurred to him that anything of even remotely the same kind could happen in London—which he saw as a plate of very thick pea soup.

Having got over his surprise, he was quick to sense that he had been all wrong about the possibilities in London, and that if he could only get the publication he had in mind off the ground, he knew now where to find enough air currents to keep it aloft without the money most people said would be required. "Don't you understand," he said to anxious friends, "that a glider doesn't *need* a bloody engine?"

Claud was never a patient man. For instance, the mere idea of having to stand in a queue for anything seemed to affect him with a kind of physical nausea. (During the war, when I would mention on his return from his office that I, like almost every other woman in the country, had had to queue for some commodity or other, he would commiserate with me as though I'd told him I'd spent the day in a police cell under third degree. The fact seemed to excite his sympathy far more than the news that I had been only just out of range of the blast of a V-1.)

Claud's haste to get started on his big little project alarmed even those of his friends and well-wishers who had been persuaded that there "might after all be something in it". They suggested, rightly enough, that at this stage he hardly knew what he was talking about.

They explained that a whole lot needed to be done before the "glider" could even be got off the ground with any hope of staying up. There would have to be a properly constituted committee of people whose names would give some authority to the affair. An expert would have to be called in to examine, in hard business terms, what would now be called the "viability" of the undertaking. Then must come a careful assessment of the personnel required, and the job of selecting them. And after all that, time would have to be spent in the production of experimental, trial issues.

Claud was all too obviously inclined to regard any advice running counter to his own uninformed ideas as a sort of sabotage.

The late John Strachey was one of those who wasted their time trying to give Claud advice. That was a couple of years after Strachey had discovered that Sir Oswald Mosley was a Fascist, and had violently broken with him. When Strachey first talked with Claud he was either finishing, or had just finished, his book *The Menace of Fascism*. He was trying to create on the Left the sort of movement which, in earlier days, he had sincerely believed Mosley's New Party would become. (Strachey began to associate with the Communists, and a lot of people would have been greatly surprised if they had known that a few years later he was going to be a minister in a Labour government.)

Strachey had heard rumours of Claud's plans, and was anxious to help in putting things on a proper footing. Of his first conversation with Claud he told me later, speaking with a certain bitterness. Although I hardly knew him (Claud had introduced him to me as a friend) he almost immediately invited me to a dinner *tête-à-tête* at the Café Royal. This turned out to be, at least in part, for the purpose of warning me against Claud. A young woman like myself, it seemed, should have absolutely nothing to do with such a dangerous, not to say poisonous, adventurer.

Knowing that Claud liked him, enjoyed his company and, as I say, described him as a friend, I was taken a little aback.

Aware that I had myself not known Claud very long at that time, Strachey thought it only right to give me an extensive précis of that dangerous man's career. Perhaps if I had been the sort of person Strachey seemed to think I was, I might have finished the dinner with the conviction that Claud was about the most sinister man in the country; certainly not desirable company for the likes of me. It was a long story, and it started with the occasion when Strachey was seeking to help Claud think clearly about how *The Week* was to be launched, and how it was to operate.

Strachey had taken a great deal of trouble to think out a sensible plan. He had carefully marshalled all the arguments about the need for a broadly representative committee, collective editorial guidance, and so on.

Claud had listened not only politely, but with every appearance of earnest attention.

"He gave me the impression," said Strachey, "of being, if not quite convinced on all points, at least open-minded about what I had to say. But then, after all that, he went off and started the thing without even trying to carry out any of my suggestions. I've often thought since that he may have already been in touch with . . . well, you know what I mean."

"What?"

"Moscow."

Claud has admitted since that when he mentally dismissed Strachey's plan on the grounds that it would cause intolerable controls and delays, he had no alternative plan in his head at all. Later, when an alternative did occur to him, he hesitated to disclose it. He thought his more serious acquaintances might consider it ridiculous.

The alternative presented itself as the result of a conversation with a friend, Archie Harding, who was then regarded as an up-and-coming man at the B.B.C. They had been at Oxford together, and Claud was now staying with Archie and his wife, Crystal, at their house in Chelsea.

Claud asked Archie what had happened to a third man who had been a friend of theirs at Oxford. This was a colourful figure who, after coming down from Oxford, had spent most of his time in Paris. He had written one, possibly two, novels of the kind described as brilliant but immature. He had then suddenly retired to a Berkshire village. He was hardly seen about any more.

Archie, who had the gift of "total recall" and could mimic

perfectly voices and gestures belonging to conversations held years before, once gave me an account of this talk.

Claud asked what the man was actually doing there in Berkshire.

"Simply vegetating, so far as anyone can see."

Claud was genuinely shocked.

"But he can't *want* to vegetate, can he?"

Archie said he thought the man didn't want to vegetate. He probably would like to move to London, and "meet people".

"So why doesn't he?"

"First, because he's been away so long he hardly knows anyone. And then he thinks people would despise him if he just drifted about London without doing a job."

"And he can't get a job?"

"Well, he probably could, but he's lost confidence. Last time I saw him he said he could get a job all right, but he doesn't think he's competent to hold one for more than a few weeks at the outside."

Claud pointed out that the man was a lot luckier than most people. He had a little money. He could at least afford to live in London without a job. But Archie repeated that the man was sensitive on that point. If he were to come to London it must be to a job.

Claud pondered this situation for some time, then said:

"Look, why don't you go down and see him. Tell him if he really does want to come to London, I can give him things to do. Quite a lot of things. But I can't give him—not yet at any rate and probably never—a cent of money. In fact quite the opposite. Unless he can put up a little money there won't even be any work."

Archie said there must be some misunderstanding.

"But you know," he insisted, "he hasn't got a *lot* of money. I mean nothing like the sort of money you need for your project. I don't suppose he could raise a thousand pounds."

Claud said, "I don't want a thousand pounds. I want forty pounds."

"But where," Archie asked, "are you going to get the rest? I mean so as to start your thing and give him this job?"

"There doesn't have to be any rest," Claud said. "Forty

will do." (Of course, forty pounds then was worth three or four times as much as it does today.)

After considering, with much scepticism and apprehension, some figures which Claud had scribbled on a paper table-napkin (they were having a meal in a restaurant at the time), Archie agreed to the mission.

Just before they parted he said, "But exactly what is this job? I must be able to tell him that."

"Manager," Claud said. "And you can promise him that he certainly will meet some people."

No doubt if Archie had been less of a friend, or more of a business man, the figures on the table-napkin might have lacked persuasive effect. It was not true that they had been invented on the spot. But it was true that that was the first time they had positively been written down. And though they had been the subject of increasingly enthusiastic mental arithmetic for nearly a week they were by no means the result of anything that could pass for a thoroughgoing "survey".

Certainly, the items included "rent of office". But the estimated rent was based simply on a reading of small advertisements in—I think—*Dalton's Weekly*, and on a mental note of the lowest figure being asked for an office anywhere within a mile or so of Whitehall and Westminster. When it was pointed out that if one went some distance beyond this radius one could get a better office for the same money, or the same sort of little dump for less money, the answer came pat.

"You forget that what you save in rent you are going to spend on taxis."

"There are buses, and the underground."

"That's worse than wasting money. You waste time."

I was often reminded of Vincent Sheean's motto, which he came out with whenever his wife tried to get him to economize on hotel accommodation in London.

"You'll find," he would say sternly, "that it's always cheaper in the end to go to Claridge's."

The list scribbled on the napkin included "rental, or instalment payments, for duplicator". This item rather shook Archie, who had assumed along with everybody else that Claud's publication, however modest, would at least be printed.

He was, of course, treated to the familiar lecture on General Schleicher and his duplicated sheet. "Furthermore," he was told, "I've been looking into the libel laws they have here. Do you realize that whenever you commit a libel the printer is equally liable for damages? You can see what that means. It means that if you decide to libel someone the printer is going to refuse to print it. You're censored almost before you start. A hopeless situation."

Archie said he had heard somewhere that newspapers could insure themselves against libel.

"And who," Claud asked unanswerably, "is likely to insure *me*?"

2 Forty Pounds

Archie Harding, more than ever apprehensive, scanned the figures on the paper table-napkin. He noted that two of the items listed, those for cost of paper and cost of postage, were followed not by figures but by question-marks. Was this, he asked, quite precise?

"The point there," it was explained, "is that obviously the amount of paper and the number of stamps we use depend on how many subscribers we get. If there are very few subscribers, there'll be very little to spend on paper and stamps. As and when the number of subscribers rises, the more we have for paper and stamps."

"What about the telephone? Even without a magazine or whatever it's going to be, you never stop telephoning." (A lot of the telephoning was done from Archie's generous home.)

"Telephone bills here are not payable until the end of the quarter. And by that time . . ."

The simple word "miscellaneous" completed the "estimate". Twenty-four hours after the talk about the man in Berkshire, Claud joyously accepted an offer from Dorothy Woodman, then Secretary of the Union of Democratic Control, to sub-let him a tiny attic room. It was adjacent to the UDC offices on the top floor of 34 Victoria Street. He had heard of this vacancy at one of the weekly lunches given by Kingsley Martin, who was then growing in fame as the editor of the *New Statesman*.

"I was seated," he told me, "between Tommy Balogh and Leonard Woolf and their conversation was fascinating—not only in its content but in the contrast between the two of them. Seen together like that, each seemed a vividly stimulating caricature of his own nationality and national way of thinking. The one so English. The other so gloriously Hungarian. But I have to admit that when I overheard someone, Kingsley perhaps, casually mentioning that office and the tiny sum they were asking for it, I began to twitch to get away. I answered brilliantly searching questions about the United States and

The Times in the dullest, most perfunctory way. I was sure someone else was at that moment struggling to sign a lease on the place."

When he got there, nobody had. But Claud himself, at that moment, was in no position to take up the lease. A small sum had to be paid down in advance and it was still too soon to hear any news of the forty pounds. However, partly out of sheer good-heartedness, partly because the audacity of the little venture appealed to her, Dorothy agreed to wait for a week before letting the office go to anyone else.

Claud assured her that barring sudden death there was no possibility of his not being in a position to make the necessary down payment well within that time limit. I am sure he sincerely believed this. In Claud's somewhat over-heated imagination, the proposal then being made to the man vegetating in the country would obviously be irresistible. Assuming that the man really had got forty pounds to spare, and enough to live on besides, what could be more alluring than the prospect of finding himself bang in the middle of an enterprise so novel that it was not only nameless, but did not even exist?

Two days later, Archie telephoned from his office to his home, where Claud was an entirely non-paying guest. Loyally sympathetic with Claud's sense of haste, he had, at much personal inconvenience, dropped his own and the B.B.C.'s affairs and hurried into the west country. (In this case I prefer to rely on Archie's "total recall" rather than on Claud's memory. Claud seems to have forgotten that it was Archie who made the first contact.)

"It's all right," Archie said. "Ben's absolutely wild about the idea."

. Throughout his life Claud has sometimes (though not, I must say, very often) been afflicted with a kind of "remorse in advance"; with the feeling that just possibly he is getting people into water which is not going to be too hot for him, but may be so for them. He had such a feeling then.

"Are you sure he *understands*? I mean that he can't make any money out of it, and the office is a squalid little room with hardly space to sit down? I tell you there isn't even a window in it, just a skylight. I'm not sure there's even any heating.

Five or six storeys up, it is. And I believe the lift doesn't work half the time. Did you tell Ben all that?"

"Considering I didn't know you'd even looked at an office, how could I?"

"But he may be horribly shocked and disappointed."

"Don't worry. Knowing you, I was able to give him a pretty grim picture of what conditions of work would be like in any place you organized. It didn't bother him in the least. He really wants to come. He's absolutely blazing with excitement. He says he can make it fifty pounds if necessary."

"Better not. If I let myself think beyond that forty pound budget I'll be needing sixty before he even gets here."

"That's the other thing. He wants to know when he can start."

"Day after tomorrow."

"And when will the thing itself start?"

"Wednesday fortnight."

This last really was a date established on the spur of the moment. It was the product of a conviction long held by Claud that unless you announce publicly that you are going to do a thing on or before a certain date, you never do it at all. (However, not even that method works during the periods of extreme lethargy or indolence that Claud is subject to from time to time.)

Just before he rang off, Archie gave expression to an afterthought.

"Has it occurred to you that even if Ben can stand you, you may not be able to stand him?"

"Why not, for God's sake? I've known him for years. Admire him. Love him. Splendid man."

"Well, it was just that I noticed, staying with him down there in the country, and talking to him, that he has developed an extraordinary sense of tidiness. Everything just so. He keeps the books and magazines straight on tables. At close quarters he might get on your nerves. Sort of trying to straighten your tie for you. Metaphorically. Perhaps even actually."

"Nothing better. Just exactly what's wanted. He'll compensate. Keep order in everything."

"God help him."

"Well look, I'm in a rush. You've got a telephone handy.

Let's start by saving a few bob. Ring him up from the B.B.C. and ask him to meet me at 11.45, day after tomorrow, saloon bar, the pub on the corner of Victoria Street and Buckingham Gate. We can talk, and I can show him the office."

Claud arrived quarter of an hour late, to find ex-vegetator Ben reading the literary page of the previous day's *Figaro*, and drinking brandy and soda. He seemed unaware that he was being looked at askance by the bowler-hatted regulars in the bar.

They were looking, in particular, at the enormous cameo rings on his fingers, and the gold-rimmed monocle, with black silk ribbon attaching it to the buttonhole of his jacket. His suit was of the kind which a smart French tailor at Deauville used to advertise as *très chic, presque cad*. This outfit, together with the fact that he was a young man of absurdly good looks, must have caused the bowler-hatted patrons to have him "taped" right away as a particularly flamboyant pansy, whose presence amounted practically to an insult.

In which conclusion they would have been wrong. Ben was not only a "hetero", he was even rather more than averagely hot-blooded where women were concerned. Once in a while people would suggest to him that he might be doing himself unnecessary harm by going about looking so queer, in both senses of the word.

He said they were mistaken. He pointed out that so far as women were concerned he could demonstrate his "normality" in the first five minutes. Equally, in the London of that period, he argued, there were considerable advantages in being thought by pansies to be pansy. Their illusions were a matter of indifference to him. But at the same time everyone said they wielded enormous secret power in all sorts of unexpected places. In the misplaced hope of rewards to come they might somehow, some time, conspire to do him good.

Considering that Ben, with his forty pounds, was the financial founder of *The Week*, it is odd to recall that he was very far indeed from being that "political animal" which Claud calls himself. Some people got indignant about this. They thought that the manager of a publication like *The Week* ought to be a person with *some* kind of political background. He ought, at the very least, to be somebody who read the newspapers attentively, and was informed about the political affairs of the day. Ben, when he walked into Victoria Street, hardly knew the name of the Prime Minister.

To criticism of this kind Claud would reply, "He'll soon find out. He is a man of good will. In short, he is a *Dreyfusard*."

In the simple type of Western, characters are divided neatly into goodies and baddies. Claud at that time mentally divided people according to an only slightly less simple system. He thought of them as *Dreyfusard* or *anti-Dreyfusard*. Were they or were they not the kind of people who, regardless of all other considerations, would, in Paris during the 1890s, have signed petitions and demonstrated on behalf of Dreyfus? This criterion of judgment explains, I suppose, why Claud genuinely liked all sorts of people whom many of his contemporaries on the Left regarded as "impossibly reactionary". It explains, too, not only his hatred of Fascists and near-Fascists, but also his contempt for people with impeccable records in the Labour party whom he considered to be anti-Dreyfusard at heart.

In addition to being by nature satisfactorily Dreyfusard, Ben had, during his years in Paris, been a member in good standing of one or other group of *surréalistes*. This training, if that is the word, was now to stand him in good stead. The political objects of *The Week* meant almost nothing to him at the time, and the technical aspects of its publication meant even less. Soon after the conversation in the saloon bar, inquisitive persons were seeking him out, in the vain hope of getting details of what was planned. Ben flashed his rings at them in ample gestures and informed them that "it was all delightful, purely delightful".

The inquisitive ones thought he was holding out on them. He was not. He was concealing nothing. To be asked to notice, let alone remember, the facts, figures, and political analyses flowing towards him across the bar table was like being asked to put an agreeable but highly complicated piece of music into words.

What was being explained to him was, first, that Dorothy Woodman had been promised the down payment before one o'clock that day. And she for her part was already having some superfluous furniture—one kitchen-type table and four kitchen-type chairs—moved in from the offices of the Union of Democratic Control. The man was coming about the dupli-

cating machine at 4 p.m., and "if it comes to haggling about
the instalment payments, we shall be in a stronger position
if there's some sort of furniture about."

"I wonder," said Ben, "why they call it shooting the moon?
I mean when people have to decamp suddenly, leaving
everything unpaid? There's an odd French phrase for it, too.
For the moment it escapes me. I ought to remember it, because
when there was all the business with poor Louis Vergeot, and
that adorable wife of his, and they had to leave that studio
they had out by the Place d'Alesia, I had to . . ."

In "Pinterish" style he told a long story of whatever it was
that had happened. With publication due in not much more
than a fortnight, most embryo editors might have become
impatient. But unlike many people who are fond of telling
stories Claud likes other people's stories to be as long and as
minutely detailed as his own. They should have a recognizable
beginning, middle, and dramatic end. "Generalizations can
occasionally be boring," he thinks. "Details hardly ever."
Perhaps his capacity to listen, possessed by one of the most
loquacious of men, had something to do with the success of
The Week. "Don't keep missing out bits," he would often say
to someone who had begun to fear that the story he was giving
Claud was growing too long. "What happened between eleven
and eleven-fifteen?"

Ben's style of conversation and Claud's habit of listening
must between them have slowed up the pre-publication
preparations quite a lot. On this occasion it was at least an
hour before they returned to the question of what the paper
should be like.

It must, Claud said, be striking to look at. Since it could not,
for financial reasons, be strikingly lovely, it had better be
strikingly unlovely. He had therefore decided that it would be
duplicated on buff-coloured paper in a nasty shade of brown
ink. ("Of course people will make coarse lavatory jokes about
that. So much the better. A talking point.")

Some time was then spent explaining to Ben the late Lord
Northcliffe's theories on the subject of the "talking point".
Which, naturally, led to a short disquisition on another of
Lord Northcliffe's insights. Claud had read somewhere that
when the then Alfred Harmsworth started the *Daily Mail* he

did so as the result of a simple social-mathematical calculation. The Education Acts had been passed so and so many years ago. The newspapers during the intervening years had hardly changed. But there must have grown up a literate public for which the newspapers weren't catering. A vacuum that he, Harmsworth, could profitably fill.

It has since been said that this story about Harmsworth's calculations was a myth. Myth or not, it served its purpose so far as Claud's own venture was concerned. The idea in this case was that as the newspapers came to need bigger and bigger circulations in order to attract the advertisers, they had, of course, to make their appeal wider and wider; small groups of people with specialized interests could no longer be much considered. The resulting vacuum could not be filled by any daily newspaper, or by an expensively produced weekly, dependent upon advertising and thus on a fairly general circulation. Which was just where Claud's new publication came in.

Ben, looking like an enormously amiable, large and handsome cat, expressed his great enjoyment of this exposition. Then he said, "What we really need now is a filing cabinet."

This early indication of a wish for order and keeping things just so was received with approval.

"I believe there's a place that sells office equipment almost next door."

Ben took out his monocle and polished it. "I don't know a great deal about that sort of thing in London, but my father always said if you wanted something sound and solid the place to go was the Army and Navy Stores. Which, as you know, is just across the street."

Infected by the atmosphere of haste, Ben urged that the purchase be made immediately. He selected a metal filing cabinet of moderate size but impressively business-like appearance, and was now much concerned that it be delivered to number 34 in sufficient time to have its effect on the man from the duplicating-machine company. He was unwilling to rely on the salesman's promise of speedy delivery.

"We can easily carry it between us," he insisted. "After all, it's certainly no heavier than an empty coffin. You know the rue St. Jacques, of course?"

As they lugged the filing cabinet along and across Victoria Street, Ben explained the circumstances under which he and a young woman had found it necessary to carry an empty coffin from the rue St. Jacques to somewhere on the south side of the boulevard du Montparnasse. Luckily it was a longish story. Because, as usual, the lift was out of order. The story lasted long enough to distract Claud's attention from the, for him, detestable muscular effort of manhandling the cabinet all the way up the stairs. Ben was as strong as a horse, and the exertion in no way impeded his descriptive flow.

With the cabinet dumped on the landing, they prepared to call on Dorothy, make the necessary payment, and get the office keys.

Ben paused to look critically at the office door.

"It doesn't," he said, "look very nice to have a door without a name on it. We ought to get hold of a man right away and have a name put on. By the way, what is going to be the name of this thing you're going to do?"

"It will be called *The Week*."

Ben stood absolutely still for some seconds, considering. Then he softly clapped his hands.

He said, "From what I gathered, vaguely, of what you were saying there in the pub I was afraid it was going to have some ghastly name like *The Arrow* or *Onwards* or, do forgive me, *The Corpse Reviver*. *The Week* is, of course, perfect."

Claud likes flattery as much as the next man. He expressed entire agreement with Ben's judgment.

"My idea," he said, "is that a title should be as totally colourless as possible. The colour must come from inside. The title shouldn't try to impose a picture on the reader. On the contrary, the contents ought to be such that, after a little while, the title itself takes on a unique significance for the reader. It immediately implies the whole character of that paper, and no other. In that way, it has an impact of its own. Think of *The Times*."

Ben softly clapped again. He said, "Of course. It is like abstract as distinct from representational painting. That's what you're saying, aren't you?"

"Perhaps. Anyway, after we've got the key we'll see about a sign or something on that door."

Money and keys changed hands. Ben eagerly set about arranging and re-arranging the positions of the table, the three chairs, and the filing cabinet. "He managed," Claud said afterwards "to convey the impression that he was an expensive interior decorator called in to put the final exquisite touches to the layout of somebody's drawing-room." Ben looked at the bare table with distaste. The need to impress the man with the duplicator had come to occupy the forefront of his mind.

He pointed out that there ought to be pens, pencils, writing paper, blotting paper. "And what about a typewriter? Don't all journalists have typewriters? Where's yours?"

"Sold. That's what I'm living on."

"I thought you were living on the Hardings."

"I usually lunch out. I have to buy a lot of drinks for myself and a whole lot of people. And taxis are a fearful expense. You've forgotten what London's like."

"But why didn't you pawn it?"

"Have you ever tried pawning a typewriter?"

"No. I've never even tried using one."

"The last time I pawned a typewriter was when I ran out of money gambling in a place in Nevada. I didn't even have enough to cable *The Times* for supplies. They gave me eight or nine dollars on a brand-new 150-dollar machine. They said they could give me more on my gun. But I had no gun. They didn't believe that, and it made them thoroughly suspicious."

"You must borrow one, a typewriter I mean, at once from next door. Meantime, I'll step across the road and get the other necessaries."

By the late afternoon some financial agreement had been reached with the man from the duplicator-machine company. He promised that a man would deliver it three days later and demonstrate its use.

Ben went off to see a girl. "I feel like dancing tonight. It's literally months since I've been in a night-club." Claud hurried away to announce all the good news to his long-suffering hostess, Crystal Harding. From her point of view, one of the best bits of news was that Ben was not going to be added to the strength of the unpaying guests in her hospitable little

Chelsea house. At that time she hardly knew him. He was thus simply one of that vague but slightly menacing category thought of as "Archie's old Oxford friends". And anyway, Claud alone was, I should think, enough to preoccupy anyone trying, without much money, to keep a quietly well-appointed home running smoothly.

Apart from being punctual at breakfast, Claud's ideas of what the perfect house-guest should do were limited. He felt he was fulfilling this role particularly well whenever the Hardings gave, as they did at least once a week, a small party. On these occasions he would insist on presenting a bottle or two of whisky. (It must be remembered that in those days a bottle cost only 12s. 6d.) But in that economically depressed year of 1933, it was the sensible custom of young people with smallish incomes to drink only sherry at little gatherings of the kind. In fact, after a couple of years of the Depression, sherry had become the drink most of them preferred. The result was that the house-guest's gift really benefited nobody but the donor. I must say that this was not at all the objective he had in mind. He just could not believe that anyone in his right senses would actually want to drink sherry if whisky were available. He would press it on the guests. When they refused it he was saddened as though he had pointed out a fine view and they had failed to look.

Crystal had been more than a little daunted when, on his return to England in 1933, Archie had invited this particular "old Oxford friend" to stay. Especially unnerving was the fact that Archie had not asked him to stay for any definite period. He had simply said, "Stay till you get fixed up somewhere." But from the moment he moved into the Chelsea house Claud's time and energies were absorbed in the "project". The possibility of his taking any steps towards getting "fixed up" in a place of his own were dim.

Some of Crystal's "socialite" friends used to commiserate with her on having "that garrulous bolshie with the whisky bottle" constantly in and out of the house. There were certainly times when she must have looked forward to an end, some visible end, of the visit. And in fact the merest hint would have done the trick. For her guest, however tough he may have seemed to those friends, had in such matters an almost morbidly sensitive skin. The idea of intruding where he was "not wanted" (unless of course it was among chosen enemies) would have greatly upset him. The trouble about this sensitivity of his was that he found it difficult to imagine that he might not be, so to speak, wanted quite that much. He could not picture himself as possibly being considered "intrusive" by anyone (except, of course, by the aforesaid enemies). He thought, or rather he took for granted, that anyone he liked, liked him in about the same degree. I suppose that that attitude was in itself a form of insensitivity.

No such hint was ever dropped. This was a tribute to Crystal's adaptability and sense of humour. Nothing in her upbringing had prepared her for the experience of giving house-room to anyone possible to describe as a "garrulous bolshie". As a child I had met her, her two elder sisters and her mother, Lady Blois, on holiday at Dinard. She was the sort of woman I had often seen in English drawing-rooms, though a phenomenon less common among us in Ireland. In fact, as I gathered later, she was one of that large number of people of her age and class who not only hoped but expected that the modern world would pretty soon "blow over". By the modern world was meant everything that had happened between, say, 1916 when World War I stopped being the sort of war one's father and uncles used to have, and 1930 when, what with the schemings of the Bolsheviks and the panicky behaviour of the Americans, one's dividends began shrivelling fast.

This being Lady Blois's general view, it was natural that she should prepare her daughters to meet the return of the pre-war world in good social trim. She laboured arduously to this end. I don't know whether Crystal was ever a débutante in the formal sense of the word, with presentation at Court and so on, but she had certainly been well-groomed for such ritual formalities. "And for not much else," she would admit sardonically.

But the time came when she started to "grow up". This was due partly to the influence of Archie, partly to the realities of the world situation. Far from blowing over, the modern world appeared to have got its barometer stuck at "Storm". Sometimes cheerfully, sometimes wryly, Crystal began to realize that possibly it had not pleased God to call her and other young women of her class to that state of life to which their mothers had thought they should be accustomed.

Archie's liberalizing influence on Crystal's political outlook was of a general nature; Archie himself did not exactly hold strong "radical" views. Indeed Claud, having got his political education in Central Europe and the United States, found his old friend's political views curiously unformed, "soupe à l'Anglaise". But *Dreyfusard*, in Claud's sense of the word, Archie certainly was. And his work at the B.B.C., where, in those days, a gifted and purposeful individual could play a larger role than he probably could in the enormous organization of today, kept him stimulatedly alert to events.

Archie was, I believe, the original inventor for radio of that type of on-the-spot documentary reportage which was the grandfather of such TV programmes as *24 Hours* and many others. The occasion for the first broadcast of this kind which he arranged was, I think, the abdication, in 1933, of Alfonso XIII, and his dramatic departure from Spain. The broadcast apparently stressed popular, Republican enthusiasm. It would, I expect, seem very mild stuff today, but it caused much offence in some places of power, as lacking due reverence for Royalty. Had the B.B.C. forgotten, people asked, that the ex-Queen of Spain was a grand-daughter of Queen Victoria?

Archie was repeatedly the centre of storms, large or small, of this kind. The same sort of pressure groups that operate today, operated then. It would appear that then, as now, a large proportion of the British public spent a large proportion of its time being shocked by something or other.

Archie used to recount with exquisite pleasure the story of the row there was when the now well-known song "Ain't it grand to be blooming well dead" was first let loose on the sound waves. People wrote accusing the B.B.C. of "encouraging suicide". And a high official remarked to Archie (who had nothing to do with the song department but was keenly interested in the row) that "although people like ourselves may find it merely amusing, I very much question whether, in the present state of the country, it can have otherwise than a lowering effect upon the public morale."

Archie was what is called a "compulsive talker". He often

simply talked for the purpose of clarifying his own ideas. He did not require, or even expect, to be wholly understood. And like many Englishmen brought up mainly in England, he thought a woman was on the whole likely to understand about half as much as a man. Men with that outlook are particularly apt to take happily for granted that their own ever-loving wives are really not taking in more than a fraction of any serious, or at all abstract, discussion.

He talked continuously to Crystal. And when Claud went to stay with them talked more than ever. He was naturally astonished when, a few days after the forty pounds had been banked and the "project" was getting up steam, Crystal quietly remarked that what she would really like to do would be to go and work, in some capacity, for *The Week*.

3 *The Alien Eye*

CRYSTAL's friends thought her behaviour in joining *The Week* at best quixotic. At worst it could be seen as somehow menacing. People of her sort did not do that sort of thing. Or, if they mysteriously did, then it could mean that the social scenery might be a good deal shakier than it looked.

As I have said, I was far away from England at the time *The Week* started. But I had been there for longish periods in the previous couple of years. And, even had I chanced to hear of Claud's project at the time it was being launched, my reaction would no doubt have been very different from hers. It would, I think, have seemed to me to have little relevance to the England I had seen.

By hindsight, historians of the period often wrote as though members of London "society" were not only "dancing on the edge of a volcano", but were conscious of it. There were some politically-minded "dancers", and no doubt they had an eye on the lava-level. True, too, that members of what are roughly defined as the upper middle and the upper professional class, were being squeezed by the slump. They could deduce that, since their bank accounts were tottering, the whole social structure might be tottering too.

But that was not, in my experience, the conclusion drawn by people in the "top income-tax brackets". Naturally they complained, on suitable occasions, of their poverty. More often they complained that England, in a general way, was poor. That was why it was so regrettably essential to cut unemployment benefits. But they rarely regarded (in the way a good many rich Americans did) the system itself as being at all near the rocks. Those people were still very rich, and, in practical terms, they knew it. Not only financiers, and what were later called business tycoons, knew it. So did large sections of that "old aristocracy" which had been loudly lamenting the ruin of the system ever since the Reform Bill.

Their most commonly held belief was that, after the first

shocks of the Wall Street crash, things in England were slowly, but wholesomely, getting back to normal. They thought of the people of the 1920s as having danced foolishly, and above all vulgarly, on the volcanic edge. These foolish, vulgar ones were contemptuously summed up as "the bright young people". It is hard to believe that any group would have applied so nauseating a phrase to itself. They themselves usually claimed the label had been pinned on their backs by the newspapers.

The notion of a return to "normality" was based on the idea that the 1920s had been a passing interlude in British life. It was a phase of the modern world which would not just "blow over" but could, and should, be puffed along on its way with the help of the leaders of "Society". Thus it was not only a pleasure but a duty to play a part in re-establishing old "standards of value". The effort implied a new emphasis on decorum and formality. Pomp and circumstance were not to be derided.

The "real grandees", in a phrase used by Siegfried Sassoon of a quite different historical set, did not shrink from what their critics denounced as gross ostentation. To assert in this way the solidity of the structure cost a great deal of money. But it was desirable in itself. A Mallful of furs and diamonds on the way to a presentation at the Palace was not a dangerous provocation to the populace. It was a proclamation of confidence in the system, and so of benefit to the nation.

I do not recall that I, or anyone of my acquaintance, found anything to feel guilty about in sitting down, quite often, to supper at a ball where four or five hundred guests ate as much caviare as they needed before getting on to more solid nourishment. They had no serious objection to such facts being mentioned in the newspapers. Such get-togethers were surely a pointer to the fact that England stood where she always had.

I had other reasons for not thinking that the English had much cause to listen to alarmist critics.

I came from Ireland. Compared to the poverty I had seen there among fishermen, farmers, and others in and around the town where I grew up, conditions in England looked astoundingly easy. Naturally, my reaction was to what I saw, which was London rather than South Wales or Jarrow or Fife.

But even when the grisly privations and sufferings of those
areas were discussed, almost everyone combined to treat
them as strictly temporary results of "the general economic
situation". The people concerned were like victims of a flood
or other "Act of God". With some drainage and dam-repair
the waters would be put under control again.

There were beggars in London. Banks of unemployed
ex-servicemen marched along the gutters of Regent Street,
playing for pennies and sixpences. They marched in single
file, as required by the police, so as not to impede traffic or
shoppers. It was a sufficiently miserable sight. But it was
viewed as the result of an "Act of God". In Ireland, on the
other hand, beggary and kindred miseries had not been sudden
nor abnormal nor due to causes that could not be seen and
explained. The causes were easily identifiable as the political
acts of men. Young Irish people, unless they lived in a vacuum,
identified them still more precisely. They were the end-
product of centuries of English occupation of Ireland.

In consequence I tended to look at England with an eye not
much less foreign than that of a visiting French person.
Sometimes an eye is blind to whole areas of life which the
natives see, and take for granted. Sometimes it may detect
important features which, for the natives, are too familiar
to be properly noticed.

Years later I came to think that *The Week* owed its successes,
as much as its failures, to the fact that Claud, too, was looking at
England with an alien eye.

Apart from those formative years in Europe, there was
Scotland.

At the time of starting *The Week* Claud had not spent more
than a total of five months in Scotland during the whole of
his life. And the first visit, lasting three months, occurred on
his arrival from Peking as a baby in the arms of his Chinese
nurse. For all that, he was a very consciously Scottish Scotsman.
Occasionally English friends were irked by his unspoken, but
evident assumption that every good-hearted Scot must feel
some decent compassion for non-Scottish people. They
accused him of being a "professional Scotsman" and even
a crypto-racialist.

"Scotland," he would be good enough to explain, "is

neither a piece of geography nor a blood-group. It is an attitude of mind."

And as the climax of a long crescendo of abuse directed against the late Ramsay MacDonald, or any other prominent Scot he detested, he would appear to clinch the matter by declaring that the man had delinquently allowed himself to be brain-washed by corrupting English influences. Alternatively, he suggested, it would probably be disclosed, on enquiry into the fellow's pedigree, that he was not Scottish at all. It was, he said, notorious that the most English Englishmen were often absurdly eager to emphasize that they had had a Scottish forebear somewhere along the line.

These somewhat extravagant sentiments were expressed in Claud's customarily somewhat extravagant language. Many people thought that what they called Claud's "Scottish thing" was an affectation. They were wide of the mark. His father, with equal lack of affectation, thought of himself as primarily Scottish, and (though more gently than Claud) would firmly correct anyone who loosely classed him as an Englishman. He had been born in Bombay. After a short period at Edinburgh Academy, he was educated at the University of Bonn. At the age of eighteen he went to China and, with very brief intervals, remained there for nearly thirty-two years. Thereafter he lived partly in England, partly in Hungary. But if asked what was his native town he would reply, without the least sense of contradictoriness, "Edinburgh". To be Scottish, and from Edinburgh at that, was for him too an "attitude of mind", and one to be glad of. It was also, he felt with occasional qualms, a challenging kind of gift of the gods which required some living up to.

He once admitted to Claud that when, in English churches, they intoned, "Let us now praise famous men and our fathers that begat us," his thoughts turned to the Covenanters, and to Border-raiding bandits. He was glad that the other members of the congregation were not mind-readers.

Claud's "Scottish thing" was greatly reinforced by his admiration for the writings of his great-grandfather, the Scottish judge, Lord Cockburn, who in the 1840s wrote the incomparable *Memorials of his Time*. "A book," Claud would say, "not only masterly, earnest and hilarious, but like all classics, singularly relevant to what people keep calling the 'dilemma of our age', usually speaking as though we were the first age to have one."

What Claud found particularly fascinating in the *Memorials* was his great-grandfather's sometimes bitter, sometimes comical depiction of the effects of the French Revolution upon the thinking of the upper class of Edinburgh Society in his youth. The analogy with the impact of the Russian Revolution upon the thinking of Claud's parents and their friends was at times so close as to seem almost incredible.

Once being threatened with a libel action by a man who, Claud had said, had murdered a Nazi spy, he made what he thought was a helpful suggestion to his lawyer. "Write and tell him," he said, "that I used the word 'murder' in no pejorative sense."

Similarly, I use the term alien eye descriptively and not pejoratively. R. Palme Dutt, for many years a leading figure in the British Communist Party and the Comintern, could in this sense be said to have turned an at least partially alien eye upon the British scene. Not long after *The Week* began to get talked about he met Claud and they conversed. Having had a good deal to do with British "intellectuals" of one kind and another, Dutt was naturally interested to know how much of a Communist Claud was. Dutt remarked on the fact that of all the British intellectuals showing some sympathy with Communist ideas and aims, an astonishingly small number had lived wholly in England. For such sympathies to be aroused, it seemed to be almost *de rigueur* for a person to have had a chance to look at England from the outside.

The outside from which Claud had been looking in was not just geographical, it was mental, too. The political books young men read furtively but eagerly in Hungary, and openly in Berlin, were not the kind generally popular at Oxford. Persons in any sort of public position, from school teachers to civil servants, who declared themselves Marxists were viewed as unsound cranks, or dangerous, or both. If they were in the B.B.C. they would be sacked immediately.

That much was taken more or less for granted. But in his task of trying to organize an information service for *The Week* he came up against a more serious difficulty than that of his identification with the Communists. He found that a great many of the people in the City, Fleet Street, and in Whitehall who were anxious to tell such a paper what they knew, in fact knew very little worth telling. Caginess and cunning deception were to be expected from dubious or hostile elements. Ignorance on the part of people who ought not to be ignorant was a more baffling problem.

As I have said, he had been much surprised by the number of supposedly informed people who were ready, even eager, to talk with him. He had supposed that during *The Week's* brief period of gestation these people would be accumulating enough milk to give the baby ample nourishment when it got born. Now the date of birth was uncomfortably near. And the prospects for a generous "milk-giving" appeared quite unexpectedly meagre. In a moment of unusual depression, he remarked that "it's as though these people's powers of observation had actually atrophied. Perhaps they have become so used to the futility of opening their mouths that when they get a chance to do so with some small effect, they find they've lost the power of speech."

The answer to the problem was paradoxical. If you really wanted to see the English landscape, the thing to do was to tour it with a lot of foreigners, other aliens in fact. They would at least know when it's raining, or freezing. The Englishman may be so habituated to it all that he will hardly think it necessary to warn you that part of the road is going to be under water, and the pipes of the house due to burst any day now.

The American newspaper correspondents in London were the most obvious companions for that sort of touring. In New York and Washington Claud had always found a majority of American newspapermen particularly *sympathique*. The American press of those days was certainly a good deal less cautiously tight-lipped than it is today. It was under continuous, often justified attack from American radicals. It was depicted as the obscurantist tool of "the interests". Yet it was less inhibited, more frankly informative and ribald about goings-on even on its home front, than the British press was about British affairs. Claud was of opinion that it offered the journalist a much better training ground and chance of development than the British press.

And, of course, in those days American correspondents reporting on Britain, France or Germany, were even less inhibited than their colleagues trying to tell some truth about Chicago. Today things are a little different. The American involvement in British and European affairs is immeasurably greater. American correspondents have had to start "thinking diplomatically". Much more than in the Thirties they face the same sort of supposed responsibilities which oppressed many British correspondents in Paris or Berlin.

However, even in the Thirties Claud had to conclude that a good many of his American journalist friends were not going to be entirely suitable people to go sight-seeing with.

One or two were already as discreet as ambassadors and other diplomatic types are often pictured as being. (I must say that in my experience this is a libel on diplomats. Many of them are the most humanly effervescent and warmly indiscreet of men.) Others seemed to have been at some time over-exposed to American comedies with damn-fool Englishmen as the butts. Royalty, peasants tugging forelocks, and Beef-eaters filled their view-finders. Bertie Woosters abounded. But Jeeves was there, too. He was the trickily cunning Britisher who by devious means foiled honest acts of American policy.

But the best of these Americans—some already well known and writing under by-lines, others relatively obscure staff members—formed, in Claud's opinion, the best corps of foreign correspondents anywhere. Among them, the ones he personally and professionally liked and esteemed the most were Frederick Kuh of the United Press, and Negley Farson.

Frederick Kuh had only just arrived from Berlin where he had headed the United Press Bureau until Hitler made it impossible for him to remain. Negley was a well-established London Correspondent of the *Chicago Daily News*. At that time the *Chicago Daily News*'s foreign service was generally considered the best in the United States.

As his autobiography *The Way of a Transgressor* makes plain, Negley had been many other things in his life besides being one of the finest journalists of his day. He had fought for the British in World War I before the United States came into it. Flying one of those primitive aeroplanes, he was shot down in Egypt with a wound which took a big chunk out of his leg.

The bones were injured in such a way as to cause him intermittent hours of pain for the rest of his life. He had also been
an engineer. And he had been actively engaged in armament
traffic in Russia in 1917. He was everything that is meant by,
in its best sense, the word adventurer.

As I have said, Claud's resignation from *The Times* had earlier
caused a stir of interested gossip in journalistic circles. Then,
on the grapevine, Negley heard of the still embryonic project.
He instantly thought, as he told me later, "this was the kind
of man I might do a bit of tiger-shooting with." Unwilling to
waste time waiting for an introduction *à l'anglaise*, he sent
Claud a characteristically modest note, leaving, as they say,
"all options open".

"In case you would care for us to meet," it said, "I shall be
standing by the cashier's desk in the Café Royal at 10.15
tomorrow evening. I shall be wearing a dark blue suit and
carrying a copy of the *Chicago Daily News*." Of course since the
staff at the Café Royal knew Negley very well and Claud
fairly well, this procedure was really unnecessary. But Negley,
with a long experience of plots and plotters, thought it possible
that Claud might be engaged in some conspiracy. He might
have some mysterious but valid reason for not wanting to
meet, or be seen meeting, the Correspondent of the *Chicago
Daily News* and President of the Foreign Correspondents'
Association in London.

Though he had no such reason, Claud for his part much
appreciated the thoughtfulness and understanding behind this.
Even in advance of their actual meeting it suggested to him,
too, that this might be a "man to go tiger-shooting with".
As for the blue suit and the newspaper, they were, Claud
recalls, quite needless identifications. Even if Negley had
forgetfully dressed in brown and carried a copy of *The Times*,
there could have been no mistake. One glance at the rather
leonine head, and large, alertly moving blue eyes, above a
big figure which was both solid and vibrant, was enough to
remove any doubt that this was the man he might "care to
meet".

They talked for hours, first at one of those marble-topped
tables in the Café Royal which Claud used as a kind of sub-
sidiary office, later in some club. Claud's recollection of the

latter part of this encounter was that they had to break off a discussion of the situation in North China "because we thought the waiters looked so tired". Others have reported that they were thrown out into the dawn for riotous behaviour. Knowing the men concerned, I feel that both versions could be true.

Negley was a fast mover. It happened that one of the then owners of the *Chicago Daily News* was touring Europe. He had fetched up in London, avid for entertainment of every kind. Among other things, he wanted visible proof that the paper's representative was really "getting around", meeting informed and representative people. Negley regarded him with a mixture of amused affection, boredom, and occasional contempt. Since he had to ask him to a lot of lunches and dinners, he decided to make one of these dinners a dual-purpose affair.

He would introduce the Big Chief to some interesting people. At the same time he would introduce Claud to these same people who, he thought, would help to make the "project" as stimulating and useful as possible.

There were two intelligent and talkative M.P.'s—one Conservative, the other from the recently diminished ranks of the Parliamentary Labour party. There were a couple of European journalists, two visiting officials of the French Foreign Office, and the Counsellor of the Russian embassy in London. The presence, and conversation, of these last three incidentally gave Claud his first intimation of the Franco-Soviet Pact which less than two years later caused civilized Europe to hope that the West had at last found a means of containing Hitlerism. It also, ironically enough, profoundly shocked the orthodox Western Communists, who found it almost intolerably hard to understand how the U.S.S.R. could have made a treaty of that kind with a capitalist state.

The dinner party did, as Negley had expected, provide a starting point for a more regular operation, conducted in London and Paris, and indirectly in Berlin. The contacts had not been made in vain.

The nature of the operation was explained to me a good many years later in a blackberry patch on the Cornish coast by Mr. Stefan Litauer, who was involved early on in *The Week*'s activities.

He, Claud and I were guests of the Farsons at a seaside

house they had there. Negley was doing a cure which involved total abstention from alcohol. Since he was normally a man who liked a drink, Claud and Litauer felt it would be unkind to drink in his presence, or even to announce that they were going out for a drink. Litauer had noticed richly-fruited blackberry bushes a mile or so from the house, about half-way to the village. He proclaimed that it was essential that these should be picked for jam, for puddings, for eating with cream. He and his fellow guests would make it their business to pick large quantities. (Negley's leg was troubling him, and he could only hobble about the house and on the beach.)

I thought they were carrying delicacy to an absurd extreme. But they insisted. So that soon afterwards while Claud, who had the longest legs, secretly strode on out of the blackberry bushes to get supplied at the village pub, Litauer and I found ourselves diligently picking to justify the trip.

It was hot and tedious work, and we rightly suspected that Claud, once inside the pub, would be in no great hurry to return with his bagful of bottles to be consumed, as they say, off the premises.

To pass the time, Litauer told me the story of the early days of *The Week*. Two, three, even four times weekly a group of three or four foreign correspondents in London met in Negley's office at Bush House. It was not always the same group. But Negley was almost invariably there.

These little gatherings were of the utmost informality. A not-specially interested outsider listening could have supposed them to be more or less casual chats between gossip-loving men with not much to do of a morning.

But of course, as Litauer pointed out, if you looked at the thing mathematically, the total of information gathered in that room was really prodigious.

You could rightly assume that each of those men talked more or less intimately with at least half a dozen well-informed men in London daily. So that a couple of dozen good sources of information were on tap for the use of those assembled at Negley's.

And two or three of them were in positions which caused their embassies, and representatives of their national banks, to treat them with more than usual regard. They were not the sort of people who could lightly be brushed off or intimidated.

Litauer, for instance, was head of the Polish National News Agency. Another of the little group was London Correspondent of one of the three most influential newspapers in Germany. Neither the Polish nor the German governments could successfully fob such men off with superficial answers to probing questions.

On top of that, these particular foreign correspondents were experienced and intelligent men, each having, as Claud used to say, a "certain philosophy" of the situation, although their "philosophies" were widely varied. They were not grubbing for unrelated bits and pieces. They recognized where the bits and pieces of the daily and weekly jigsaw would fit.

I asked Litauer whether people had not, after all, tended to keep their best stories to themselves. It appeared that this was not the case, or not usually so. Each concerned (it was a carefully selected group) could see that in the long run it was to the interest of all to put the maximum into the pool. That was the way to get the maximum out.

In the early stages, Claud's contribution was probably less than that of others. But even then, before he had had time to extend his own contacts, there was a particular function which a publication such as *The Week*, and only such a publication, could perform. It could deal with stories which were, as the saying goes, too hot to handle.

In other words, in those grisly and claustrophobic early Thirties, there were a lot of unpleasantly true stories which even a leading correspondent did not care to take responsibility for transmitting direct to his newspaper or agency. But if such a story were to appear in *The Week*, it could be quoted from that source. The situation was then quite different. If high authority, in the shape of an Editor or Foreign Office or Embassy were to take exception, the correspondent was in the clear. Since *The Week* had published the story, it was common property. In fact it would have been a dereliction of duty on the part of the correspondent not to send it out, when rivals certainly would.

Naturally no one member of this loosely constituted group was starry-eyed enough to assume that all the others were saints, let alone martyrs. There was always the possibility that

someone, some time, was going to plant a supposedly confidential story with the object of getting it wide publicity.

As everyone knows, the whole purpose of a person who says
"don't tell this to a soul" is to ensure that the story be immediately spread far and wide.

There were certainly some members of the group who did
implicitly trust one another not to play this game knowingly.
On the other hand, there was always the possibility that one
or other might himself have been the victim of a planted
"confidence". Mr. X, representative of the X-land press,
might have been told a very interesting story by the Counsellor
of the X-land embassy not because it was true, but because it
was a lie which the X-land government wished to have
generally believed. And the X-land government rightly
thought it more likely to be believed if it appeared to be a
leak, than if it had any smell of officialdom about it.

That, of course, happened. But, as Litauer pointed out, if
one came to the conclusion that one's friend X had been the
victim of such a false confidence, that in itself was of interest. It
helped one to find out what the X-land government was up to.

Naturally these little gatherings at Bush House were themselves supposed to be confidential. But like all such confidential
arrangements, news of the gatherings and rumours of them
spread about the place. At an early date the German and
Japanese embassies in particular began to attach perfectly
ludicrous importance to certain stories in *The Week*. They
supposed that all *The Week*'s stories emanated from what they
variously described as "that devil's cauldron" and "lie factory"
at Bush House. All of which naturally did *The Week*'s circulation
a lot of good.

Between the first of those gatherings and the date set to
issue the first number of *The Week* there was very little time.
Also, the difficulties of launching what most people had
estimated as at least a £5,000 enterprise on forty pounds
became more and more apparent.

Whom, for instance, were they to circularize with copies of
the first issue? Everyone explained that there were agencies
which specialized in providing "sucker lists" for any desired
purpose. But the very cheapest of such lists was going to cost
at least a couple of hundred pounds.

Then the Union of Democratic Control said they could lend a list of former subscribers to their old journal *Foreign Affairs*. There were over a thousand names on the list. All of them, obviously, were names of people likely to be interested in the kind of thing *The Week* was going to be interesting about.

Claud took it for granted that the circulation problem was thereby solved. For this absurd naïvete, which alarmed everyone else concerned, there were two reasons, neither of them good. There was Claud's native over-optimism. But there was also his extreme dislike of everything connected with what is called "admin". And this dislike was not, as he supposed, due to his feeling that admin was a tiresome interference with serious work. It was due, also, to the fact that he was always extremely bad at admin. This, of course, he would freely admit, and even with a certain pride. It was as though the ability to handle commercial affairs were in itself a badge of intellectual inferiority. Claud's attitude was typical of British university-educated intellectuals of the period. It is, I think, significant that this attitude was rarely found among European or American intellectuals. It may well have been a product of the particular British class set-up.

Claud, it is true, used sometimes to annoy a few stuffy people at *The Times* by referring to himself and them as members of the working class. But that sincere assertion did nothing to make up for his lack of proper education on the subject of admin.

His attitude to admin was also in large part due simply to laziness. Since he had never been taught anything about it, except perhaps to look down on it, it was going to be an exertion to learn now. Then as now, his energy was accompanied by a great deal of lethargy. The news-gathering and the writing got the energy. Admin was left with the lethargy.

As so often happens when a person is wrong, someone or something turns up to justify his attitude. In this case, it was a man who was, he said, from Vancouver. How this man entered the act was a mystery. Claud had met him somewhere and been touched by the fact that, in Claud's description, "he had mittens on his feet."

The man had been apparently well-dressed and well-shod. He had also shown intelligent interest in some rumour he had heard about the project. He had proposals to make for getting *The Week* a lot of money through advertising. He was no confidence trickster. He was obviously sincerely solicitous for the success of the project. But since Claud was determined to reject any advertising that might, improbably, be offered, the man from Vancouver might have been shaken off. Then Claud noticed that despite his otherwise prosperous appearance, the man's socks only went down to the top of his shoes. When he moved in an ill-advised manner it could be seen that his feet were naked in the shoes. Evidently his last pair of socks had worn out in the soles and he was doing the best he could to keep up appearances.

The man's calmness and assurance under these trying conditions endeared him to Claud. Claud realized that for this man *The Week* was a last port of call. The man was assured that he could get no money in the foreseeable future, and perhaps never. But he was a believer. He clearly felt that if he could personally survive long enough for *The Week* to take advantage of his business know-how, the future was bright. Indeed, he convinced everyone else that, if only Claud would listen to him, the bright future might be nearer than it could be so long as Claud was allowed to disregard admin.

Naturally everyone went on urging Claud to listen carefully to this man. Then a few weeks later, meeting Claud outside the Army and Navy Stores on his way to the office, he fell on his knees and made to worship Claud as his Brother in the Sun. He called upon the passers-by and shoppers to join him in a general act of reverence. He had to be driven to a nursing home. Claud said, with some smugness, that naturally he was very sorry for anyone who went off his head, but it was, he felt, something of a warning to all those who might allow themselves to take admin too seriously.

But on the occasion of the first production of *The Week* the man from Vancouver was among those present. As he jumped about the tiny office in high excitement, the fact that his socks were mere mittens was visible to everyone. He continued, nevertheless, to explain ways in which money could be made. At the same time he was busy helping Crystal, Ben, and Claud with the actual production.

At that time Crystal could not type. It was one of those

skills her mother had never supposed might some day come in useful. Claud had the job of cutting the stencils. Here was a double hazard. On the one hand Claud was used to typing at considerable speed but without any regard for neatness or accuracy. He had been accustomed to correct his own typescript by hand before sending it to cable-operator or printer. But this stuff about to be rolled off from the stencil was the final product, going direct to the consumer.

The other part of the hazard was that as he laboriously cut stencils from his own typescript, Claud kept thinking of ways in which his original could be improved. With time running shorter and shorter he would distress everyone by muttering, "By God we could sharpen this up a bit," tearing the stencil out of the typewriter, and starting the sheet again.

The paper was to go out strictly by post. It was to be posted on a Wednesday, so as to get ahead of the existing weekly newspapers. Claud, Crystal, Ben, and the man from Vancouver had spent the early part of the night before, addressing the foolscap envelopes to the addresses on the list of 1,200 persons to be circularized.

Claud insisted on leaving the actual writing and hence the stencilling of the material until after the arrival of Wednesday morning's newspaper. He was determined that the deadline must always be as late as possible. "This is," he kept saying, when anyone urged that he was running things a bit fine, "supposed to be a *news* sheet." He was also haunted by the fear that some story he had supposed exclusive would have somehow leaked to one of the daily newspapers. In that case, for the story to appear in *The Week* as being somehow confidential or "inside" would make *The Week* look ridiculous.

Claud claimed that he was worried, too, by Crystal's showpiece Pekingese dog, named Pig. Crystal had explained that she had to bring it to the office because there was no one at home who could be trusted to look after it properly. It was said that a maid had been seen trying to kick it. Claud, for whom unusual-looking dogs and cats have an almost hypnotic fascination, was delighted by the arrangement. Also he felt that the presence of a dog whose pedigree intimately connected it with his own birthplace would be auspicious. He therefore not only welcomed this Peke but, when taking time off to brood on his next paragraph, watched it with attention.

But the dog's attitude, it seems, was the reverse of encouraging.

"As you know," Claud said to Ben when they went out for a quick drink, "I am the reverse of superstitious. Still the fact remains that that dog looks at me with an air of scepticism I can hardly bear. It looks at us all, the whole outfit, with scepticism. Its expression suggests that we are a lot of loonies."

Ben said, "You're being anthropomorphic. A mistake, surely, to attribute thoughts of that kind to the dog. What does that little brute know about the state of the world, the purposes of *The Week* and so on? Pekingese, I grant you. Well-bred, too. Could be a winner, no doubt, at Cruft's. But that's no reason for you to pay attention to the expression it has on its face. It just wants to be at home on the sofa instead of lying on our bare floor there in the office. We'll take it some nuts and chips from the counter here, and it'll cheer up. It'll soon be wishing us all Chinese good will."

They did so, but it was already a little late. Pig had watched Crystal and the man from Vancouver squeezing viscous brown ink out of tubes to ink the duplicating machine. Other tubes lay about the office within reach. Out of hunger, boredom, or a general notion of drawing attention to its discomfort and thus getting taken home to the sofa, the dog attacked the tubes. It chewed them up. It covered itself and everything else within its reach with this particularly thick brown ink. There was a delay while more ink, more paper, more envelopes had to be sent for, and quite a number of new envelopes addressed for the second time to the former subscribers of *Foreign Affairs*.

When things seemed at their worst, Claud would seek to comfort his friends and helpers with a quotation from *Alice Through the Looking Glass*. Alice speaks to the Red Queen of a hill. "When you say hill," said the Red Queen, "remember that I've seen hills compared to which that would be a valley." "A hill can never be a valley," said Alice. "Oh yes it can," said the Red Queen.

Whether the thought was as reassuring to others as it always was to Claud is doubtful. Still, the hill, or valley, was finally passed. With the whole 1,200 copies safely posted, Claud suggested that they all go to the Café Royal and drink champagne.

The man from Vancouver was well aware of the financial situation of *The Week*. He suggested that it would be just as agreeable to go to the neighbourhood pub and drink beer.

"And who," Claud asked, "will pay for the beer? At the Café Royal, where they already know me quite well, they will put the champagne on the slate. Our entire celebration will cost us no more than the taxi fare."

II

4 Nasty Jar

IT is probably difficult for anyone today to conceive of the jarring effect *The Week* had upon the reader whose mental lungs, so to speak, were accustomed to the atmosphere of the early 1930s. One subscriber, indeed, used to state that he enjoyed reading *The Week*, but found it so acrid that he felt the need of some sort of gas-mask while doing so. Or, as another put it, "I know it's good for one, but my God it gets on one's nerves."

Some of the nerve-rasping effect can, naturally, be only imagined by the reader of today. He is used to a press which, with some glaring exceptions and limitations, is in general a great deal more outspoken than the press was in the days of *The Week*. With those same exceptions and limitations, it makes a greater effort to treat its readers as being of at least average adult intelligence.

It may be, too, that the shock-effect is to some extent reduced by the simple fact that the picture presented, however startling, is still a picture of events which occurred some time ago. I say "may" be. For just because the Thirties are so lurid a piece of the history of our times, the result of seeing them in close-up through the lenses of *The Week* can be jolting. A back number of *The Times* or the *Daily Mail* or the *Daily Worker* for 29 March 1933, the date of *The Week*'s first issue, is of evident interest. But the lenses are oddly opaque. Changing the metaphor, one has a vulgar impulse to ask them please to take the mush out of their mouths.

Nobody had to ask *The Week* to take the mush out of *its* mouth. On the contrary, as will be seen, a lot of people were constantly wishing it would use more mush before it spoke. And occasionally they tried to force it to do so.

The special impact of the paper was in part due to the fact that it was saying in public what a great many people were saying or thinking in private. Some of the topics of discussion among informed people were not factual but speculative. In a personal note soon after *The Week* appeared, Kingsley Martin wrote to Claud saying that "a good many of the stories have already reached me in the form of rumour." He explained that having been unable fully to confirm them, he had not felt able to refer to them in the *New Statesman*. Claud took the view that there are many occasions when the existence of a particular rumour is as significant and worthy of mention as a proven fact. Regarding this as a vital principle of journalism, he was often attacked by people who supposed, or pretended to suppose, that he made no distinction between fact and rumour. This was nonsense. But he did believe that the speculations, and even the gossip, of informed people ought to be reported too.

The jar, or shock-effect, was also in part due to *The Week*'s peculiar style. On this point, the editor, at a late stage of *The Week*'s existence, offered some explanation. In April 1940, paper rationing compelled it to reduce its size from six to four sides of foolscap. An editorial note, announcing this, stated:

> Subscribers can be undisturbed. Despite drastic cuts, stylistic changes enable wordage per issue to remain scarcely reduced, news coverage not at all. *Week* returns to the compressed style wherewith it was launched 7 years ago; when it set a fashion subsequently imitated *tant bien que mal* by innumerable British publications. In deference to objections of subscribers who declared our style over-abrupt, inelegant, we deliberately adopted more traditional Anglicisms. With war, rationing, these are done for. By stylistic compression, plus elimination of type and spacing variations, we calculate same word and news meat is packable into the smaller egg. To those preferring elegance to information —our regrets. The subscribing majority will prefer our decision.

On the style of the "elegant" period there is shrewd comment by Mr. Cyril Connolly writing years later in the *Sunday Times*. "This equation of rumour with fact made *The Week* an intoxicating newspaper; written for the knowing by those in the know, it was genuinely diabolical in the sense that it never put anything past its opponents. Motive was peeled from motive, betrayal found under betrayal, bribe upon bribe, and always in the august and persuasive language of *The Times*.

I am sure it was his *Times* manner that spared Mr. Cockburn a single libel action—not, as he thinks, the poverty of his organization. His victims literally could not believe their eyes."

However, it will be seen that the first issue was rather far in style from the august language of *The Times*.

When chided for his prodding impatience to get this first issue out, Claud kept monotonously repeating, "But this is a critical moment of history, don't you see that?"

To which Ben, irritated by all this fuss and urgency, replied by asking, "Do you suppose there'll ever be a moment you won't regard as critical in history? If there was no crisis you'd certainly find it necessary to invent one."

But in the 1930s it was never necessary to invent a crisis. A genuine one occurred every month. The old joke about the newspaper-seller shouting "nothing *bona fide* but the murders" came grimly true.

This situation, and the varying states of mind it produced, have possibly been blurred in retrospect by the violence and magnitude of the crisis which ultimately blew up the Thirties. History, I think, always subtly suggests to one that the earth-shaking thing that happened was the thing that was bound to happen. And history hints that it was not just bound to happen, it was bound to happen just when it did.

So that there is some danger, perhaps, of considering the period of the Thirties, at least unconsciously, as running along a clearly evident straight line from point to point. A line from, say, the financial crash of late 1929 (though it did not really hit Britain until a little later) through Hitler's seizure of power and Mussolini's and Japan's aggressions, to hit the buffers punctually at World War II.

Looked at like that, the period has the quality of a neat detective story, the interest of which depends entirely on what the denouement is going to be. But if an officious friend who has read the book is so unkind as to tell anyone in advance how it all came out, the book is not worth reading.

But only the most primitive determinist supposes that history is pre-determined like the plot of a detective story. A devout person can; certainly nobody else does. In other words, looking at History, nobody is in a position to assert that things might not have happened, or been made to happen, otherwise than they did.

I am not here playing the "if" game, let alone the "if only" game. In the Thirties, people sickened by the number of "if's" and "if only's" they heard all around them, brought the game to an end by asking, "What would have happened if Hitler had been twins?"

But to deny that the "if's" mean anything, is to deny that what people do or think means anything. It amounts to saying that someone bought them their ticket on a non-stop train and they could not have got off it if they tried. In the matter of the Thirties the facts are that some people tried to stop the train and others tried to jump off.

Because they all failed to stop the train, and most of those who tried to jump got mangled, it is too easily assumed that there was no point, ever, along the line where the train might not have been switched, or, at least, de-railed.

But in reality there were many such points. A determined hind-viewer perhaps thinks not, because he believes that history had the whole business sewn up from the beginning. But then it is still important to record that the people living in that distant decade did suppose that they, like ourselves, had choices open to them. They did not see themselves as characters in a story of which the end is already known to the inventor. They thought there were things to be done. They jockeyed and jostled to do them.

The Week, from its very first number onwards, recorded the jockeying and jostling.

A lot of what it thought important at the time turned out, in the final result, to have been less important than supposed. When I remarked, perhaps unfairly, to Claud on this point, he said, "You're watching the Cheltenham Gold Cup and half-way round there's a horse lying third, and is coming on well. And then it falls at the next fence but two. Is it wrong to say, in the minute before the fall, that it's lying third, is coming on well, and has a good chance? Or are you supposed to know in advance that it's going to fall, at the next but two?"

Quite a number of the horses *The Week* tipped over the years might have been said to have fallen or even (as a result of later investigation) to have been doped.

This is obvious. It is also not entirely relevant. Everyone knows that the reports of, say, the Spanish Ambassador and other envoys to the Court of Queen Elizabeth I were full of misapprehensions. The *Letters* of Cicero seem to show that his ideas of what was likely, or possible, at the moment of the demise of the Roman Republic and the bloody start of the Roman Empire, were usually shrewd, often mistaken, and sometimes, by hindsight, purely absurd. This is true of most commentators seeking to comment on what is going on right under their noses. They lack, of course, perspective.

And it is just this lack of perspective which gives them value and interest for us. Even if we think we know the way things really were, it is important, too, to know the way informed onlookers thought they were. Important, also, to realize that a lot of the informed onlookers, and even participants, thought at the time that things might be changed.

In its first issue *The Week* refers to a war scare. It took several years for the scare to become a reality. That reality, as I have said, can obscure the fact that the scares of the early 1930s existed, were considered much more real than mere nightmares, and deeply affected people's thinking and actions.

The moment of crisis when the first issue of *The Week* appeared, came at the end of the second month after Hitler's seizure of power. Communists took literally the slogan "Fascism means War". Claud, questioned by a Conservative M.P. as to whether he shared this view, said he did not.

"War," Claud irritatingly remarked, "could quite easily be postponed. One can always surrender. If the white flag trade is short of supplies, a reasonably clean handkerchief will do."

He was then of course not thinking of the possibility that someone else, i.e. Stalin, might ultimately have a whiter handkerchief than the British could fumble out of their pockets, and wave it on the end of a more noticeable pole than the British could do their rather over-used bit of linen.

At the time the first issue of *The Week* appeared, there were still a lot of options open.

The war scare, resulting from Hitler's seizure of power, was the product of the notion that the Powers determined to maintain the principal provisions of the Treaty of Versailles, including those Powers established by that treaty, would now face a showdown.

At the same time, action on this old-fashioned national front was affected and often quite paralysed by the situation on another front. It was thought and spoken of at the time as the "class" front. It might be more illuminating now to speak of the "vertical" and the "horizontal" fronts.

Right from the outset, there was the situation in which Hitler was seen as a menace "vertically", but the Russians, with their Comintern, appeared to be a menace "horizontally". The Russians were stirring up class war and ultimate revolution.

Snide critics of the military constantly quote the hoary adage that the generals are "always preparing for the last war". It may be true of generals. It is certainly true of politicians.

"When it comes to Russia," Claud said, "a lot of them, including a lot of men of good will, are really living somewhere around 1920."

Certainly there were quite a number of people who made a serious effort to evaluate Russian policy by a genuine study of what the Russians actually said and did. In Claud's experience, there were more of them in the Conservative party than in the Labour party.

(In the same way, there were people who, sometimes in close co-operation with, or identical with undercover correspondents of *The Week*, tried genuinely to evaluate German policy. Like the producers of *The Week* they had, for instance, read *Mein Kampf* and taken it seriously.)

But a majority were still fuzzy with the hang-over from the early years of the Russian Revolution. They had never, Claud angrily alleged, really studied the speeches of Lenin at the time when the New Economic Policy was being introduced. In consequence, they missed the fact that this was an event as crucial as the Revolution itself. It was certainly so in its effects upon Russian attitudes to the rest of the world. It was clear, or at least, according to Claud, it ought to have been, that Lenin was talking about what was later called "co-existence". And Lenin was saying that it was not only a possibility but a necessity for Russia. He called it "a certain equilibrium".

The possibility of such an equilibrium over any lengthy period was denied then by Trotskyists and "left deviationists" in Russia. It was denied equally by Right Wing extremists in the West. In the 1960s it continues to be denied in Peking, and to be proclaimed in Moscow.

If, Claud maintained, the New Economic Policy and its consequences had been properly studied and understood in London and Paris, it would have been obvious that for a very long time from then on, Russian foreign policy was going to be totally, almost recklessly defensive. It had to be. It was not based on abstract or pious general beliefs in peace. When the Russians talked of peace and non-aggression they meant it. They had to. Westerners hoaxed themselves into the idea that all this was a mere smoke-screen. But they could have seen, starting with Lenin and the New Economic Policy and following through, that it was no smoke-screen. The economic condition of Russia absolutely required not only peace but the maximum possible co-operation with the capitalist states in terms of trade and concessions to foreign capital operating in Russia itself.

People would argue that Lenin's policy was intended as a very brief *reculement pour mieux sauter*. The jump could come any time. But it is fairly easy to deduce that Lenin already had in mind the likelihood, though not the certainty, that this period of slowly shifting equilibrium would have to last a very long time indeed. And his successors certainly acted on that assumption. The policy of defence, of paying almost any price to postpone or prevent a united capitalist attack on Russia, reached its climax in the Russo-German Pact of 1939. It was, in fact, very much in the orthodox Bolshevik tradition of the Treaty of Brest-Litovsk which Trotsky opposed and Lenin insisted on. His opponents saw it as a monstrous betrayal of Russia to the German imperialists. Lenin argued that it was not a choice but a necessity. A vast and seemingly catastrophic retreat was essential if anything were to be preserved at all.

"He felt, you see," I once heard Claud explaining to a youthful enquirer and critic, "that it's always better to have forty per cent. of something than 100 per cent. of damn all."

Those who in the early Thirties still saw Russia as an aggressive menace could always produce plenty of evidence. It was provided by agents inside Russia, men worthy to be believed because they were on the spot. In fact, of course, a great many of these people were drawn from Russian or Russian-speaking circles bitterly opposed to the régime. Not many of them could bring themselves to treat the "philosophy" of Bolshevism seriously. Many of them often believed their own wildest stories.

But so far as Britain and the West in general were concerned, the doctrine of "equilibrium" could be considered in a different and, in a sense, more realistic way.

You could believe that Russian policy was defensive, and that reports of Russian aggressive intentions were hot air. You could go further. You could examine the views of people who agreed that a direct military attack from the east was a nonsensical idea. But the Russians, it was said, would achieve the same ends by subversion. The Comintern would be their instrument. They would be at it, particularly in India, but also in Britain and France through the medium of the Communist parties. But there were also long-sighted observers who believed that as and when it came to the crunch, Moscow would carry its defensive policy to the logical extreme. It would, if the compensations were big enough, always in the end restrain the Comintern and its parties, rather than allow a situation to develop in which their activities could be used as a *casus belli*.

So the equilibrium would be maintained. But, as Lenin had pointed out in the early 1920s, it would be an equilibrium always shifting gradually in favour of Russia. Every year gained for Russian reconstruction and economic development was going to tilt the balance that way. From which the conclusion could very naturally be drawn that the thing to do was to go for the Russians at the earliest possible moment. Or at least to get someone else to go for them. Someone else, meaning, without any need to spell it out, Germany.

In that way, the tilt of the balance would be stopped. And an internecine war in the West would be averted.

It was a perfectly intelligible conclusion. It seemed to make quite a lot of sense to a lot of people in London and Paris. Equally realistic people in Moscow also saw that it made sense to a lot of leading British and French politicians. In fact, it was so easily intelligible and so apparently sensible, that it was the dominant factor in the thinking of some of the most politically powerful thinkers in all three capitals right through the Thirties, through the Russo-German Pact, and up to the moment of the final German attack upon Russia.

For obvious reasons, this notion, however realistic, was not one which the British press much liked to present without the use of a great deal of mouth-mush. Occasionally articles or speeches by Ukrainian refugee leaders in London or Paris were reported. It was desirable to offer them some little open encouragement in addition to that provided behind-the-scenes.

But these utterances were usually too frank, too "harshly realistic" to be exposed to the British public view. There was a consensus that they somehow tended to give the game away.

As Claud put it, this was not exactly a conspiracy of silence. It was a conspiracy conducted, like deaf and dumb language, by signs supposed to be intelligible only to the conspirators. For this reason the first issue of *The Week* drew emphatic attention to this type of realistic design.

The date towards which all concerned with *The Week* had so fast, so furiously and, as many people declared, recklessly moved, was 29 March 1933. The first story in the issue which on that day dropped for the first time onto the breakfast tables was "Black-Brown Plan". It read:

> Dominating all international developments of the week are the plots and counterplots now going on in London and the European capitals over the Mussolini-Hitler four-power plan, billed as a plan for co-operation between Italy, Germany, Great Britain, France: its announced object to "improve atmosphere", postpone war, revise treaties. First impressions were that the big ballyhoo of MacDonald's visit to Rome was an indication that the plan was just another "gesture". Investigation of behind-the-scenes activities shows that the plan and the negotiations arising out of it are opening moves in a new phase of the present pre-war situation in Europe.
>
> Essential are the facts (1) that this is primarily a Black-Brown-Fascist plan arranged between Hitler and Mussolini some time before MacDonald got to Rome, and (2) that as a result of it Great Britain has come out officially for the first time on the side of Treaty revision.

Most sensational and significant of the proposals now being discussed is that put forward in private negotiations last week by Arthur Rosenberg, former Editor of the Nazi newspaper *Völkischer Beobachter* and Hitler's principal liaison man for dealings with foreign governments, foreign financiers, industrialists, newspaper owners. Rosenberg has definitely proposed in Warsaw and London that the question of the Polish Corridor, most spectacular stumbling block to Treaty revision, should be settled—as between Germany and Poland—by giving to Poland, in exchange for concessions to Germany in the Corridor, a slice of Russian Ukraine. This idea has for years played a prominent role in all attempts to form a united anti-Soviet front among the capitalist powers. In an article published just before his accession to power, Hitler himself strongly hinted at the dismemberment of Russia as a solution of the acute rivalries between the European powers. At the present moment Rosenberg's proposal is of peculiar importance and immediacy: the rivalries between the European powers have entered upon an acutely dangerous stage. War between the revisionists and the anti-revisionists is everywhere discussed as an early possibility. In this situation Rosenberg's plan and others similar to it are being actively discussed in London, Berlin and Warsaw.

It certainly cannot be said yet that the Rosenberg plan has reached the stage of "official" consideration in London. The British Government is however seriously exploring the possibilities of lining up Poland with Germany, Italy with Great Britain.

Present indications are that the Four Power Pact as proposed by Mussolini in Rome is likely to be expanded under pressure of the Little Entente and Poland to include other powers besides the four originally suggested. Such expansion will give full scope for the further extension of the manoeuvres at present going on. Hope of aligning Poland with the Fascist bloc is based largely on the comparatively recent weakening of the connections between France and Poland. The present Polish Government knows that Poland can no longer rely definitely on French support in the event of serious trouble with Germany. Important elements in the present French Government profoundly embarrassed by the Polish connection are known to be anxious to cut the connection altogether. It has been suggested publicly that the existing agreements should be denounced, and a new one made in which military action

would be expressly ruled out. A member of the Cabinet was heard
to remark at a private gathering in Paris recently that France
would certainly be obliged sooner or later to terminate her
engagements to Poland. On the other hand French relations with
Soviet Russia are better than they have been at any time since
the revolution.

It is now definitely known that when MacDonald came through
Paris from Rome on his way to London last week, the French
Government immediately suggested to him that Russia should be
invited to take part in any conversations arising out of the
Mussolini proposal. This MacDonald refused. And now that it
seems probable that other powers besides the original four will
have to be asked to join the discussions, the French Government
is again pressing the British Government to include Russia. At the
moment of writing the British Government is steadily refusing to
do any such thing.

MacDonald himself is still considering using the supposed
"improvement" of the atmosphere in Europe after the hysterical
war scare prevailing just before his visit to Geneva and Rome as
an occasion for announcing that now is the time to take advantage
of this more agreeable atmosphere to call together the World
Economic Conference. It is not improbable that an announcement
of this kind will be made shortly.

It seemed clear, at the time, to the simplest mind that
conflict over Treaty Revision between the Powers west of the
Russian frontier was a genuine possibility. Perhaps it really was.
Perhaps not. In any case, it was equally evident that in such
circumstances it was desirable to consider whether the charge
could not be exploded in another direction, eastwards.

Since calculations of this kind were nicely balanced, every
overt row, or mere cause of friction, between the British and
Russian governments assumed a special importance. Most
people who lived during that period may have only a dim
memory of what the "Metro-Vick" trial in Moscow was about,
if, indeed, they remember it at all. But it was perhaps a crucial
testing of strength. Or, to return to the question of co-existence,
a probe of the state the equilibrium had reached.

The great British engineering firm of Metropolitan-Vickers
had got a big contract with the Russians for engineering con-

struction work. For a while, things went well. Everyone was satisfied. It seemed to be agreed that this type of concession could, as Lenin had predicted, be granted to capitalist firms by the Russian government.

Then some of the British engineers engaged on the project were accused by the Russians of wrecking and spying. One of them confessed, and two were convicted and imprisoned.

But the trial of strength had started a little earlier. Making realistic calculations, the dominant people in the Foreign Office thought this was a good opportunity to probe. They decided, as *The Week* reported in its first issue, to do a little something to exacerbate the affair. The intention was to force the Russians to show a bit of their hand.

Metropolitan-Vickers was in a different position. It was trying to do business. And since its chiefs had certainly not been born yesterday, they saw nothing at all startling in the news that some of its engineers had been caught acting beyond the line of strictly commercial duty. Perhaps a majority of the British public could still be led to believe that British engineers do not get up to that sort of thing, but the executives at Metropolitan-Vickers knew different. To them it was all in the game.

And if the game were played the Foreign Office way, there was more than an even chance that Metro-Vick would lose quite a bundle of money.

The result of this was that right in the middle of the hullabaloo over the arrest of simple-minded British technicians, an executive character from Metro-Vick made contact with *The Week*. Since he still lives and prospers, it is evidently impossible to give his name here. Perhaps one of the reasons why he lives and prospers is that he, like the editor of *The Week*, took for granted that telephones were tapped, mail intercepted. As a result his precautions were admirable. And when the two of them met, which they did several times during the trial and subsequent uproar, they were not observed.

A lot of what Mr. X told the editor of *The Week* was, in the nature of the case, confidential. The editor did, however, have an authoritative assurance that the Russians quite certainly had a good case, that those involved should take what was coming to them without too much international rumpus, and that the desirable thing to do was not to let Anglo-Soviet trade be interrupted by the wild men (or "hawks" in the jargon of today).

The probe was not quite conclusive. When the Foreign Office, as disclosed exclusively by *The Week*, tried to get the Russians to release Russian citizens involved in the affair, the Russians felt strong enough to refuse. Ten years earlier they would probably have thought it wiser to knuckle down.

That was round one to the Russians. They also sentenced two of the British engineers to imprisonment, winning round two on points.

The British government, to the anger and embarrassment of the traders at Metropolitan-Vickers, imposed a trade embargo between Britain and Russia. Some of those opposed to this course claimed that it was like friends of the prisoner, following the judge's verdict, retaliating by slashing the tyres of the judge's car.

However, though everyone lost money, and the international atmosphere was made rather more than usually sulphurous by the embargo, it could be held that this round went to the British government. The Russians released the British prisoners.

The Week, appearing for the first time at a moment soon after the affair had begun, was the only publication in Britain to deal with the matter without flags waving. It had, in this momentarily lonely position, the comfort to be derived from the friendly co-operation of the big man from Metro-Vick.

The Foreign Office, it reported, is "playing high".

The shouting and the tumult over the arrest of British engineers in Moscow somewhat subsided over the weekend. The press lay relatively doggo: but in spite of this lull in the publicity gale, the affair has in fact taken an exceedingly grave turn. Outstanding development of the weekend was the intervention of the British Foreign Office between Metropolitan-Vickers and the Soviet authorities: an intervention directed not towards conciliation but towards stiffening the attitude of the British company.

It will be remembered that on Thursday the Soviet Embassy in London issued a statement offering to release on bail three of the English engineers and indicating that in the case of the fourth the investigation was still proceeding, and that he would probably be released on bail. It is now known that Metropolitan-Vickers were perfectly prepared to accept this proposal and to put up bail. A high official of the company had actually arranged to go to the Embassy to talk the matter over.

It was at this point that the Foreign Office intervened. It was the Foreign Office which dissuaded Metropolitan-Vickers from accepting the Russian offer and the company official cancelled his visit to the Russian Embassy. At the suggestion of the Foreign Office the company now framed a very different communication from the one it had intended to send. It informed the Soviet authorities on Friday that the company could not accept the offer of bail for the British subjects concerned alone: either the Soviet authorities must release all the prisoners—including Russian subjects—on bail or else the company would not bail out the four British engineers. As basis for this striking request, the company offered the fact that it was confident that all the accused of both nationalities are equally innocent.

The point which gives serious political significance to this is that, at the moment when the Foreign Office intervened and suggested this form of demand upon the Russians, the authorities at the Foreign Office were fully aware that the Russians could not accept such a demand. A further fact of somewhat sinister significance, is that within twenty-four hours of the despatch of the company's demands to Moscow, the Foreign Office allowed it to be known that it was seriously considering placing an embargo on Soviet imports to this country. During the weekend the Foreign Office attitude moderated slightly: partly owing to a definite and unambiguous statement by the Soviet authorities to the effect that the trial of the arrested engineers in Moscow would be held regardless of attempts to exert pressure from abroad, and partly to the agitation expressed on behalf of certain German banking interests which feared that if Russian exports to England are barred, the Soviets will be unable to repay their German banking credits.

Present indications are that the Foreign Office attitude is again stiffening. The complete rupture not only of trade relations but of diplomatic relations is a definite possibility of the next three or four weeks.

Regarding the background of the arrests themselves, one story which has reached London is worth recording as it seems to offer a fairly reasonable explanation of the situation. This is that the engineers in question were technically guilty of some form of sabotage but that they were innocent in the sense that they were the unconscious dupes of other interests. Instances of foreign engineers being used without their own knowledge for purposes of sabotage are known to have occurred on several occasions in the life of the Soviet Union.

In this connection the sensational but well vouched for piece of information which has reached us from an exceedingly well posted and cautious source in Berlin regarding the activity of certain foreign oil companies in Germany is worth recording. According to this source, the burning of the Reichstag was regarded by these foreign oil interests as an excellent opportunity to attempt to force a breach between Germany and the Soviet Union and thus remove from the German market the active competition of Derop (the Russian oil agency operating in Germany). How far these foreign oil interests acting in concert with certain elements in the Nazi government actually helped to plan the fire is unknown. Certain is that persons previously connected with those oil interests were connected with the planning of the fire and that within an hour or two of the outbreak of the fire a lightning raid was made on the office of Derop. The police paid especial attention to searching of the lift shaft in the Derop office building and it is understood that they had expected to find there some incriminating document planted by the hostile oil interests in question. Three or four days ago the Derop offices in Cologne were raided and the employees arrested.

(A good deal later, Sir Henry Deterding, then head of Royal Dutch Shell, and a most enthusiastic anti-Soviet operator, saw fit to issue a denial of stories originating in *The Week* to the effect that he had any hand in the burning of the Reichstag.)

Turning to the home front, *The Week* saw signs of movement in a situation which the press in general could have led one to suppose stagnant. Admitting that the paper had the facts about right, critics maintained that it was regarding them with starry eyes. Perhaps the critics were right. *The Week*, as its editor often acknowledged, had a tendency to imagine that more was happening, and happening more quickly, in Britain than was actually the case.

Negotiations—it wrote—on the proposal to form a united front of British Labour to resist wage cuts, reduction of social services, the Means Test, war preparations, and other manifestations of the preliminary stages of Fascism, overshadowed in importance all other domestic political events of the past week. First phase of these negotiations came to an end late last week leaving the Independent Labour Party definitely lined up with the Communist Party on most important questions of immediate policy, and the Joint Council of the TUC, Labour Party and Parliamentary Labour Party definitely rejecting proposals of Communists for a meeting to discuss common action. The attitude of the Joint Council was more or less of a foregone conclusion. Its policy was decided by about half a dozen quick thinking bosses at Transport House, above all Citrine, General Secretary of the Trade Union Congress. New and significant, however, is the fact that there was serious opposition to the policy finally adopted within the innermost circles of Trade Union Congress and of Labour Party. Several highly conservative members of both bodies expressed the opinion that a mistake was being made. The replies of the Labour Party Executive and of the TUC to the first overtures from the Communists indicated clearly a distinct divergence of opinion between them, the Labour Party being a great deal more friendly in its manner of address than the TUC. The Parliamentary Labour Party is on the whole still more inclined seriously to consider the Communist proposals than the Labour Party.

At the present stage of the negotiations the following facts emerge. First, there is strong opposition to the Joint Council's decision developing within the Labour movement both among the rank and file and among Labour candidates and officials. Strenuous efforts are being made effectively to organise this opposition. Expert opinions on the outcome differ: present indications are that the opposition movement will develop strongly, will be effective in encouraging local united action by the rank and file, but that it will be a long time before it is able to reverse the policy of the big bosses. Secondly the statement of the Joint Council explaining its attitude shows clearly that no difference of principle separates the official heads of the Labour movement from the left wing Liberals. The statement was heartily endorsed by *News Chronicle*, leading Liberal newspaper. Possibilities of some sort of amalgamation between the right wing Labour and left wing Liberal people have long been discussed and numbers of Liberal Members of Parliament are known to regard such amalgamation possibly under the leadership of Lloyd George as an eventual certainty.

Proof of the seriousness of the strength of the opposition to the right wing bosses within the labour movement is afforded by the fact that this opposition forced the machine into following the Communist lead in protesting against the outcome of the Meerut Case, and into organising on a national scale a demonstration in Hyde Park on Sunday May 7. [This was a case in which British and Indian citizens were condemned for allegedly subversive activities in India. An attempt to organize Trade Unions in India was part of their supposed crime.] There has been no demonstration of the kind in Hyde Park for several years, and even then the demonstrations used to be organized for May by the London district alone; it is much longer since there was a May demonstration in Hyde Park organized on a national scale. Communists and ILP are organizing a militant demonstration for May 1. They are protesting strongly against decision of Labour leaders to hold their demonstration on 7, pointing out that May 1 is traditional day of labour demonstration. Nevertheless it is extremely significant that the labour movement's demonstration is going to be held at all, even on May 7.

The tail-piece of this first issue struck an exceedingly sour note. It concerned both the international and the domestic fronts.

It had one absurd but unfortunately quite predictable effect. Predictable that is to say by everyone except the editor. He had been warned of this particular effect, but shrugged it off. He said that even in London people could not be quite so foolish as that.

But they were. And a number of earnest people who, though not bothering to subscribe, had been shown the paper, wrote to protest that *The Week* was evidently anti-Semitic. Claud noted with interest that none of these letters came from Jews. They were all from earnest Gentiles.

"They have," he suggested to friends, "a guilt complex about the Jews. And how well-justified they are in having it.

But it leads to this absurd result. They are saying, in effect, that it is all right to criticize rich men, on condition they are not Jews. It is all right to expose selfishness and pusillanimity provided no Jews are accused of those very general defects of character. Yet everyone knows that Jews themselves are the first to expose and deride their own weaknesses. They are a great deal more capable of self-criticism than the English, and in this resemble the Scots. In my opinion it is the type of Gentile who writes these letters who is really guilty of anti-Semitism. By desiring that ill-behaved Jews be treated differently from ill-behaved Gentiles, he is already, subconsciously, discriminating against the Jews."

This was the story which caused the protests:

Widespread boycott of German goods by Jews as protest against Fascist persecution of the Jews has given rise to stories of joint action by big Jewish financiers against Germany. These stories are at the moment nonsense. The vigorous moves at the beginning of the anti-Fascist campaign among the London Jews were in large degree due to the activities of the British Anti-War Council established as a result of the Anti-War Congress representing around thirty million manual and intellectual workers at Amsterdam last August. Delegates to Amsterdam Congress pledged themselves to fight against Fascism on ground that Fascism leads to war. Board of Deputies of British Jews meeting last Sunday adopted much more cautious attitude than that taken at earlier meetings in East End. Back of this caution was the fact that so far from being anxious to line up for common action, the big Jewish financiers, notably Rothschilds, are extremely alarmed remarking plaintively that the debts owed them in Germany are now so large that it is now the creditor not the debtor who has to watch his step.

5 *"Little Liar"*

THE immediate outcome of the first number of *The Week* was startling in the most negative possible sense.

"Unfortunately," Claud wrote in later reminiscence, "no one had warned me that the *Foreign Affairs* list was years old. Forty per cent. of the people on it were dead, indifferent, or had radically changed their attitude to world affairs. Also there had been a serious miscalculation regarding the mentality of the British public—its readiness to jump for something new or love the highest when the editor saw it. The number of paying customers secured by that first circulation was seven. Just seven." (He had reckoned on a minimum of 800.)

"The news," he records, "spread rapidly among my friends and acquaintances that my big idea had misfired. Personally, since I regarded the existence of the 'pool' as a mathematical certainty, I was not discouraged, although I could think of no convincing reason to offer anyone else as an explanation of my continued optimism."

(The "pool" is a reference to the idea of the "unfilled vacuum", derived from real or supposed calculations of Lord Northcliffe.)

Claud's light-hearted, not to say, flippant, explanation of the low response to his first issue was partly inaccurate and totally inadequate.

It was not, I understand, true that anything like forty per cent. of the people on the circularization list were either dead, or indifferent, or had changed their opinions. The list was not as old as all that.

Claud was right in supposing that he had over-estimated the public's readiness to jump for something new. He did not understand that their hesitation was in part due to the very newness of *The Week* itself. The stories, the approach, the angle of vision, the tone of voice, were, at the time, such as to leave a good many potential readers merely numb.

Apart from that, there were certainly a lot of people prepared to jump for something new. The subsequent success of *The Week* proved it. But they, being serious people, were not prepared to jump through a hoop. And, as many of them stated later, they thought that was approximately what they were being asked to do. Claud, knowing the authenticity of his own sources, had a starry-eyed, childish desire to warn as many people as possible of the horrid doings in the woodshed. It never crossed his mind that the outsider might question the authority of this unknown bearer of dire tidings. He expected to be attacked for venturing to bear such tidings and thus upsetting officially fostered complacency. He did not expect to be simply disbelieved. When he cried "Fire! Fire!" he was quite unprepared for a situation in which the only answer was "Little liar!"

The potential readers wanted to see some sort of credentials. They were offered absolutely none. The "nasty-looking bit of work" was, after all, entirely anonymous. Not a name, known or otherwise, to be seen. No mention of editor, correspondents or sponsors. And, to complete the generally disquieting effect, the issue was dated, but not numbered. Surely, it was thought, if these people were genuinely proposing to publish a weekly news-sheet, and asking for an advance subscription of twelve shillings per year, they ought to have put "No. 1" on their first issue. The omission was seen as significant. Naturally, those circularized had no way of knowing that the idea of numbering the issue had somehow slid into the "admin" category and been entirely forgotten.

This initial meagreness of response to *The Week* proved to Claud that the British intelligentsia was as conventional in its thinking as he had supposed; it was conditioned to believe that, after it had read at least two daily newspapers and a couple of weeklies, it must be in possession of an adequate supply of relevant facts. It was certainly true at that time, and possibly is still true now, that even alert and intelligent people found it extraordinarily hard to believe just how much they were taking for granted concerning matters outside their own immediate field of knowledge.

As Claud often pointed out at the time, you could sit in a club talking, say, to a judge and a couple of other leading lawyers. They would disclose, almost as a matter of course, astounding miscarriages or perversions of justice behind some affair which the newspapers were treating as perfectly straightforward and above-board.

But if, as conversation proceeded, you mentioned that some major event on the diplomatic front, or behind it, was being totally misrepresented by the press and the official spokesmen, those same lawyers were apt to be sceptical. In that field they were inclined to believe what they were told. Part of the purpose of *The Week* was to enable people to look over the hedge from the field they knew to the one adjacent.

Another under-water snag of which Claud was almost entirely unaware until he hit it, was the prevailing British attitude to the Communists. It was, in fact, a characteristic and revealing feature of the early 1930s in Britain. But nothing in Claud's experience in Europe or America had prepared him for it.

In Europe, above all Central Europe, Communism was of course a major issue. The Communist party was a factor in domestic politics that it would have been idiotic to ignore. Any serious political discussion which failed to take into account the relationship of this or that political group to the Communist party was merely frivolous.

Odd as it may seem now, in the early 1930s thoughtful Americans, too, discussed Communism and Communists openly and seriously. These were subjects, that is to say, neither for conspiracy nor for taboo. The American Communist party was tiny. It was also rent by dissention. And hardly anyone read the *Daily Worker*. But, at least at that time, the Americans were a volatile people. Until October 1929 a considerable majority of them had believed that the existing economic system was probably going to solve all life's material problems; and even if it failed to do that, it was still the only way of life anyone between the Rhine and the Pacific could be expected to take seriously. With the stock market crash and the subsequent economic earthquake all that changed. Far more than in Britain, Americans almost immediately began to ask fundamental, if often naïve, questions about the basis of the whole system. One might perhaps say that while an Englishman would go so far as to admit that the world slump indicated some lapse on the part of the Almighty, the Americans at once began to wonder whether the Almighty was there at all, or to turn Manichaean and think the Devil must have been in charge for some time.

As a result of his European and American pre-conditioning, Claud quite failed to understand that there was anything more than very mildly explosive matter in, for instance, the story "United Front". He did not until then grasp what was really a quite elementary fact of life in the Britain of the day. To report sympathetically on anything whatsoever which chanced to be favoured by the Communists was virtually to proclaim oneself a Communist, or at best a Communist sympathizer. And to be a sympathizer with the Communists on any issue was in some ways worse looked upon than to be an actual Communist.

An ironic feature of the situation was that if Claud had at that time had any contact with the Communist party he would no doubt have been advised by some skilful strategist in the party to tread more carefully. It was his total lack of contact with the Communists in those early days which paradoxically caused him to write in a way that got him immediately suspected of being a Communist, long before he actually became one.

Asked point-blank whether he was not, at the very least, a Communist sympathizer, he replied truthfully enough. He had not, he said, had any opportunity at all to study the goings-on of the British Communists. As for sympathy, he certainly sympathized with some of the things they seemed to be trying to do. Rashly, considering the atmosphere in Britain at the time, he would talk about the Comintern or the Soviet Union in the way he had been accustomed to do in New York or pre-Hitler Berlin. He would freely explain, for instance, that he thought an international organization such as the Comintern had advantages which outweighed its obvious disadvantages. He thought it a matter for discussion and argument. But in London in the early Thirties it was not, except in a rather limited intellectual circle, a matter for argument at all. Hardly anyone not a Communist could think of the Comintern as in any possible way beneficial. And no Communist could admit, except to closest intimates, that it might in any possible way be noxious.

If the public at which that first issue of *The Week* was aimed were a little slow on the uptake, the British Security Services were a great deal quicker.

As early as its fourth issue, *The Week* had to complain in an editorial note that it was being held up for as much as 36 hours in the post office.

In those days a document posted in Victoria Street early on Wednesday afternoon was supposed to reach London addresses late on Wednesday evening, and country addresses by the first post Thursday morning. If it failed to do so, there were reasons to suppose that something unusual was going on.

By an accident which some will think extraordinary, Claud happened to know a girl who later became engaged to a man who was an intimate friend of a man who had just resigned from the Security organization. Claud was thus fairly well-informed as to the attitude of the C.I.D. Special Branch of M.I.5.

Given the situation at the time, the position of the Security people was simple and intelligible. The whole point was that the position of *The Week* was neither simple nor intelligible. If any Intelligence Officer can report that this or that organization has started a new publication and is saying such and such, all he has to do after that is to keep a file of the publication and report on anything particularly subversive it may say.

But *The Week* could not be fitted into any of the ready-made slots. Its editor had resigned from *The Times* for, it was understood, leftish reasons. Probably, therefore, a Communist.

But then the man comes to England and, so far as can be ascertained, makes no contact at all with the Communists. True, he rents an office from the leftish Union of Democratic Control. But he is far from following the general line of their propaganda. Moreover, he is very little seen in those intellectual circles of the Left where he might be expected to circulate. Most of his associates seem to be professional people of one kind and another. Above all, he seems to be on excellent terms with numerous bankers and stockbrokers.

I suppose that all Intelligence Services provide a kind of distorting mirror of the general anxieties of the society they work in. What is felt by people in general (I am not speaking here of the very rich) as a more or less nagging uneasiness, becomes, in the minds of Intelligence men, a state of acute nervous tension. And of course it is always true that an Intelligence Service, living largely on secret funds, feels a particular need to justify itself. It cannot stage anything like a Trooping of the Colour to prove to the gaping public that the public is getting its money's worth.

Because of the mystery and uncertainty surrounding *The Week*, the Intelligence people mounted a very thorough operation. Claud at the time had taken a flat in Ebury Street, and this, as he learned from his private contact, was for a time under a 24-hour watch. At that time, and perhaps still, it was more or less routine procedure for people doing such a watch to use as their cover the sort of road-mending job always going on somewhere in London. Residents at the Victoria end of Ebury Street were naturally not surprised to see just at that time evidence that some work of the kind was about to be undertaken in their section. Poles and trestles appeared, and also one of those little wigwam-type tents which are used by night-watchmen on the site of road-mending operations. The night-watchman was in this case not watching anything except Claud's flat.

In the normal course of entirely unpolitical affairs, Claud had a good many visits from young women and girls. Their times of arrival and departure were scrupulously noted by the watchman. This nearly brought disaster to the engagement of the girl I have mentioned who was to marry a friend of the man who knew someone who had just quit working for M.I.5. For this latter man, on hearing the name of the girl, and not aware that his friend was just about to get engaged to her, remarked with interest that her name was quite familiar to him. She was, he said, a member of Claud Cockburn's "organization". Pressed for details, he said that she had on several occasions been seen entering his Ebury Street flat at a late hour of the evening, and leaving it again at five or six in the morning, and once or twice at breakfast time.

The girl's parents were socially and financially prominent. She had no political affiliations whatever. And the time she spent at the flat was not devoted to readings from the Marxist scriptures or attempts to convert her to any other political creed. But the Intelligence people considered it hopelessly naïve to assume that this was the case. They were convinced that she was being primed as an agent of someone or something. Or, even if they were not convinced of it, they felt it their duty to behave as though it were true.

As a result the girl herself became the object of what the army later termed "suspicious alertness". She was suspect. Her social contacts, many of them débutantes and the kind of young men who took débutantes dancing, were suspect, too. The dossier on her and her friends became quite fat.

A good many other girls, of the most total political innocence, got their names into the night-watchman's notebook. One of them was the niece, or ward, of some highly respectable landed gentry in the West country. The Intelligence people somehow got the idea that their respectability, and their commodious country home, were in reality a cover for subversive goings-on. The family interests did not, in fact, extend much beyond hunting, shooting and fishing. As a result of unusual clumsiness on the part first of a sleuth and then of a friendly chief constable, they learned to their extreme astonishment that they, and the guests at their frequent and innocuous house-parties, had attracted the suspicions of authority. The girl, who quickly guessed how the suspicions had arisen in the first place, was naturally far from eager to explain the matter.

The hold-up at the post office while the Intelligence people examined *The Week* was naturally vexatious. But Claud's complaint was not that *The Week* itself and all incoming correspondence were interfered with. It seemed to him the natural and inevitable thing for the authorities to do. What he noisily objected to was their leisurely manner of doing it, which caused, he said, quite unnecessary delay.

As for the surveillance of himself and his friends, and the fact that his telephone was tapped, these too appeared to him the perfectly natural and predictable reaction of people in power to their critics. He was more irritated by two different types of reaction among his own friends and acquaintances.

There were those who became furiously indignant in a liberal-minded fashion. They declared these invasions of privacy outrageous. And they were visibly shocked by Claud's taking the proceedings as a matter of course.

Much more annoyingly, there were others who, unable to believe that such things could possibly happen here, said, or at least hinted, that Claud must be suffering from persecution mania. Since he had quite irrefutable evidence that these things really were happening here, this incredulity exasperated him. It was personally irritating to be disbelieved. But he saw in this incredulity a more important meaning. It was, he felt, just because the British public at the time refused to believe in the ordinary realities of political battle, that people whom he considered villainous were enabled to get away with so much villainy.

"It isn't," he insisted, "that I mind my telephone or anyone else's being tapped. It would be ridiculous for the Intelligence people not to tap telephones. What I do mind is the hypocritical pretence that the high-minded British government wouldn't dream of doing anything so terribly un-British."

The appearance on 20 April of the fourth issue convinced a few of those who had thought *The Week* was to be a once-only affair, that it might stagger on a bit longer. They felt that it was at least trying to carry on.

On the other hand, the editorial note complaining about post office delays caused a good many to think that hostile forces were closing in and that the end would come sooner rather than later.

One development was, I suppose, significant of the oddly nervous state of mind among sections of the public. A number of the existing subscribers wrote asking that their names be removed from the subscription list. They judged, from the note about the post office, that *The Week* was deemed subversive by the authorities, and they had no wish to be connected in any way with such an enterprise.

The issue itself suggested that if the paper was already in hot water, it certainly was not trying to cool the water by saying anything likely to bring a smile of approval to powerful official and political faces. It appeared at a moment when preparations were being made for the World Economic Conference. Everybody who knew anything knew that Anglo-American tensions were more than usually tight-drawn. As a result both of the New Deal in the United States and the new Conservatism of the National government in Britain, the economic theories on which the two governments were being run were in fact in total contradiction. As often happened then and still happens today, even supposed insiders in London were quite ignorant of the real line of thought in Washington. There were people in London who seriously believed that the Americans were interested in somehow bailing Britain out. They had genuine faith in what later came to be called the "special relationship".

Personal questions were also involved. For Roosevelt it was a question of perpetually keeping up the momentum of the post-Hoover months in early 1932. For Ramsay MacDonald the aim, ludicrous though it may now seem, was to present himself as some kind of reincarnation of Woodrow Wilson who, with a mixture of Celtic idealism, sweetly diluted pink socialism, and rugged realism, was going to save the world from the result of its past sins.

Sweetness and light shone through the British press like the weather in the Garden of Eden just before they saw the apple.

It was thus startling for the still tiny but growing band of subscribers to *The Week* to read on 11 April a story headed "Beginning to Commence".

The heading was itself an ironic quotation from a remark by Ramsay MacDonald fuzzily designed to express optimism.

MacDonald's visit to U.S.A. [*The Week* wrote] is the result of (1) flanking movement smartly executed by Roosevelt immediately after Davis conversations with British Government (2) last-minute compromise between two factions in British Government itself. It will be remembered that at the moment of our going to press last week, proposal under discussion was that a *delegation* of British Ministers should go to Washington. As reported then, the idea was that such delegation should work out preliminaries of the World Economic Conference, hope being that these preliminaries would reveal readiness of British to make valuable trading concessions at the Conference: Roosevelt indicated that on the strength of such revelation, he might be able to use his influence with Congress in favour of a moratorium on debt payments due June 15. Snags to this plan were *unwillingness* of British to make any concessions, *determination* of dominant section of British Government to make no concessions at least until moratorium was in the bag.

Roosevelt refused help for moratorium until concessions were in the bag. The result deadlock.

MacDonald persuaded *The Times* to send up a big kite, suggesting desirability of a visit to Washington by Prime Minister. Wind proved unfavourable. Roosevelt made no response; hard-boiled members of British Cabinet became alarmed, suggested there was danger of MacDonald giving away too much if he was allowed to go alone, suggested at least somebody ought to go along with him as keeper. Lindsay, British Ambassador at Washington, visiting London, told the Cabinet from Roosevelt that a mere goodwill tour would result in nothing but hot air. Roosevelt could do nothing about the debt question simply on the strength of friendly talks with British Prime Minister. The whole plan lapsed. Then when negotiations with Davis for sending a ministerial delegation reached deadlock, Roosevelt took *The Times* off the shelf and issued his invitation to MacDonald.

Latest advices from Washington show sharp recrudescence of activity on the part of the manufacturers' lobby, directed chiefly against the British being allowed any concessions on the debts without guarantee of stabilization of the pound, cessation of exchange dumping by British, Japanese in foreign and American markets, powerful groups will push for special tariff against goods from depreciated currency areas. This represents answer from anti-inflationist industrialists to inflationists, who propose to meet situation by devaluing dollar, undercutting British Japanese that way. Significantly Garet Garrett, crusading mercenary on behalf of American heavy industry, publishes savage article along these lines *Saturday Evening Post*, highly influential American weekly entitled "The Economic Drive Against America".

By hindsight of course it might be possible to have headed the article "America's Economic Drive Against Britain".

At the end of 1931 [*The Week* continued] and at beginning of 1932 Garrett's articles were of first-class political importance in influencing American opinion in the direction of nationalism. One was reprinted as a pamphlet by the American Chemical Industrialist and circulated free by the hundred thousand as propaganda against the German Dye Trust and ICI.

This chilling analysis was followed in the same issue of *The Week* by a story entitled "Misgivings".

MacDonald's state of health is now a serious political factor. Colleagues watch it closely: Beaverbrook, anxious to get MacDonald out of the way and Baldwin into centre of his target, loses no opportunity to drop broad hints that MacDonald is unfit to carry on. MacDonald has stated on separate occasions that he is suffering from (1) loss of memory, (2) below par feeling or invisible lack of health. [This remarkably characteristic phrase was used by MacDonald himself to one of Claud's informants.]

On the occasion [*The Week* continued] of his last big speech in the House on unemployment, he spoke disjointedly, kept peering over his shoulder while speaking. He stated afterwards to a member of the Cabinet that the strain of the circumstances had somehow translated itself into a curious impression that there was a man in the gallery aiming to shoot him in the back. Incidents of this kind, together with steady falling off in the quality of his speeches, are giving ample ammunition to MacDonald's political enemies, some of them belonging to the extreme right wing inside the Cabinet. His friends in the Cabinet and those who consider his presence as head of the government politically indispensable, are anxious he should take a long rest to recover from the strain which seems to produce these occasional lapses in his powers of concentration. They are afraid, however, that in the event of too long a rest his enemies will succeed in ousting him anyhow.

I have already said that at the outset Claud was staggered by the extent to which people who might be supposed to be in the know in fact knew very little. As his range of acquaintance and information extended, his amazement and irritation tended to shift to a different target. He began to become increasingly maddened by the extent to which people who really did know a lot of the facts considered it perfectly reasonable that these same facts be withheld from public knowledge. Because no doubt of his long experience of Washington, he was particularly exasperated by what he considered the deliberate or unconscious blurring of the real state of Anglo-American relations. Upon many English people he made the impression of having an absurdly exaggerated affection and admiration for America and Americans. They were all the more surprised by the fact that he wrote about American policy in relation to Britain in terms which, had they appeared in an ordinary British newspaper, they would have considered most uncivilly hard-boiled, not to say insulting.

Thus, following up the earlier story of MacDonald's visit to Washington, he wrote a story under the title "Warning Shots". Indeed the title itself seems to us today even more prophetic than it did to people who read it at the time.

Of predominance and importance in the international situation, and sharply increasing the growing Anglo-American tension, is yesterday's decision of the American Government to prohibit the export of gold and the announcement that there will be no further attempts on the American side to stabilize the dollar on the international exchanges. We learn on good authority that this move was deliberately undertaken to coincide with the arrival of MacDonald in Washington today. It constitutes a warning shot in the economic skirmishing which is now developing into a pitched economic battle. Specifically, the fall in the dollar and the decision not to support it either by shipping gold or by any other means, is a means of bringing pressure to bear on the British representatives at Washington in order to force trading concessions.

Friends and well-wishers wondered sceptically whether the small voice of *The Week* could ever make itself heard above the din of official propaganda. To cheer them up Claud drew their attention to the question of blasphemy and swearing. He urged that an oath which in an unbelieving period or century lacks all force can be detonated with offensive vigour at other times and in other places. "Go to hell" is not in our place and time a forceful expression. On the other hand in a place or time where the person addressed really believes in hell the remark can have the effect of a dangerous curse. In, for example, Catholic Spain, there are innumerable oaths of which the basis is some obscene reference to the Virgin Mary, the Host, or the Lord God. Used by simple Catholic believers to another of the same persuasion, these oaths have a certain impact. In relatively pagan England they are at the best childish and at worst meaningless.

In other words, you cannot break a taboo unless the taboo exists. But if it does exist, however idiotic it may be, to break it in the slightest degree has a startling effect. The analogy with the situation created by the suffocating silences of the press in Britain was obvious enough.

"They have produced," Claud would tell his friends, "a situation in which the merest squeak has the effect of a scream."

As things turned out, the scream penetrated, with electric effect, to a rather unexpected quarter. Claud admitted that this effect took him entirely by surprise.

As the session of the World Economic Conference approached, and finally opened, *The Week* continued to shed disconcerting sidelights upon the affair, and upon MacDonald himself.

Illuminating—it wrote on June 14—is the fact that at the present moment the principal adviser on economic policy to MacDonald, Prime Minister and President of the World Economic Conference now in session at the Geological Museum in South Kensington, is Sir Arthur Salter, K.C.B. Salter is in high favour with MacDonald, is regarded by him as one of the most valuable and far-sighted of economic authorities and is likely to play an important role at the conference. Characteristic of Salter is a book called "Recovery" written by him and published last year. Although comparatively few individuals are mentioned in the book, which deals rather with more general economic factors, Salter came to the conclusion that he could not let the book go to press without special mention of one heroic figure, suitable to be classed with the outstanding "constructive" phenomena of the period. So he wrote as follows: "Some countries have declared a moratorium of their foreign obligations, others are likely to do so. Good constructive loans like those arranged by the League or the Central Banks or a man of such creative vision as Mr. Ivar Kreuger, are threatened with the bad." This was written within a few weeks before the suicide of Kreuger in Paris. By the time the discovery was made that among other creations of his vision were numbers of forged bonds, and that large numbers of his operations were not merely grossly fraudulent but actually illegal, Salter learnt to his distress that it was now too late to withdraw the book or to alter the unfortunate passage.

This paragraph naturally delighted Sir Arthur Salter's fellow economists. At least two of them took out subscriptions to *The Week* on the strength of it. There is no record that it

did more than pin-prick the eminent economist himself.
MacDonald however felt as usual that he had been personally
insulted. In conversation not only with friends but with others
who were, as MacDonald himself would have said, "disloyal"
enough to report his remarks to *The Week*, he blabbered about
the matter at some length. Naturally most of his hearers thus
learned of Sir Arthur's deplorable slip for the first time. They
noted with interest that MacDonald appeared not in the least
bothered by the fact that his favourite economist and trusted
adviser had so recently regarded the late Ivar Kreuger as a
model of all that a modern financier should be. What bothered
and enraged him was simply that anyone should have drawn
attention to Sir Arthur's attitude in this unseemly and, as it
seemed to MacDonald, virtually blasphemous manner.

At the time Claud was aware of only one person who to his
certain knowledge was regularly, and with gleefully malign
intent, drawing MacDonald's attention to *The Week*. Later it
emerged that there had been several who had amused themselves in this fashion. They were aware after close observation
of the Prime Minister that he suffered not only from delusions
of grandeur, which everybody knew, but also from a tendency
to persecution mania. This being so they thought *The Week*
was just the thing to make him hop and quiver. As the sequel
showed they were right.

It was not only the nasty little frivolities such as the Salter
story which upset MacDonald. It was also *The Week*'s running
commentaries, both serious and ribald, on the realities behind
the conference. Thus in the issue of 5 July its main conference
story was headed "The Good Old Daze".

The panic jitters into which what remains of the World
Economic Conference has been thrown by flat American rejection of stabilization of the dollar, are partly the result of a series
of misunderstandings and miscalculations regarding the absolute
and relative importance of the personalities round Roosevelt in
their relation to the President, to one another, and to the general
situation. Hence when Moley, heavily publicized head of the
"brain trust", had agreed to a formula in London, its rejection by
Roosevelt came as a shattering surprise. Part reason for this was
the failure to grasp the present importance of the big speculators

in America (headed by Bernard Baruch) who for a moment are a much more practical factor in the situation than clever Professor Moley, recently described by one of the best living observers of affairs in Washington as a "Mussolini and soda". It is the considered opinion of several members of the American delegation that Baruch has definitely exerted his influence with Roosevelt not as had been expected by some in the direction of stabilization, but rather in the direction of ensuring a maximum fluctuation of the exchanges peculiarly useful for speculative purposes.

For a considerable time after the incoming of the new Administration, Bernard Baruch was under something of a cloud, the cloud being about the size of the hand of Owen D. Young. Baruch's varied and important governmental and political activities had never diverted him from his principal life work which is speculation in everything from wheat and copper to marks and dollars. Two weeks ago someone referred in a conversation with a highly conservative London banker to "Mr. Baruch the international banker". The British banker was horrified. "My dear sir," he cried, "we don't call Mr. Baruch a banker over here; we call him a speculator."

Everyone knows now that the conference broke up in disorder and dismay. It not only failed to achieve any positive results. Its collapse and the collapse of the hopes which MacDonald and his associates had, for their own political purposes, caused the general public to build on brought about an actual worsening of a situation which had been bad enough in the first place.

From the standpoint of *The Week* an interesting aspect of the whole business was the fact that almost up to the last moment the British press was still purveying the preposterous pieces of optimism being peddled from No. 10 Downing Street. As so often happened in the Thirties, this type of deception boomeranged. In this particular case it boomeranged much to the advantage of *The Week*. The list of its subscribers was still of course pitifully small. On the other hand it had got itself talked about. And then the kind of thing happened which makes one feel that if *surrealisme* had not existed it would have been necessary to invent it. MacDonald himself suddenly gave *The Week* world publicity.

There was as there usually is in such situations a dotty kind of logic about the way things turned out. And to Claud at least it was a confirmation of his theory that the more people tried to suppress the facts, the greater is the explosive effect of even the smallest detonation, disclosing reality. MacDonald came to the conclusion that all the *sotto voce* rumours about impending disaster at the conference, all the cynical chat which never got into the columns of the British press, were in fact inspired by *The Week*. One morning he went down to the Geological Museum and called a special conference in the crypt. Leading journalists from the press of the entire world were present. A special conference of this kind naturally suggested that something momentous was about to be said.

As though under the guidance of some peculiarly diabolic theatrical director, MacDonald placed himself on a small temporary podium against a background of the bones of prehistoric animals, so worn, broken or unidentifiable that they were useless for exhibition in the museum itself and had been relegated to the crypt. After a few opening words of hope and glory MacDonald swept himself into a tirade against evil influences which he said were gnawing at "the very foundations of the noblest aspirations". He then reached into his pocket and produced a document. He waved it above his head. He held it in front of him and punched at it with his fist. "This, this," he choked, "is where you will find that all of this sort of thing is coming from."

He even read a line or two from the document and then paused to give an elaborately sarcastic laugh.

Claud could barely believe his eyes. For the document consisted of the familiar brown-on-buff pages of *The Week* which he had himself written only a few hours before. Since the passage which MacDonald had chosen to read exactly expressed what was known or suspected by at least a majority of the journalists present, his laughter did not get the response he had expected. Only a minority had up to that time even heard of *The Week*. They jostled forward to peer at whatever it was MacDonald was holding in his hand and to ask questions. MacDonald was only too happy to hand out not just one copy but two. The second he had apparently brought along for this very purpose—that is to say to give the journalists of the world ocular proof of the kind of villainy which was being manufactured in an obscure office in Victoria Street.

The journalists of course were not trying to read *The Week*, there was no time for that. They were simply scribbling down its address and the rates of subscription. By late that evening or the following morning the circulation of *The Week* had trebled. But more important and interesting from Claud's point of view was that the quality of the subscription list had also been profoundly changed. It now included the London bureau of every principal newspaper and news agency in the world, the press secretaries of most of the embassies and legations in London, and the representatives of a large number of foreign banking houses in the City of London.

6 Tin King

PERHAPS it is not true that *The Times* once ran the headline "Heavy Fog in Channel. Continent Isolated."

It certainly is true that when Britain crashed clumsily off the Gold Standard in 1931, Americans in London found sudden difficulty in changing dollars into pounds at their favourite bars.

The pound was fluctuating like a fever chart. It fell from a value of 4 dollars 86 cents to below 3 dollars 30 cents. An American newspaper correspondent, accustomed to change his dollars in his hotel bar, thought that in the circumstances the hotel people would be positively glad to get their hands on a sound currency.

He was gently rebuffed. They were sorry. But they really could not handle dollars any more. Too unstable. "Jumping up and down and all over the place those dollars are."

To Claud's sort of alien eye this insularity was not more than briefly amusing. In the circumstances of the early Thirties it was distressing. It reminded him unhappily of the dreadful scene at the end of Conrad's *Under Western Eyes*. The miserable central character confesses to treacherous behaviour. A villainous brute breaks his ear-drums with blows from his fist. Outside, the victim finds the Geneva street absolutely quiet. He does not hear the roar and clang of the approaching tram.

Even after the street-car named Depression had actually struck, a majority of British observers seemed to act as though they too suffered from broken ear-drums and myopia. The situation, it seemed, appeared to them as unpleasant, certainly, but essentially abnormal. And, as the former President Warren Gamaliel Harding found in his time, millions of people are happy to believe that there is such a thing as "normalcy". Their wish to return to it is like the longing to return to the womb. A vote-catcher who promises to take them there, catches votes. And anyone who denies it ever existed, and thus that there is any way of getting to it, is looked at askance.

Many looked very askance at *The Week*.

It would have been a ludicrous conceit for anyone to suppose that this little box of tricks was immediately going to persuade those millions that the abnormal situation was here to stay. So far as the great mass of newspaper readers was concerned, its effect was never going to be other than indirect. First, it would try to get more or less taboo subjects talked about by a few people in a way that formerly had seemed more or less taboo too. And, with some management and a lot of luck, it would even get these subjects written about in the magazines and the big press.

It might be able to do this, according to the calculation, because some people did not suffer from split ear-drums. And they knew, too, that "normalcy" had always been an illusion. They would start the talking.

Archie Harding sometimes felt that this calculation was over-optimistic. He admitted he was influenced by the low state of mental health and energy shown by the writers of letters to the B.B.C. He would add gloomily that this condition was apparently shared by the B.B.C. authorities themselves. Certainly a good many things that happened around the B.B.C. during the Thirties seemed to confirm his pessimism. His spirits reached a nadir at the time when the brilliant cabaret artist Ronald Frankau was invited to sing over the air. For this mass public he chose a song which had been very popular among cabaret audiences, called, I think, "Let's go wild". After various suggestions as to how to go wild, it had the line "Let's find Hitler and kick him in the pants". The B.B.C. chiefs read the script. They consulted the Foreign Office. Following these deliberations Frankau was officially informed that he might sing the song only on condition that for the name of Hitler was to be substituted "Carnera". Pathetically, Frankau argued that, apart from the fact that the change tended to take the point out of the song, the name of the mammoth boxer could hardly be made even to scan. It was no use. The original version was just the sort of thing that could bring a sharp protest from the German Embassy.

In the attic in Victoria Street this estimate of the public was enthusiastically denied. "Just because a lot of fuddled people write to your organization, which is partly responsible

for befuddling them in the first place, there's no reason
whatever to suppose that the majority of people are suffering
from arrested development any worse than we are. And most
of your bosses aren't fools. Some of them are just scared, and
most of the rest are intellectual and political delinquents. We
must not judge the public by them."

"So how will you reach people?"

"Through the alert, anxious, inquisitive minority."

"And how will you reach even that little lot?"

"By jolting them with surprising facts, told in language
they're used to in the public prints, not to mention your gas-
filled air. Where possible we must, however, proceed from the
known to the unknown."

This last principle was basic to the philosophy, if that is
not too pompous a word, and the strategy of *The Week*. The
paper would certainly have to write a lot about *la haute politique
internationale*. And some of that would seem to some readers a
sort of news from nowhere. Top-level politics was at best a
flickering film, a game being played according to rules which
it was tricky, not to say tedious, to master. There would be
informed and knowing people who understood the rules and
the tricks. They would be delighted, or horrified, as the case
might be, to see the game described the way they saw it, in
terms they used among themselves. They would by no means
be dumbfounded to see the Prime Minister depicted as being
on the ragged edge of certifiable lunacy.

But there were others outside this group of real or soi-disant
insiders. They were, in fact, the people on whose account the
annual subscription to *The Week* had been held down to 12
shillings, including postage. Particularly for their benefit,
though for the pleasure and edification of all, *The Week* must
as often as possible give space to a different kind of story.
Preferably about money.

The idea was that people, as a rough general rule, may be
taken to be a little more understanding, a little more realistic,
about money than they are about politics. Everyone has been
involved in some transaction or other involving money.
Naturally, high finance, like high politics, has for most people
an air of unreality. They feel, when reading about it, like non-
mystics reading of someone's mystical experience. Comparatively

few people in the West have had even indirect contact with
genuine mystics. But huge numbers have at least known a man
who knew a man who nearly saw a ghost. At least, while
naturally not believing in ghosts, he saw enough to convince
him that something pretty peculiar was going on in that house.
This kind of experience makes it easier to go a bit further and
get some sort of focus on mysticism.

In the same way, it was held, a story of high intrigue centred
on money was easier to grasp than one centred on long-term
international diplomacy. This was part of the "known to
unknown" process. People would move from what they knew
about money, to an understanding of what was going on in the
financial stratosphere. And that trip, in turn, would help them
to see as realities the facts, mostly dismaying, about things in
the political and diplomatic stratosphere too.

It was with this sort of consideration in mind that *The Week*
in an early issue turned its attention to the conflagration of the
French super-liner *Atlantique*. This enormously costly ocean
greyhound, pride of the French merchant marine, was swiftly
and mysteriously destroyed by fire. Some people were surprised
to find the editor of *The Week* taking a keen interest in the story.
It was not, they said, a political story. The editor said that, for
a start, all stories are in one way or another political. Secondly,
this was a perfect occasion to go from the known to the unknown.

"Whenever anything burns down," said the editor, "anything from the corner shop to a warehouse, everyone's first
thought is that somebody fired it for the insurance money. It's
one of the things people know that other people do. In this case
we have to find out from all sources in Paris and London
whether it's true and if so why. That will make a story everyone
can understand."

The Week ran the story in one of its earliest issues, under the
heading "Fire and Smoke".

The case of the burning of *Atlantique* is now before the French
Courts and stories of sabotage as cause of the burning are being
sedulously spread. We learn that true reasons for this fire well
known or suspected by shipping men are concealed under these
stories because (1) the French shipping interests and complicated
oligarchy of iron masters and industrialists wish to divert attention

from bad construction, corrupt and inadequate inspection (2) newspapers in France and elsewhere, fearing loss of shipping advertisements, are refusing to publish the fact that the construction of all model luxury liners is such that fire is ever-present menace. . . . Following is significant. M. Philipper is Chairman of *Chantiers de la Méditerranée*: also Chairman of the *Messageries Maritimes*: also powerful member of the Inspection Committee of the Bureau Veritas (Bureau which passed *Atlantique* as seaworthy). Thus he is able to order ships from his own dockyards, run them and have a hand in certifying them. Similarly interlocking appointments are common. We have in our possession an authenticated instance of a vessel passed by the Bureau Veritas as new and seaworthy which actually had large rust holes, with light shining through them, in plates just above the waterline.

In a later issue, *The Week* followed up at greater length. Since that early account was published, the paper reported, the case had developed into a first-class international financial battle involving the leading British insurance companies, the leading French shipping, insurance and steel interests, and the French government.

The prize in this knock-down and drag-out fight, which will reach its climax in the course of the next few weeks, is approximately £2,000,000 of insurance money.

The owners are trying to collect the whole amount. The insurance companies are withholding the money in an attempt to play for time while their agents in France collect sufficient evidence to support in a court of law their present sensational conviction, which is that the *Atlantique* was the victim neither of accident, nor of sabotage by workers, but of an arson plot carried out with the object of collecting the insurance money. . . .

The *Atlantique*, built at enormous expense, soon proved to be a white elephant. The ship, it turned out, was unable to enter her home port of Bordeaux, and had extreme difficulty in manoeuvring in her South American ports of call.

At the end of last November an enquiry was held at Bordeaux to determine what would have to be done in order to surmount these difficulties. The result of this enquiry was summed up in what is known as the Haarbleicher Report, an unpublished document of crucial importance in the case. The conclusion was that only by the most extensive and expensive alterations of the harbour at Bordeaux (widening etc.) would it be possible for the *Atlantique* to use the harbour properly. It was quite clear as a result of the Haarbleicher Report that the *Atlantique* was going to have to remain a white elephant for a long time to come. It was less than a month after the final preparation of the report that the *Atlantique* caught fire in a manner never publicly explained, and was reduced to a total wreck.

The British insurance companies were not at the time convinced that the vessel was really beyond repair, and made strenuous efforts to have her brought to an English dock for repairs. They were unsuccessful. Then the maritime enquiry was held at Bordeaux, and the results summed up in a report by M. de Bouraye. Despite constant and noisy demands for its publication, the contents of this report have been held carefully secret.

The report was, however, seen by a correspondent of *The Week*, and with the expenditure of a good deal of money was seen, too, by agents of the insurance companies concerned. The tendency of the report was to cast the strongest possible suspicion on an official of the *Atlantique*. It was at this point that the British insurance companies first began to believe that the fire had been arranged by the company for the purpose of collecting the insurance money.

The naming of names, the disclosure of the content of secret reports, and the absence of expected counter-action by those under fire, did a good deal to get *The Week* talked about. Evidently part of the story could have been supplied by Leftists in France, which surprised no one. But it was also obvious that much of it must have come from strategically placed informants in the City of London and in Paris. This did surprise many, and was unnerving for some.

As I have already indicated, Claud always paid special attention to his contacts with the City of London. "After all," he would say, "you can fake practically everything but you can't fake the Stock Market closing prices." It was his view that were he to be suddenly isolated on a desert island or in a hospital with nothing to read whatever but the *Financial Times* or possibly only the financial pages of *The Times*, he could still produce an issue of *The Week* which would be more informative than most of the national daily newspapers and the weeklies.

Money, he thought, was like the camera. People suppose that the camera cannot lie. This is untrue, because the camera is highly selective. And it is also true that financiers will lie their heads off in order to mislead you. But in the end there are those fatal stock market price figures, and financiers are more vulnerable to reality than politicians. According to the editor of *The Week*, this was the reason why there were more financiers in jail than politicians.

It is, regrettably, impossible to describe even today the City contacts of *The Week*. The disclosure could ruin their official positions, or at least embarrass them in their present activities.

I have often asked Claud to particularize somewhat about these people. After all, I have pointed out to him, it was a long time ago. To which he replies, reasonably enough, that "a confidence is a confidence, and should last for ever." I agree, rather disappointedly, with this view.

On being pressed to be a little more precise, Claud admits that among his principal sources in the City were two merchant banks, and a stockbroker whose brother-in-law was a very high-powered official of the Treasury. One of the principal partners in one of the merchant banks was the man who, with tears in his eyes, almost compelled the bank to lend a lot of money to an inventor whose invention subsequently proved invaluable to Britain in the early stages of the war. The man at the other merchant bank was, by origin, Italian. Under a long-assumed name he became—and already was when Claud knew him—an unofficial economic adviser to the government of the day.

Claud very much preferred the atmosphere of the City to that of Westminster. It seemed to him more genuine, more closely in touch with undeniable fact. Accordingly, he spent a great deal of his time there.

The City to some extent reciprocated. And on at least one occasion reciprocated to an extent which Claud found embarrassing. He had been invited to lunch at the City Club to meet a few important financial figures. He found himself seated between his host and a leading broker. I say leading because he was later ennobled, so I assume that he must have been a leader in his time. He did not catch Claud's name as they were introduced and sat down to lunch. After some general conversation, the broker said, "By the way, do you ever read a paper called *The Week*?" Claud said cautiously that he saw it "from time to time".

The broker said, "But you ought to read it *all* the time. It is the best-informed news-sheet in London."

Claud had just come from a terrible row with his secretary about the number of typing misprints which occurred in *The Week*. Still hot under the collar from this shindy, he said to the broker, "Well, if these fellows are as well informed as all that, why would they not have enough money to hire an efficient typist? I simply do not understand how people who are supposed to have that kind of information would be so inefficient in their product."

The broker looked at him with scorn.

"But you don't understand," he said, "about the misprints."

"But I do understand," Claud rashly said. "I think they are absolutely lousy."

"That's what you think," said the broker. "But if you were one of those who really knew things, and know what *The Week* is up to, you would understand that these misprints, as you call them, are a kind of code."

"Code?"

"Yes indeed, the misprints are supposed to indicate to some of us that the information is a piece of news between the lines of which we should read."

"You read between the lines?"

"Certainly. For instance, when they say that there is liable to be a fall in the forward price of the Dutch gulden and misprint the word 'gulden', this means that the date they have suggested is in fact supposed to be a little further off than it really appears from what they have written. And the same thing is true about their misprints in political reports."

The editor, thinking of the recent row with his secretary, began to feel quite nervous.

"Do you," he said, "often play the market on the basis of these misprints?"

The broker said that yes he did. This made Claud more alarmed than ever. He said to him, "But do you in fact make a profit on those particular transactions?"

"Good God!" cried the broker. "Of course I do!" And Claud was able to relax, feeling that evidently all was somehow well with the general system.

Its persistence in unearthing and reporting goings-on in the City brought *The Week* a lot of trouble. During one such storm, across a glass of burgundy at the Café Royal (you could buy the stuff at 3s. 6d. a bottle then), Claud remarked to his guest, "You seem pensive, preoccupied." The friend replied that this was indeed the case. "You see," he said, "I have just read your latest issue. The question I am pondering is simply this. First, how long after we part at the end of this splendid lunch will it be before you are arrested for criminal libel? Secondly, will you receive a sharp jail sentence or is there some loophole by which you could settle for a crippling fine?"

It was a question often in the forefront of the minds of the friends and well-wishers of *The Week*, but when it had been running for nearly two years without that sort of disaster occurring, many of them felt calmer. Some had simply accustomed themselves to the idea that *The Week* was possessed of some mysterious, not to say magical, sleight of hand which enabled it, so to speak, to saw people in half on the public stage and escape any evil consequences.

There were those who had a different explanation. Claud, familiar enough with Communist thinking by this time, was quite aware that some simple and rigid minds saw in this immunity of *The Week* a sinister significance. It was obvious that *The Week* was being secretly protected by M.I.5 for devious and noxious purposes of its own. Long afterwards I asked him whether he had not found it embarrassing to be constantly in company with people some of whom supposed him to be a spy of the Intelligence Service. He denied that it had been embarrassing. "After all," he said, "if I had been of the same upbringing and background, if I had suffered the same type of police persecution and espionage as they have, I should draw the same conclusions that they do. I would very much rather go tiger-shooting with a man who is over-suspicious, even of me as his fellow hunter, than one who is over-credulous, as most of the Left in Britain seems to be."

However, at about the end of this two-year period *The Week* plunged into a campaign which even those who for various reasons had acquired a faith in its total immunity thought must finally be the end of it. It was this campaign which occasioned his friend's gloomy speculations over the burgundy.

Long before, Claud had laid down as a principle for *The Week* that one should never, if possible, pick on anyone less than twice one's own size. This time the figure, and the forces, singled out for uncompromising attack were not only enormous but since they were not a foreign government but based upon the City of London, had every opportunity to retaliate directly and crushingly.

It was supposed also to be a principle of *The Week* that one should never make personal attacks on individuals unless their personal behaviour or character in some way affected larger issues or public interests. I say was supposed to be, because there were several instances in which the principle was more or less blatantly infringed.

However, in the battle against Howeson, the Tin King, there was no infringement whatever of this principle.

The Week broke the story after the City of London had been shaken by the spectacular collapse of a multi-million speculation on the pepper market, and the shares of companies concerned with pepper.

The issue of 13 February 1935, opened the attack.

Behind the shouting and the tumult over the crash of the great pepper gamble, lie facts, factors and figures of national, also international importance. Since the local press, for reasons which will become obvious, is handling the situation with about as much delicacy as one would use for a new-born child or a live bomb, it appears worthwhile to report at some length on the position which is going to have important political repercussions.

Dominating the London commodity market, with half the City muttering and whispering and no one saying anything very loud, is the figure of John Howeson . . .

John Howeson whose original name was Ernst Hausen occupies the position of the World's Tin King. He and his associates are a power in world politics, and particularly in British imperial politics, compared to which a good many of the better publicized figures of the capitalist world are pygmies.

It was the absent figure of Howeson which really held the centre of the stage at the recent enquiry in Washington by the Foreign Affairs Committee of the House of Representatives which met to consider the position of the United States in regard to tin, with special reference to the fact that tin is an essential war material.

In important matters of policy John Howeson has virtually dictated to five governments: the British, the Dutch, the Bolivian, the Siamese and the Nigerian.

People who have retained somehow a certain naïveté regarding how and why the wheels go round in imperialist London, have occasionally expressed surprise at the fact that the Colonial Office should sometimes appear to act as though it were a sub-department of the office of Mr. Howeson and at the further fact that efforts from the most "respectable" quarters to get questions asked about Mr. Howeson in the British Parliament have rather consistently failed to get on to the order paper.

The Week noted the awe with which Howeson was treated in the City of London, describing how one of its correspondents had had to spend fifteen minutes circling upstairs and downstairs in a City restaurant trying to find a table sufficiently isolated to encourage his knowledgeable companion to mention the man at all. Howeson was clearly not a man who liked a great deal of publicity. To a newspaperman who was supposed to know quite a lot about him he remarked, "I would pay £2,000 for the news of your death." *The Week* continued:

The field of the Howeson operations was at one time Calcutta and the subject matter was jute. But then something went wrong with a jute pool or something and things did not look so good in Calcutta and that ended.

The Indian connection was not utterly severed. In 1928 was formed in London the Anglo-Oriental Tin Corporation, a holding company of Malayan and Nigerian producers, absorbing the whole issued capital of the Anglo-Oriental and General Investment Trust Ltd. The first directors were two knights, plus the Hon. Lionel Holland, Richmond Temple, and John Howeson. Then everyone except John Howeson quit, and the directors came to consist of John Howeson, Oliver Hoare, brother of the present Secretary of State for India, and two others.

The original auditors of this company were Messrs. Fitzpatrick, Graham and Co., but in 1932 their report stated that this firm having dissolved partnership Messrs. Graham Robinson Dignasse & Co. were appointed auditors, and then in 1933 Messrs. Graham Robinson Dignasse & Co. dissolved partnership too and Messrs. Fuller Wise Fisher & Co. became the auditors.

Typically of London in the present period, Anglo-Oriental was approximately the first serious rung in the ladder which brought John Howeson to a position where he actually exercises considerably more influence on the policies of the British Empire than most politicians and even many millionaires.

At about this time Howeson was closely connected with a Mr. Bishirgian, the currently publicized pepper operator.

It was in 1928 that Howeson and his associates started the first tin pool. They began buying Stand Tin heavily on the London market at about £235 per ton. The stocks of tin were then very low, and it looked as though it would be pretty easy to corner the market and skyrocket the price of the metal. And skyrocketing the price of the metal would have been a good way to help the quotation of tin companies which was a profitable thing to be up to at that time, and Howeson and his friends were up to it. Unfortunately for the tin Napoleons there happened what often happens when people start to corner anything. Amazing sources of tin, unheard of and undreamed of, began to discover themselves. People who hadn't produced tin produced it, and other people produced more tin, and people who were not known to have any tin suddenly had tin and so on as usual.

By the summer of 1929 things began to look pretty bad. So they formed the Tin Producers Association which was to put into effect a voluntary restriction scheme to cut down the production of this useful metal and thus help the pool to get out.

The Week ironically described the Association as a "patriotic affair". Membership was confined to Empire producers and the chairman was Sir Philip Cunliffe Lister. (Lister remained chairman right up until the time he became Minister for the Colonies.)

The scheme in spite of excellent auspices and the collaboration of some of our best people flopped. The pool was in acute danger of losing a very great deal of money. Tin was on its way down towards a price of about £100 per ton. It was in this perilous situation that there began to be talk of "planned capitalism" which then as later—when it has been dressed up with all the trimmings of Fascism, New Deal, etc.—turned out to be a good way of getting the government to rush in and hold up the roof while the bull pool got out from under.

It was somewhere about this point that the audacious Howeson succeeded in interesting the Right Hon. Reginald McKenna, Chairman of the Midland Bank Ltd. and former Chancellor of the Exchequer. Whether because McKenna was quite won over to planned capitalism, or for other reasons, McKenna became interested and things began to move. The amount of his personal fortune which McKenna "invested" in tin ran into six figures, and with McKenna known to be so interested things began to go more smoothly and doors opened. The Midland Bank was one of the chief bankers for the activities of the "group".

The Colonial Office it appears was not instantly susceptible to the planned capitalist idea. But the pool had by this time a rather persuasive argument for planning. It was explained to the Colonial Office that unless the Colonial Office would put through a compulsory restriction scheme, the pool would most unfortunately have to dump its stocks on the market. Whereupon the whole market would crash, the price of tin would go to approximately nil, and a chief industry in Malaya, that important section of the far-flung imperial battle line, would collapse in ruin.

The Colonial Office saw the point.

As *The Week* observed, the other governments which saw the point after a time were those of Holland, Siam and Bolivia, plus Malaya and Nigeria. In other words the governments of all areas of the world producing tin. And Simon Patino, the Bolivian tin millionaire, who owned a great part of all Bolivia's tin, was for a long time one of the most powerful associates of the less rich but more active John Howeson.

At The Hague in April 1931 [*The Week* continued] the compulsory restriction scheme was signed and the pool which now amounted to 21,000 tons was as part of the scheme held and financed until such time as a rise in the price of tin justified its sale.

Even so things did not immediately go too well. Walter Henry Barnard, Howeson's chief broker on the Metal Exchange during 1928, failed. Lewis Lazarus and Sons were then employed as one of the "group" brokers and then they failed too, disclosing the fact that among those who speculated in tin through this firm was Sir Samuel Hoare, the present Secretary of State for India.

During the years which followed the "group" led by John Howeson succeeded to perfect its hold on the world supply and distribution of one of the modern world's essential commodities.

A spectacular feature of the campaign was the encirclement of the world's one big independent smelter, namely the Straits Trading Company. The Straits Trading Company was apparently under the impression that it could get protection from this international group by appealing to the patriots at the Colonial Office. Oddly enough although many permanent officials in England and Malaya were of the opinion that the two governments should support the independent company and thus save the one free tin market in the world at Singapore, higher powers intervened and the Straits Trading Company found little or no protection.

The Week noted a curious fact in this connection: the passage of a law in Malaya entitled the "Disclosure of Smelters' Stock Bill" which forced the Straits Trading Company to disclose its tin stocks. The Bill was fought violently by the unofficial members of the Legislative Assembly. Oddly enough there was no forcible disclosure of the stocks of the Williams Harvey Smelter at Liverpool which was of greater importance from a statistical point of view but was one of the "group" smelters.

In the circumstances [observed *The Week*] it was not surprising that the restriction scheme was kept going without serious interruption, that Howeson and his associates got richer and richer, and that people who still retain a pathetic belief that in England as opposed to the scandalous United States there is a gulf fixed between the Government and the Government Departments and the operations of private financiers got some unpleasant shocks.

Private moves against the Howeson group were frequent but the crusaders tended to fade away mysteriously, apparently snatching defeat from the very jaws of victory. People in the City would get together groups to attack Howeson and collect a lot of data and then quite suddenly find something better to do.

Efforts were made to get people on the Government side of the House of Commons to ask questions. At least one prospective questioner went to Sir Philip Cunliffe Lister as the Minister concerned and asked if there was any objection. And Sir Philip

Cunliffe Lister, who, by the way, has figures to prove that he sold all his tin interests before he went into the Government, said that he was out of touch with the situation and that the question looked all right to him but it had better be shown to Sir George Penny. Sir George Penny, who since 1931 has been Vice-Chamberlain of His Majesty's Household, knows a lot about tin and is in fact a co-director of Consolidated Tin Smelters with John Howeson. Sir George Penny indicated that it really would be better not to ask that question: and it was not asked.

An example of the excellence of the relations existing between Howeson and the Colonial Office was indicated by the retirement in 1933 of Sir Samuel Wilson who for some years previously had been Permanent Under-Secretary of State for the Colonies. Shortly after his retirement he became a director of Consolidated Gold Fields and of New Consolidated Gold Fields at a salary of £1,000 per directorship. Howeson is a director of both these companies.

January of last year he became Chairman of the Tin Producers Association.

Equally remarkable were the events of last year, when Howeson was pushing the idea of the famous "buffer pool" in tin. The scheme met with strong and general opposition from Malaya as well as a letter of protest from the London Metal Exchange. A referendum was to be taken in Malaya and the forms were printed. And then quite suddenly the Malayan members of the International Tin Committee which regulates the Tin Restrictions Scheme received a direction or instruction from the British Colonial Office to vote for the Howeson scheme and they did and the scheme was approved by the Committee just before the referendum papers could be sent out.

The situation at the present is that with the assistance of the British Government and some of the most powerful banking interests in the country Howeson not only dominates the tin market but other commodity markets too.

It is noted that the leading operator in the pepper pool is a man who has frequently acted in a very big way indeed on behalf of the Howeson interests. It is noted that among the shareholders in the suspended firm of James & Shakespeare is Reginald McKenna.

In an effort to use the pepper affair as a weapon, numbers of people have attempted during the past few days to re-open the attack on what they now regard as a sort of capitalist Frankenstein. To this there had been dropped in reply sad hints that the United States might perhaps be kinder to Mr. Howeson than Great Britain and that it would cause unemployment in Liverpool if anything were to happen to cause Mr. Howeson to transfer his activities across the Atlantic.

And overhanging the whole remarkable scene is the factor which in the long run is perhaps the strongest defence of all for the tin Napoleon: namely the approach to and preparation for war.

One of the objects of the resolution—God-fathered by none other than the eminent Bernard Baruch—which the United States House of Representatives had to consider last year was "whether acquisition by the United States of foreign tin sources would improve the present costly and dangerously dependent position of the U.S. with respect to an item essential to the national defence".

It may well be that Mr. Howeson has already been listed by the British Government, along with Vickers Ltd., as an "essential of national defence" and therefore worthy of the earnest protection of all patriotic and right-minded persons.

Since nobody previously had got around to talking much about Mr. Howeson and his powerful, semi-official associates before, and had certainly not spoken of them in the terms used by *The Week*, the ground-swell which followed *The Week*'s publication of the story was considerable. It was much strengthened by the fact that people in the know who could read between the lines immediately understood from *The Week*'s story that *The Week* knew a great deal more than it had seen fit at the moment to publish.

The Week resumed the theme in its next issue, that of 20 February 1935.

The political repercussions of the pepper gamble, forecast in the last issue of *The Week*, are already beginning to rumble around London. A curious feature of the situation was that on the day when *The Week* appeared, the tin pool for the first time for years stopped buying quite suddenly and did not buy for several days. The price of tin fell at one time around £6 per ton on the London market, indicating vividly the prevailing nervousness in certain quarters.

[The "quarters" referred to were of course precisely those people who actually had read between the lines of the previous story and saw the prospect of a lot of unpleasantness to come.]

It is now certain [the report continued] that the attack on "the men behind the pepper pool" will be heavily pressed in the House of Commons. Answers to questions being in general unsatisfactory, it is probable that the Opposition will raise the matter on the adjournment in the course of the next week or two, whereupon any facts produced in the privileged House of Commons will become available for a press which so far has distinguished itself chiefly by its acute recollection of the details and possibilities of the British libel laws.

It is noteworthy that within the past two months, Mr. Howeson was able to approach Mr. Brendan Bracken, owner of the *Financial News* [later Minister of Information and finally Lord Bracken], and inform him that he did not care for the habit of the newspaper regularly producing every month an article highly critical of the operations of the tin restriction scheme . . . Howeson informed him that his company advertising was worth a lot of money and that it would be withdrawn in the event of these critical articles continuing to appear. The articles have ceased.

Commenting on the present situation, Montague Norman, Governor of the Bank of England, spoke in somewhat violent terms of the men behind the pepper crash, remarking that the only one of the whole lot who had had the courage to come out in the open and face the music was "that bloody Armenian". (Meaning Mr. Bishirgian.)

It is noted that the Right Honourable Reginald McKenna, now arrived in Capetown, has told the newspapers that he cannot imagine why his name should ever have become mixed up in the affair, that he was just an ordinary shareholder in the firm of James and Shakespeare, and that he did not think, at the time he bought the shares, that they were dealing in pepper.

The statement throws a somewhat peculiar light on the situation of the Manager of one of London's leading banks, especially since only a few months ago Mr. McKenna was actually advising his friends to buy certain shares on the ground that what they would actually be buying would be not the shares but the pepper that was behind them.

In the circumstances, *The Week*'s stories seemed to laymen and lawyers alike to be nearly dripping with obviously libellous references to the doings of Mr. Howeson in particular and quite a range of other important financial and governmental characters too.

That they were damaging was equally obvious.

The Week was passed nervously from hand to hand in City offices. "They keep it," one observer remarked, "like a whisky bottle in the desk drawer. They like to take a swig at it themselves. And if they are sure they are quite alone with reliable friends, they will offer them a quick swig too."

In its issue of 27 February 1935, *The Week* noted:

As one or two of the local newspapers have already pointed out, the crash in the price of tin has been largely affected by the fact that in the face of the attacks now being launched on the tin pool, and the disclosures made, no bank is willing to advance money to the group concerned for fear of looking pretty silly if anything should, as the saying goes, happen.

That something may in fact "happen" is a fear that is worrying not only the tin operators concerned but the government itself. Specifically what is feared is that either the government and the banks will have to involve themselves even further in the tin business than they are now with all the risks that that implies, or else that there will be another market crash which will explode what is left of the "confidence" which every government newspaper has been frantically trying to promote, with more or less disastrous effects, during the past ten days.

As attacks on Howeson increased, so did the certainty of many that *The Week*, however important its City connexions might be, had this time walked into a mine-field. It was even suggested that the paper had allowed itself to be used as a fall guy, or patsy, by and for some of the City interests concerned, who were too nervous to attack Howeson themselves. Threats and genuinely friendly warnings poured in.

But *The Week* operated on the principle that in situations of that kind the most dangerous thing to do is to retreat, or even hesitate. To do so in this case would immediately convince Howeson that *The Week* was less sure of itself than it pretended to be. On the other hand, the longer Howeson remained passive, the bolder his enemies would become.

The calculation was correct.

It was not the editor of *The Week* who was taken to court, but Howeson. Almost exactly a year after *The Week*'s first attack, Mr. Howeson, after a long trial at the Old Bailey, was found guilty of wrong-doing and sentenced to twelve months in the Second Division.

7 Civil Liberty

A CANDID visitor to Victoria Street said: "Trouble with you people is that half the time you complain that people in England aren't raising enough hell, and the other half you spend exaggerating how much hell they're raising."

As such observations go, it was true enough. And the fact that this was so, was itself a reflection of a general situation existing in the mid-1930s.

In the last couple of years there have been signs of a trend among economists in the direction of showing that the Thirties were really quite a prosperous decade. Conditions in Britain, it appears, were nothing like so bad as the people living in them thought they were. They were on the up-and-up without knowing it. If they had read the right statistics they would have been a lot happier.

At the time, to get a receptive audience for that kind of talk you would have had to call out the Horse Marines. *The Week*, certainly, was quite unaware of how well things were, statistically speaking, going. In April 1934, it was the first to publish news of the establishment in London of a "Committee against Malnutrition". The Committee was composed of doctors and other experts in the field. Its establishment, *The Week* noted, was a consequence of

the extremely serious repercussions—resulting in the largest political revolt to date of the Government's conservative supporters, which occurred partly under the pressure of the facts about starvation conditions in this country brought out at the time of the Hunger March. Apart from the immediate parliamentary revolt, it is now agreed by all members of Parliament from industrial constituencies that the question of malnutrition has become a dominating factor in the political life of the country. The new Committee has as its aim "the giving of numbers of persons throughout the country the opportunity of centralizing their information, and co-ordinating all efforts to one end—the securing of adequate nourishment for every man, woman and child".

The conditions referred to supplied one at least of the reasons why *The Week* gave the impression that the population ought to be raising more hell. In particular, its easily raised blood pressure went up fast when it saw Labour leaders more busy trying to curb hell-raising than to encourage it. This of course they were particularly inclined to do when the principal hell-raisers were either Communists or suspected Communist sympathizers trying to promote militancy among the Labour rank-and-file, and luring Labour men into suspect united fronts with the Communists. It followed that when signs of militant action did appear, *The Week* was often inclined to see a summer in each flight of swallows.

Possibly the fact that the editor twice abandoned the editorial chair at short notice in order to tramp the roads with Hunger Marchers, may have coloured his judgment of these manifestations of popular disgust with the existing state of affairs.

These sudden disappearances were naturally disconcerting to the staff. And they were the more surprising because it was well known that the editor detested all forms of physical exercise, reserving his particular horror and contempt for the act of walking. Nobody was prepared for the news that he had bought a pair of army boots, taken train to Aberdeen, and there joined a contingent of Scottish hunger marchers who were going to walk to Glasgow, via Dundee, the Fife coalfields, and Edinburgh. For the underfed little group of working men from the far north of Scotland who started the march at Aberdeen, it was an arduous walk. The editor, though a lot better fed, was in the worst possible state of physical training. And the march did not proceed along the line of a crow's flight.

Claud admitted that the march deepened his hatred of the physical business of walking. However, though his feet were sore, he found the experience uplifting. In every village and town, the working population, including a high proportion of professional workers as well as factory workers and agricultural labourers, turned out to cheer and wave and wish good luck. For them that bedraggled contingent, which swelled its numbers to several thousand on the way, seems to have been a tiny sign of hope, of something stirring. "I think," Claud said on his return, "that's the first time I really believed that there is another nation here."

At the beginning of 1934, a National Hunger March—actually a series of marches—was to converge on London. *The Week* had been repeatedly criticized, particularly by Labour party subscribers, for attaching undue importance to the event. The people affected by, or interested in, such a demonstration were, they said, only a minority. To this Claud replied that probably only a minority of people in Jerusalem gave a damn about the Crucifixion. Most of them no doubt ate their dinner that Friday quite as usual.

The authorities, however, seemed rather to share *The Week's* view; that is, so far as the importance of the affair was concerned. In its issue of 21 February, the paper reported:

Police preparations for attempting to "deal" with the National Hunger March and the huge demonstrations of sympathy which will occur when it reaches London, are on a scarcely precedented scale. They stretch from an extraordinarily increased activity of detectives and police spies operating round and about working-men's clubs in working-class districts, to the giving of bits of material for "red menace" stories to the Rothermere press. A minor but sufficiently significant indication of governmental alarm is the urgency and care with which the police remove the tens of thousands of little notices of the march pasted up on the walls and elsewhere all over Greater London. A high official of the C.I.D. a few days ago informed a correspondent of *The Week* that for ten days they had been concentratedly busy on plans for squashing the expected demonstrations. It was admitted by this officer that the main difficulty experienced by the police arose from the fact that the overwhelming majority of the working-class population of London, and a very large section of the professional and non-manual workers, are in active or tacit sympathy with the marchers.

In this as in many other instances, the paper's use of the term "a correspondent of *The Week*" may be confusing. Naturally, nobody called on a high official of the C.I.D. and stated "I'm from *The Week*. What do you think, and what are you up to?" In the first instance, the phrase meant that the information had been given by the C.I.D. Special Branch to one of the regular reporters of a respectable national news-paper. It might have been given "off the record". The police officer would know that the paper in question would certainly not publish anything of that nature. The journalist, himself after all one of those professional, non-manual workers, would ease his frustration and help to justify his existence by giving the story to *The Week*. (In this particular case the journalist concerned was an old, conscientious and reliable friend.)

There were other occasions when Claud would become obsessed with the fear that his informant, carried away by enthusiasm, was seasoning the story to suit *The Week*'s taste. This could quite easily happen, despite the fact that no payment was involved. When seized with these fits of suspicion regarding his own informants, Claud would, as sparingly as possible, make use of more direct contacts with what are called the higher echelons. For it was in the nature of *The Week* and of the atmosphere in which it operated, that such sympathetic contacts existed in astonishing places. They included the Special Branch of the C.I.D., or Political Police.

The next part of the report on the police and the hunger march did, in fact, come from such a source.

In the opinion of the highest authorities at Scotland Yard, the position of the interests opposed to the March has been somewhat strengthened by the reorganization of the police force hastily rushed into operation after the last national hunger march. At that time, the Government and its backers were seriously alarmed by reports of some fraternization between police and workmen, and by reports of widespread sympathy among the police rank-and-file for demonstrators against the Means Test and the pay-cuts whom they were supposed to be beating up. According to authorities at the Yard the reorganization carried out by Trenchard with the object of "stiffening" the police force with middle and upper middle class elements has been successful . . . in reducing the above-mentioned tendencies.

The press had reported that the police had issued notices to shop-keepers to board up windows and be prepared to barricade their premises against the marchers. *The Week* commented:

Since the marchers and their supporters are unarmed persons conducting a peaceful demonstration, this order has naturally given rise to a strong impression that the police are planning an attack on the march . . . Certain is that there are elements within and around the present Cabinet who, in discussion of the prospects of the march during the past week, have made clear that in their opinion an attack by the police and the resulting uproar would be an advantageous excuse for a sweeping attack on organizations of the Left.

The Week then reported, "with the greatest reserve, despite the reliable character of our informant," a story that a small consignment of Lewis machine-guns had been delivered at Kentish Town police station. This was at first, and naturally enough, denied with fury. But in its subsequent issue *The Week* noted that, following its own report, several leading Fleet Street dailies had investigated the matter, and one had had the story confirmed at Scotland Yard.

It also noted that careful arrangements were being made to keep the special constables, or auxiliary police force, well out of the affair. This was partly because, during the previous year's march, the behaviour of the special constables

aroused the most violent resistance from otherwise more or less neutral spectators. There was also acute tension between the "specials" and the regular police who, regarding the "specials" as a form of blackleg labour were on several occasions—notably one evening in Whitehall—with difficulty restrained from attacking the specials instead of the demonstrators. On the last National Hunger March the "specials" received special instruction in street fighting in, among other places, the Duke of York's Headquarters in Kings Road, Chelsea. This year the idea is to keep the "specials" as far as possible entirely on traffic duty, leaving the entire regular police force free to "deal" with the demonstrators.

The behaviour of the police towards the hunger marchers of the previous year had been described in terms varying from "harsh" to "outrageous". In the February of 1934, the newly-formed National Council for Civil Liberties, of which Claud was a founder member, decided to give itself, so to speak, a watching-brief. It was felt that in case the violences of the previous year were repeated, the word of a beaten-up marcher was not going to carry much weight in a London police court, against that of a policeman. On the other hand, if some more or less nationally distinguished upper- or middle-class figure were to have been present as an observer, and turn up to give evidence, the victim might have a chance.

Meeting for the first time in the crypt of St. Martin's-in-the-Fields, the Council, number at that time less than a dozen, decided to mobilize such observers and send them to Hyde Park where the ultimate gathering and demonstration of the hunger marchers was to take place. This decision was well publicized. And it was felt that the mere knowledge that all these notables were lurking about the park might actually prevent any violent action being taken at all. Claud has described that final scene elsewhere: it was his particular task to make sure that H. G. Wells arrived in time to do his bit of "observing". As on the previous occasion the marchers were perfectly orderly. And this time there was no trouble from the police. It is, of course, anybody's guess whether the presence of the observers was actually responsible for this happy outcome.

There were one or two people, later connected with the Council for Civil Liberties, who imagined their position would be largely a sinecure. And one privately admitted that he had mixed himself up with the organization so as to get to know such distinguished members of the Committee as novelist E. M. Forster. They thought that in any case the only kind of infringements of civil liberty they would be called upon to struggle against would be police interference with supposedly obscene publications, pictures and so on. They took the general view that other attacks upon civil liberty could not happen here.

These people were rather quickly disillusioned. Furthermore, whatever their own views as to the calm and docile attitude of the public, they were forced to admit that such views were certainly not shared by the government. The occasion for this disillusionment was the presentation of the Incitement to Disaffection Bill, more generally known as "the Sedition Bill".

The Week—and the Council for Civil Liberties—were at first optimistic about the chances of organizing sufficient opposition to kill the Bill before it became law. On 18 April 1934, *The Week* wrote:

According to information received by us yesterday from a source opposed to the Government but at the same time very close to several members of the Cabinet, there still exists the possibility that the Government may yet withdraw the new Incitement to Disaffection Bill in face of the unexpected storm of resentment, criticism and opposition which it has aroused. The storm is still growing, especially among all groups, societies, and organizations opposed to war, whose premises will be liable to continual invasion by the police, their personnel to arrest, imprisonment and fine if the Bill becomes law: for under the terms of this Bill mere possession—let alone publication—of any pacifist or anti-war literature becomes a criminal offence.

The storm of resentment and opposition was certainly real, though it is not likely to get much of a showing in the history books. But it was basically incoherent. And its incoherence was a particular symptom of the general incoherence of the Left during the whole period of the Thirties.

Those who may be called dyed-in-the-wool pacifists had, obviously, simple and intelligible reasons for their alarm and hostility. Their relatively small numbers were enormously swelled by people who, though they would certainly not have called themselves pacifists, would equally certainly, and sincerely, proclaim themselves "against war". The phrase, though foggy, was not in the circumstances of the time meaningless. What most people meant by it was that they were against the battle of Passchendaele and all that the mere mention of it evoked. They were against casualty lists stretching out horribly month after month, to end not in a world safe for democracy (as President Wilson had promised), or a land fit for heroes to live in (as guaranteed by Lloyd George), but in the Treaty of Versailles, followed by Mussolini, followed by Hitler. There were millions of them. And, foggy or not, they were potentially a powerful political force.

But, already in 1934, these people were beginning to find themselves in a dilemma which was to become gradually more confusing and enfeebling. It has been the subject of endless historical comment since then. It consisted essentially in the fact that they were against war, but also against Hitler and all that he seemed to imply. Were they then, they asked themselves, and were more and more vehemently asked by their critics, against preparations for war with Hitler?

The position of *The Week* was very far from pacifist. As for being against war, it was certainly against the battle of Passchendaele. But the dilemma just referred to seemed to the editor unreal. In his view the question was not: Are you for war, or against it? Or, if the question were posed, then the answer was another question: What war? Against what? Under what conditions? Above all, under what sort of government or supreme authority?

The consequence was that when *The Week* loosely used the phrase "opposition to war and fascism" the words "war and" might often have been omitted. One has the clear impression that they were there because the phrase, or slogan, was tactically convenient in uniting the aims of a maximum number of people. For there were certainly more people prepared to be roused against a repetition of the battle of Passchendaele than against the behaviour of the German government in Germany, or even against fascist tendencies in Britain.

In this connexion, *The Week*'s very free-wheeling use of the terms fascist, or fascistic, appears today inaccurate, misleading and quite often absurd. In part, its repeated use in a very loose and inexact sense is explicable only as being a handy kind of shorthand for describing authoritarian tendencies which were recognizable to everyone. And, as I have said, it was a fact that at the time there was a common and perhaps not absurd belief in Britain that the powers above were, in fact, edging the country along the fascist path.

There were a good many years in between when the consensus was that people who had harboured such thoughts were hysterical. Fascism was another of the things that could not happen here. It was not until the 1960s that some observers —from Left and Right—began to suggest that after all it could. They were recalling the familiar reply of the late Huey Long, Governor of Louisiana, to the question "Could we have fascism in America?" "Sure we could," he said "except we'd have to call it anti-fascism."

Questioned [*The Week* reported] during the last few days about the motive for introduction of the Bill at this time, members of the Government reply darkly "Ah, if you only knew what the Government knows, you wouldn't be surprised." The facts are that several members of the Cabinet were themselves very much surprised when they saw the terms of the Bill for the first time. For it now turns out that the Bill was concocted in the War Office, Admiralty and Air Ministry, with the co-operation of the political police . . . The political police are annoyed by their loss of the case brought against them by the National Unemployed Workers Movement in connexion with the raid and seizure of documents at their headquarters. The militarist and fascist wing of the Government welcomed the Bill with open arms: for with its passage the country will pass at once into a new and much more open phase of military fascism.

We gather from some of our subscribers who have occasionally written to us suggesting that we are exaggerating the rapidity of the development of tendencies towards fascism and war in this country, that they received rather a nasty shock on publication of this Bill . . .

To some members of the Government . . . and to many of the Government's supporters, the Bill seemed too blatant and aggressive a step. Seeing the uproar it has caused and the much greater uproar it is going to cause when the citizenry are generally informed of the extent to which the Bill hands over their remaining liberties to the whim of the police and the magistrates, many of them are now worried: the militarists and the fascists are confident, however, that they—with War Office and political police behind them—have the upper hand.

So far as the Bill was concerned their confidence was more justified than was the optimism of *The Week*.

It is significant that immediately the Bill was produced, the Conservative Central Office was busy pumping out to all and sundry—including numbers of foreign correspondents—the information that it was directed chiefly against the Blackshirts. [That is, the followers of Sir Oswald Mosley.] As was admitted in the House of Commons, several members of the Labour Party fell for this and, apparently, at the beginning, the *Daily Herald* did too. The *Daily Herald* had announced the Bill under the headline "Government Action against Communists and Fascists".

It was a central theme of Labour party propaganda at the time to suggest that the Communists, who were the only people visibly, and often physically, battling the Blackshirts were somehow the same as the Blackshirts who spent a lot of their time trying to beat up the Communists. The theory was supposed, at least, to be useful in coralling the middle-class vote. Privately, and sometimes even publicly, the Labour leaders would admit that they regarded the Communists as a potential menace to the Labour party, and the Blackshirts as somewhere between a joke and a handy weapon against the Communists.

The Week added:

> The Government has, and possibly still is, contemplating "taking steps" to prevent the Blackshirts, with their armoured cars and the rest of their paraphernalia, menacing by their extravagance the quiet development of governmental fascism (cf. the simultaneous opposition to, and preparation of the road for, Hitler, by Bruening, Schleicher and large sections of German Social Democracy and the Trade Union Movement). Yet it is obvious that since the Fascists are all for King and Country and big armaments, this Bill would be a feeble sort of weapon to attack them with. Startling is merely the extent to which this red herring deceived people who, with the German example in full view, might have been expected to see matters in a different light.

Possibly enflamed by his own writings, the editor carried his opposition to the Sedition Bill to the point of getting arrested while addressing a queue of unemployed outside a South London labour exchange. Someone acidly suggested that he should defend himself on the ground that since his very Oxford accent was certainly unintelligible to those addressed, he could not properly be accused of inciting them to anything. The arrest, occurring on a press day, briefly disrupted the operations of *The Week*. More serious in this respect was his agreement, about this time, to write for the *Daily Worker*. The journeys between the two offices took quite a long time. And the tapped telephones and intercepted mail at both places of business made it essential to be physically present in one office or the other whenever anything serious had to be discussed.

He much enjoyed writing for the *Daily Worker*. But, even

apart from the matter of trekking back and forth across London, he found it rather more time-consuming than anyone had at first supposed. It had been intended that he should act as a correspondent on special, specific assignments. But the staff was tiny. He soon found himself doing every kind of job. There was sub-editing, often of stories sent in by men who certainly knew what they wanted to write, but had little experience of handling pen, ink and paper. Occasionally he wrote the leading articles. He was sometimes the Foreign Editor and sometimes the Diplomatic Correspondent and sometimes the Political Correspondent. He also wrote a coarsely satirical humorous column. He had to go abroad a good deal, too. He admitted that there were two jobs on that paper which truly bored him. One was the task, which members of the staff took in turns, of snipping with scissors the advertisements of birth-control appliances out of those copies of the paper destined for the Irish Republic. To leave them in would have got it banned there. The other, also undertaken by rota, was to sit by the telephone all evening taking down the racing results from the London dog-tracks. A man at each track rang up with the results as each race finished. As the paper had to go to press very early because the Newspaper Proprietors' Association banned it from the newspaper trains, it tried to make a virtue of this necessity. The dog-racing results were rubber-stamped into the stop-press column, and the paper was on sale in the streets of London around eleven o'clock. The racing results raised the London circulation by as much as twenty-five per cent.

He had been working there quite a while before anyone suggested to him that he might as well join the Communist party. Approaches of this kind had naturally been made before. But they had been made by the sort of intellectuals who, at the time, regarded the act of joining that party as either a cure for their frustrations, or an expiation of some kind of guilt. Claud rarely suffered frustration except when impeded by the police or unable to find a taxi. And he was unaware of anything that he felt he could properly be expected to feel guilt about. In any case, he had very little to do with those circles in which, at least according to later writers and critics, Communism was "fashionable".

He has often complained that although he has devoted quite large chunks of two books trying to make clear why he joined the Communist party and why he left it, people still put those questions to him as if they were the kind of questions you can answer between one glass of whisky and the next. "It's like," he says irritably, "being asked when did you know Greek?"

The movement first in, and later out, was gradual. "People," he remarks, "still seem to find it impossible to believe that I really do not recollect just when I joined the party. They, especially American officials wondering whether to give me a visa or not, always ask, 'how long were you a card-carrying member?' The truthful answer to that is that in the first place I can't remember when I first held a party card, and secondly that since I am notably bad at keeping documents of that kind, let alone putting stamps on them at the proper time, I cannot give any precise dates. Naturally I can't tell them that. They would think I was making a joke in poor taste."

When signing articles for the *Daily Worker* he did so with the name Frank Pitcairn, Francis being one of his own Christian names and Pitcairn that of his paternal grandmother. The pseudonym only once caused serious trouble. During the liberation of North Africa, Claud Cockburn was arrested by the American security forces for allegedly passing information to Frank Pitcairn.

At that time the Communist party enforced a rule that nobody was to be paid out of the party funds more than the basic wage of a semi-skilled labourer. The pay at the *Daily Worker*, even when it could be paid at all, was subject to this rule. And although the circulation of *The Week* was rising fairly fast, its absurdly low subscription rate prevented it providing more than a minimum of spending money. Claud was therefore happy, at about this time, to be offered and accept a job as first European Correspondent of *Fortune*, the new and grandiose venture launched by Henry Luce, of *Time* magazine. *Fortune* was described as the magazine of America's top business men.

The magazine paid handsomely. And except when posses of executives came over to London and desired to be shown round and told all, the duties of the European Correspondent were not heavy. Rather the reverse was the case. A European trip, researching into something or other on behalf and at the expense of *Fortune*, could often be usefully combined with other researches on behalf of *The Week*.

One of these safaris—this time into the Nazi hinterland— was especially useful but especially trying to the nerves. It began with Claud's receiving from Paris an urgent request to call at the offices of the principal Committee of the Comintern trying to improve the lot or reduce the sufferings of Hitler's victims inside and outside Germany. "You may be sure," he said before leaving, "that whatever happens, there's going to be a bloody muddle. When dealing with that lot, you must always remember that if a mistake can be made, they'll make it."

The popular notion of the Comintern and its proliferating agencies as a powerhouse of almost superhuman though sinister efficiency, like a strip cartoon view of some outfit in outer space, seemed to him a long way from the truth.

On his arrival in Paris his expectations were immediately confirmed. The job in hand was the rescue from Germany of the two small children of a prominent Communist sympathizer. Although safe outside the country himself, his children provided a means of blackmail. They were staying with a politically neutral aunt near Hamburg. What was needed, the Committee men explained, was a man with an impeccably British passport who could enter Germany without difficulty and travel about unmolested.

Claud explained with regret that although he had such a passport, he could not use it. He was by now quite high on the black-list of the Gestapo. This was not, he made clear, just a guess. An agent of *The Week* had seen the list. He had photostated it and got it to London.

(A similar photostat, though of a slightly different list, with the editor's name prominent upon it, was found in the German official archives after the war. It appeared as the dust-jacket of Peter Fleming's book about German arrangements for, and after, the invasion of Britain.)

The short-list of undesirables was in the hands of Gestapo men at every German frontier post. "I'd be no use to you," Claud told the Committee. "I might get about 100 yards into Germany, but I certainly shouldn't get out and about again."

The Committee men pondered. Then they came up with a bright idea. "We'll forge you a British passport," they said.

"But I thought the whole point was that the courier should have an absolutely genuine copper-bottomed passport. Be in a position to call up the British Consul and all that sort of thing."

"Give us the name of someone with that sort of passport who'll be willing and able to do the job."

Claud could not at the moment think of anyone.

"Well there you are," they said. "This thing's urgent. Stay in Paris a few days and we'll get you a passport."

Very superficially it did look like a British passport. But, apart from other blemishes, the photograph was a spectacular failure. "If you looked at it directly," Claud said, "it seemed to be the picture of a middle-aged Swiss business man, with jowls. From a little further off, and sideways, the way you see passport police looking at passport pictures, it could have been a retired Nordic boxer. No feature had the slightest resemblance to any of my own."

However, since the matter really was urgent, and there did not seem to be anyone else available for the job, Claud reluctantly agreed to do his best.

By a stroke of good luck, *Fortune* had just despatched, on a special mission to Europe, a certain Captain Hilton Railey. The Captain had been a member of the American Military Intelligence during World War I and involved in dangerous blood-and-thunder escapades on the Eastern Front. Briefly but successfully he had masqueraded as a Major of the German Army. After some ups-and-downs in public relations business compared to which a trip on the grand dipper was a quiet ride, he acted as an unofficial observer for President Roosevelt at the League of Nations. Now *Fortune*, which had already run an enormously successful article on the armament business, had sent Railey to research and write a series on the British and European armament set-up, from Vickers, to the Comité des Forges, to Krupp.

It was a period when the "Merchants of Death" had just been discovered and named. Much of what was said about them as promoters of international mischief and distrust for the purpose of selling their wares was true. The belated disclosure that the guns which the Turks used to drive the British out of Gallipoli were made in Britain, had made a deep impression on the British public. *The Week* had devoted a good deal of space to the doings of British armament manufacturers. (It may perhaps be considered a sign of the prevalent naïvéte and lack of the proper public relations outlook, that in those days war contracts were actually so-called instead of being termed, as later, defence contracts.) Railey was briefed to contact Claud immediately, and Claud to give the Captain all possible assistance.

They had been working together for some weeks when the question of the mission to Germany arose. In this connexion, the Captain, apart from being a congenial companion, suddenly appeared as a potentially priceless asset. First, he not only had a faultless passport, but was very well connected in Washington official circles. And he had the backing of what was called the Henry Luce Empire. There was another point about him which, though less obvious, might come in very handy. Like a good many Americans of his type he alternated moods of deep moral earnestness with almost maniacal outbreaks of euphoria which was sometimes aggressive. Even Claud classes his drinking as heavy. The Captain knew that his mental processes were erratic. It bothered him. He made huge efforts to bring order into his life and work. He had ream upon ream of quarto sheets of paper. Each of them was of a different colour. There was blue paper, pink paper, yellow paper, green paper.

Each category of his researches was to be assigned to a different coloured paper, thus avoiding chaos and ensuring neatness and clarity. He carried a score or so of sheets of each colour in his brief-case, so that at the end of a day results could be correlated, assigned, and neatly typed on the properly coloured sheet. But it just so happened that, as the days passed, the information acquired never seemed entirely and finally worthy of being inscribed on the coloured sheets. It remained either in the heads of the two collaborators, or on the backs of restaurant and night-club bills.

Claud now suggested to the Captain that the thing to do was to stop nosing round Vickers in England, and go to Germany to take the lid off Krupp and the other notorious tie-ups between the Nazis and the armaments interests. There would

be a lot of material, and he urged Railey to bring a full brief-
case of coloured papers.

On arrival at Frankfort airport, Claud allowed Railey, who
looked like everyone's idea of a F.B.I. agent, to walk just
ahead of him to the customs counter. Behind the regular
customs examiner, stood a vigilant agent of the Gestapo. When
this agent looked over the customs man's shoulder at the
contents of Railey's case, his eyes bulged and glittered. Innocent
people simply do not go about carrying cases full of neatly
stapled sheets of coloured paper with nothing written on them
except neatly typed classifications such as A/4 in the top left-
hand corner.

Snatching the brief-case, the Gestapo man ordered the
Captain to follow him to the private investigation room for
suspicious characters. This was just beside the passport-
control barrier. Claud made as though to follow Railey into
the investigation room. The Gestapo man, supposing that some
boob of a tourist was trying to muscle in on awfully secret
and important business, pushed him back into the passport
queue, and angrily waved him to get going. The passport-
control man was also deeply interested in the nabbing of the
Captain. He stamped Claud's dreadfully false-looking passport
impatiently and without examination, anxious to get done with
the tourists and innocent travellers so as to get in on more
interesting affairs.

Claud, pretending that he was waiting for a friend's car to
pick him up and take him to the city, waited as discreetly as
possible at a reasonable distance. It took the Gestapo experts
an hour to discover that Railey's pages actually were blank,
with no trace of secret writing to be discovered by any test.
They might have taken longer. But Railey, an influential
American citizen in good standing with his authorities, was all
the time raising Cain and demanding to telephone not just to
the Consul but to the American Ambassador in Berlin, whom
he knew personally.

On their way to the centre of the city, Claud pointed out
that this had been only the first hurdle to be surmounted. It
was, for instance, impossible for them to register at an hotel.
At that time, the hotel guest had to surrender his passport on
registration. The hotel then sent the passport round to the

police. It would not, Claud opined, take even the simplest policeman, taking more than the most cursory look, to see that there was something damnably fishy about Claud's document.

It was therefore decided that they should spend all their nights in Germany in the sleeping cars of long-distance trains. So long as the train crossed no frontier, there would be no passport examination. It would be a rather expensive trip. For instead of going direct from one city they needed to visit to the next port of call, which might be only a couple of hours away, they would have to keep zigzagging across the country so as to have a reasonable excuse to be taking sleepers. Still, the enforced travel had its advantages. They covered a great deal of territory, not just in terms of geography, but of people seen. With the credentials of *Fortune* they were treated with some respect by the rich. It was assumed in many financial back-rooms from Breslau back to Essen and across again to Leipzig that they were part of the Old Boy Net of Big Money.

Naturally, nobody told the truth, any more than a British or French business man, under far less perilous pressures, would have done. But no journalist expects anyone in power to tell the truth. His business, like that of a navigator, is getting his fixes from keen observation of the lies told. And at that, as Claud said, they certainly opened up to the *Fortune* correspondents in a way which they would have been far indeed from doing if they had thought they were talking to a correspondent of *The Week*. Ironically, at least two of these supposedly fervid pro-Nazi business executives were secret correspondents of *The Week*, responsible for numerous messages transmitted through devious channels. The editor had to restrain a natural inclination to shake them warmly by the hand and thank them for services rendered to the anti-Nazi cause.

Fortunately for him, during his visit to Germany just before Hitler's seizure of power, he had hardly been outside Berlin. The chances of anyone recognizing him anywhere else were small. All the same, he spent those busy days between the sleeping-car trips in a state of permanent alarm. He was well aware of the truth spoken by Mr. Charles Peake of the Foreign Office when, after the trip was over, a mutual friend learned by an indiscretion that Claud had been in Germany and asked what the Foreign Office would, or could, have done if the Gestapo had picked him up.

"I suppose," said Peake, after some consideration, "we might have got his sentence reduced from Death to Life."

The trip to Hamburg had to be made separately. It was not an affair in which the Captain could reasonably be involved. The children and their aunt were located. But here again the Committee had made one of its habitual little slip-ups. Claud had been assured in Paris that word would have been passed along the underground grapevine to the aunt, to expect a friend who would give a certain password and legitimate himself by telling a particular story. After that, she would talk freely and the question of getting the children to the Danish frontier could be dealt with. Unfortunately none of these arrangements had in practice been carried out. To the aunt, the password and the story were gibberish. They were suspect gibberish at that. So far from being welcomed as the potential rescuer, Claud found himself treated as possibly a maniac, and much more probably some kind of Nazi *provocateur*.

Since the aunt's dwelling was certainly under at least occasional surveillance by the Gestapo, Claud was reluctant to remain in it longer than absolutely necessary. He had counted on a maximum of an hour. It took him a full hour of blarney to convince her that he really was a courier of the Committee. "In her place," he said afterwards, "I wouldn't have been convinced at all." And even after that, the discussion of the practical arrangements took a good deal longer than it need have. For the aunt, being politically neutral, kept veering from the view that the removal of the children was unnecessary, to the idea that the Gestapo were absolute ninnies, and all that Claud need do was take them along with him to the frontier, flash his British passport at the exit point, and travel peacefully across with them.

The Paris Committee, under pressure of work, had of course omitted to supply in time the essential forged documents for the children to travel on. Procuring these through anti-Nazi elements in the relevant department was going to take at least twenty-four hours. Luckily, the city concerned was Hamburg, where anti-Nazism was possibly stronger than anywhere else in Germany. Even people who would have called themselves in a general way "Nazis" were often glad to maintain the old Hansa traditions by doing anything likely to impede and annoy those gross-mannered Prussian ruffians in Berlin. For the same reason, it was not excessively difficult for the aunt, now at last convinced of the need for the job to be done, to arrange for Claud to spend the night in a place where no questions were likely to be asked. She also made what seemed to him some rather ramshackle arrangements with a man living about half-way between Hamburg and the frontier who was to do duty as a temporary uncle for the two children and get them across to Denmark under their new names. Ramshackle or not, the arrangements worked and the children did get out. It was, Claud pointed out later, paradoxical, and on the whole encouraging, that all the most dangerous practical part of the job was done by people who considered themselves neutral and non-political, but could understand a human need when they finally saw it.

He had no wish to risk trying to get out of Germany on his own, without benefit of the Captain and Henry Luce. And the Captain was in Berlin, staying at the American Embassy. There were, admittedly, two other motives for showing his face in Berlin. One was simple curiosity to see how the familiar city looked under present conditions. The other was a matter of revenge.

In order to obviate the difficulty about hotel registration, it was arranged with the embassy that they should take a room in a good hotel sometimes used by them as an embassy guest house. No individual registration would be necessary. From this cosy base, and usually in the Captain's company, it was possible to venture occasionally into the streets of the capital.

The act of revenge was necessarily left until the last moment. It was to be taken upon a former acquaintance. This man had, in earlier years, proclaimed himself an ardent anti-Nazi. Many people had confided in him. Very soon after Hitler became Chancellor, he joined the Nazi party. At first people had supposed that this was a mere cover under which he could usefully pursue anti-Nazi activities. He rose to a fairly high position in the Ministry of Interior. A few people still confided in him. But the casualties among them became startlingly high. They were arrested and shot. Finally, through a piece of clumsiness on his part, his guilt as an informer became indubitable.

Claud did not feel himself equipped to carry out the assassination which he considered would have been well deserved. But it occurred to him that there was another action he could usefully take. It might, in the long run, cause the man more misery than a bullet. The American Embassy had already been kind enough to book tickets for the Captain and his companion on the plane to Paris. A couple of hours before departure, Claud called at the office of the well-padded official. He had himself announced by his real name, not the name on the passport. Since the official had access to the black-list, this was in itself a shock for him.

What followed was for him an exceedingly *mauvais quart d'heure*. Claud talked loudly and freely expressed his anti-Nazi sentiments. He appeared to be assuming that he knew nothing of the other man's treacheries.

The official, his visitor was happy to see, began literally to sweat. Obviously his first thought was to ring a bell and have this notorious enemy of the régime arrested. But to do so would involve the Gestapo. And the Gestapo might start wondering why the visitor had so confidently called upon this particular official. Would not such a visitor have been reliably assured that, despite apparent evidence to the contrary, the man was still a secret Red? Or at least a double agent? It would only be a shadow of doubt crossing their minds. But even a small shadow of the kind, at that time and place, would be quite enough to lose the man his job, and he would be lucky to escape a spell of observation and re-education in a concentration camp. Conversely, the visitor might himself be an *agent provocateur* from the Gestapo. He could have been sent to test whether this informer was really as good as he was supposed to be at gaining or retaining the confidence of anti-Nazis. And what, in that case, was the proper procedure?

After a quarter-hour of the treatment, Claud amiably took his leave. Using a favourite phrase he said, "I hope you're as well as you look." Since, as Claud said, the man looked as though he had just seen a peculiarly nasty and dangerous ghost, the remark had a sinister ambiguity. By way of a final dose of poison, Claud, with his hand on the door handle, wished the official "all the luck you deserve". He then left for the airport. He was confident that the man would not resolve this dilemma in time to interfere with his departure. And he was fairly certain that he would not resolve it at all. He would go on living, if he did live long, in the shadow of a fear. For Claud had not only given his name to the official's male secretary but insisted on it being written down. And who knew what reports on visitors that secretary might be making?

"Considering what the fellow was guilty of," Claud said later, "it wasn't much of a revenge. Still, one must do what one can."

A judicious Englishman to whom I told this story much later said, "It goes to show what I've always said. The Scots are even more innately vindictive than you Irish."

8 Can't happen here

I HAVE no idea who first used the phrase "it can't happen here".
It was no doubt sincerely meant as an expression of belief in
the stability and decency of Western, and in particular Anglo-
Saxon, institutions. It corresponded to the schoolboy's well-
known definition of revolution as "a form of government
abroad".

By the early Thirties the phrase had taken on a derisive
connotation. It was used specifically to indicate the attitude
of people who supposed that everything was cosy in the
Western garden. But as has so often happened since, despite the
proddings of the satirists, people in the West and most particularly in Britain, were constantly being taken by surprise by the
things which not only could, but did, actually "happen here".

In the opinion of *The Week* almost anything could happen
anywhere. Given the forces loose in the world, and the enormous
loot available for seizure, that seemed a reasonable assumption.
For making such assumptions and publishing them, it was
under fairly constant attack by friends and by ill-wishers alike.
The ill-wishers of course said that it was simply seeking to stir
up trouble, or rather, to trouble perfectly calm waters in which
it could then fish. Friends shook their heads and said that
although very startling and unpleasant things did from time to
time happen, *The Week* on this or that occasion was going too
far. It was making itself ridiculous, laying itself open to counter-
attack, leading with its chin.

The frequency of this type of reaction, even by well-disposed
subscribers, to that sort of story had a more than immediate
significance. Simple incredulity of this kind was a notable
ingredient of British thinking at the time. When I saw British
thinking, I am not of course referring to the thinking of the
Foreign Office or of informed people in, say, the City of London.
I am speaking of the British public at large. Probably an entire
sociological study would be required in order to explain this
particular phenomenon. It would surely not be true to say

that the British people as individuals are less alertly suspicious of one another than individuals belonging to other nations. Their readiness to believe that the man next door, the farmer, the grocer, the banker, and half the other people at a cocktail party, are up to no good, is well developed. But when villainy or the possibilities of villainy reach a certain social or international level, it sometimes seems as though the British in general are wearing their short-sighted spectacles. This can of course lead to some dangerous states of complacency.

This complacency Claud personally found not only dangerous but almost incredible. Perhaps over-optimistically he believed that if only he could convey to the public what was happening on the political backstairs and in the underworld of Europe known to him and to a good many other people familiar with those murky scenes, some disturbance of the complacency would be achieved.

The Week made a characteristic attempt of this kind in its issue of 6 November 1934. The issue appeared not long after the assassination in Marseilles of King Alexander of Yugoslavia and M. Barthou, the French Foreign Minister.

In a story headed "Assassination Plans", *The Week* reported:

From a source in Geneva, which has hitherto proved reliable, we are informed of new discussions in Munich among members of the Foreign Department of the Nazi Party regarding the possibility of steps being taken in the present critical international situation to weaken the existing close relationship between the French and British governments.

Although several of the plans now being discussed perhaps may never be put into effect, it appears to be a matter of general interest to report at least one of them.

This was officially discussed in Munich at least seven weeks ago, that is to say before the Marseilles killings had been carried out, but when a plan for carrying them out was already well advanced.

The plan is based on the necessity of finding quickly a means of creating a coolness between English and French opinion.

It is calculated that such a purpose will be very well served by the killing on French soil of some popular British public figure, preferably a member of the Royal family or—for example— Princess Marina.

In order to carry out such an assassination successfully, it is realized that the connivance of at least some of the Chiefs of the French police force would be essential.

This, however, is not felt to present any insuperable obstacle.

It will be possible in fact to kill two birds with one stone by arranging with the Paris police that the assassin, who would be killed immediately after the murder, should be identified as a Communist.

In this way the origin of the crime could be concealed and at the same time the police and the Right wing chiefs would be pleased at the opportunity of bringing off a first-class frame-up of the United Front in France.

In this connection will be recalled the manoeuvres of the French Right and of the police in connection with the assassination of President Doumer by Gorguloff, who was at first admitted to be a White Russian emigré, and later was suddenly announced to be a Bolshevik.

To what extent Gorguloff was actually coached by the police before the shooting has never been quite clear, although at the time it was strongly rumoured that the police and the Right had organized the assassination.

As already pointed out in *The Week* and elsewhere, the killing of Alexander and Barthou organized in Berlin, Munich, Vienna and Budapest, required a certain co-operation on the part of the French authorities.

The technique and the strategy of the Marseilles murders turned out to be very successful.

Despite the customary nonsense put out for public consumption, the fact is that the murders have resulted in a very grave disturbance of Franco-Italian relations and in a strengthening of the German influence at Belgrade.

The immediate subsequent issue of *The Week*, that of 14 November 1934, was prefaced by an illuminating editorial note.

We see by the mails that a number of subscribers, regarding the report published last week on a plan by the Foreign Department of the Nazi Party to arrange the assassination of a prominent British figure in Paris as "fantastic", have jumped to the conclusion that the story must be a baseless product of anti-Fascist enthusiasm.

It is to be suggested that the same comment would have been made had we published in June news of a plan by the same department to murder the then Austrian Chancellor, or in September, news of the projected assassination at Marseilles or Paris of Alexander of Yugoslavia and Barthou.

We regret that considerations which ought to be obvious prevented and still prevent us from offering a more detailed and possibly more convincing account not of the plan itself, but of the channels through which the news of it reached us.

It is at the same time a curious and perhaps significant phenomenon that what have become the most commonplace events as strokes of international policy are still regarded as fantastic, though people continue to believe in the "impossibility" of certain events even after they have happened.

There was another broader and rather more tricky aspect of this type of story. It concerned not only stories of impending assassinations but of various other skulduggeries at various levels, international or domestic.

Pointing to the exposure in *The Week* of some such embryonic skulduggery, a friend said to Claud, "Are you really as sure as you sound that this is actually going to happen?"

Claud said: "I am not at all sure that it is going to happen. But I am entirely sure that if we don't publish it it certainly will happen."

He invented a name for this type of activity. He called it "preventive journalism". There were of course plenty of people who felt that it is no business of a journalist to go about being "preventive". He should either confine himself to reporting on events after they have occurred, or if the worst comes to the worst, to non-committal hints of certain sinister possibilities in the situation.

Obviously there is a great deal to be said for this viewpoint. The practice of "preventive journalism" is dangerous in many different ways. On the lowest and most sordid level, it certainly lays the journalist open to libel actions or, as once or twice occurred in the history of *The Week*, to fierce retaliation, by those who felt themselves exposed against those they imagined to be responsible for the leakage of information. On a different level "preventive journalism" is likely to be not merely un-rewarding, but actually damaging to the journalist. Its very success is in this sense harmful to him. If the projected sinister event is prevented from occurring, a majority of readers, as *The Week* found in the 1930s, are going to draw the conclusion that the whole thing was a *canard* in the first place. In other words, if you cry "Fire! Fire!" too early, and then stamp out the fire before the building is properly ablaze, the passers-by are once again going to shake their heads and reply "Little liar!"

There is another danger of which the journalist who goes in for prevention in this sense has to be constantly aware. Nothing is easier, certainly nothing was easier in the 1930s, than to pick up reports of one sort or another of impending crime. People attuned to the realities of the period were in no danger of light-heartedly accepting such reports. On the contrary, what they light-heartedly did was brush them off. Another sort of people accustomed to breathe the atmosphere behind the scenes and with some knowledge of, for example, the mentality of members of the Foreign Department of the Nazi party, were of course in constant danger of taking such reports too much at their face value. There were certainly numerous occasions on which Claud fell victim to this type of credulity. Just how many, it is in the nature of things hard to say. For if a plot were exposed and then fizzed out, who could possibly say for certain that it had never existed, or on the other hand that it had existed but been ruined by exposure?

Claud readily admitted the dangers involved and also the fact that he had not always successfully escaped them. This being agreed, he maintained that given reasonable intelligence, energy and general alertness, it ought to be possible to avoid most of the dangers most of the time. The alertness naturally consisted first in making a correct estimate of the reliability of a given informant or group of informants. Secondly it was necessary to develop a kind of sixth sense which told you when the informant or informants had either gone over to the enemy and were funnelling you false information on purpose, or had become tired and out of touch and in consequence had no genuine information to offer. He said that in his experience (and I suppose this is true of most people engaged in any kind of "intelligence" work) even informants who are otherwise perfectly honest hate to admit that their sources of information have simply dried up. And in the case of paid informants this reluctance is easily understood. When their sources dry up their money will dry up too. But since *The Week* very rarely paid anyone for any information, this financial motive was lacking.

I think that at the outset Claud was inclined to believe that because his informants were offering their services free they were less likely than hired men to fake their news. Experience soon showed him that this was not so. In this connection he said it was of the greatest importance to keep constantly in mind a remark of Lord Melbourne, Queen Victoria's first Prime Minister, who had been active on the political stage throughout the most lurid intrigues of the early nineteenth century. A friend said to him: "After your long and varied experience of political life, do you not reach the conclusion that mankind is exceedingly corrupt?"

"Not corrupt," said Lord Melbourne, "just damned vain."

It was therefore essential to realize that quite a number of people who could not possibly be described as corrupt might, out of vanity, even unconscious vanity, pretend that they were still on excellent terms with the Foreign Minister of whatever state they happened to be residing in, long after they had become suspected of seducing the Foreign Minister's wife and been shown the door.

These in Claud's view were simply the normal hazards of the profession. He still thought it pusillanimous to try to avoid the risks involved in preventive journalism. "Surely," he would say to anxious friends, "it is a lot better to make a public goat of myself twice running, than to let those sons of bitches," this with a comprehensive gesture indicating all the sons of bitches one could think of, "get away with anything, even one time in three."

Preventive journalism at its best was illustrated by a lurid story in *The Week* of 9 January 1935. The occasion was the plebiscite which was to decide the future of the Saar district. Under the terms of the Treaty of Versailles the Saar district, rich in coal and other industries, had been for fifteen years under the control of the victors of World War I. Now in 1935 a plebiscite was to decide whether the district should be returned to Germany. A great deal more was at stake even than the industrial wealth of the Saar. The result of the voting was going to be treated by the whole of Europe as a yardstick by which to measure some realities about the Nazi government.

Anti-Nazis, including often enough correspondents of *The Week*, sometimes cautiously, sometimes audaciously, inclined to suggest that the Hitler régime had been imposed upon the German people by the alliance of big business with the organized gangsterism of the Brown Shirts. Theoretically at least Hitler's writ did not run in the Saar. So that, again theoretically, the German population of the Saar now had an opportunity to show freely what Germans really thought of Hitlerism. If the optimists who imagined a German people groaning under Hitler's yoke were right, then the people of the Saar would certainly not vote to incorporate themselves in the tyrannous Reich. And if they did vote to do that, the result would be viewed far and wide as some sort of proof that so far from being imposed upon Germany, Hitlerism expressed the free will of the German people.

All this was particularly true in relation to the British public. For at that time at least the general British public seriously believed that free elections or a plebiscite held under the sublimely neutral supervision of an international commission must result in an expression of the voice of democracy, the true will of the people.

The Week, which believed no such thing, was at some pains to draw attention to the harsher facts of the situation and particularly to the thoroughly realistic approach of the Nazi government itself. I am not suggesting that if the Nazi government had refrained from terrorism, intimidation and trickery, the outcome of the plebiscite would have been otherwise than it was. Despite *The Week* I was always at best doubtful whether the supposed antagonism of the large majority of the German people to Hitler was much more than the product of wishful thinking. I am not quite sure just how firmly Claud himself believed in it. As I have said earlier, he did consider it of the highest importance to publicize whatever evidence was available of dissensions and weaknesses within the Reich. These existed. The Nazi government naturally did its best to suppress the evidence. For a variety of reasons, some well-meaning and some disreputable, the big press of Britain and France also ignored most of it.

Of perhaps greater importance was the press's habit of ignoring most of the uncomfortable facts of Nazi terrorist activities outside the borders of Germany. The shrugging off of such facts seemed to *The Week* a perilous deception of the public. While almost everyone else was proclaiming the free and democratic nature of the plebiscite in the Saar, *The Week* published the following story headed "On the Way to the Saar".

The steamship *Watussi*, Deutsche Ost Afrika Linie, Capetown to Hamburg, is due to touch at Southampton tomorrow or the day after. She carries one way or another some curious evidence regarding the "arrangements" made by the Nazi authorities for securing the largest possible favourable vote in the Saar plebiscite next Sunday.

Just how curious will only be known when the *Watussi* gets into Southampton, and it is seen whether a certain Hans Froelich "from Johannesburg" is aboard or not, and how he is. Here are the facts.

Hans Froelich is entitled to vote in the Saar plebiscite, having been domiciled in Brücken-Stadt, on June 28, 1919. Recently he saw by the papers that all such persons could obtain free return passage to the Saar for the voting period by application to the German Consul General.

He therefore communicated with the Consulate General for Germany who forwarded to him certain papers which when filled up were to be forwarded to the Advisory Bureau of the Deutsche Front for Persons entitled to vote in the plebiscite. In November 1934 Froelich got a letter from this Bureau informing him that he was entitled to vote and advising him of his voting number.

The Bureau also informed him he would be given a free return ticket to the Saar.

A few days after that he was notified by the Deutsche Ost Afrika Linie that the line would give him a return ticket to the Saar and that he would have to leave on the *SS Ubena* sailing November 1934.

On the 29th he went to the dock and boarded the *SS Ubena*. There on board he saw the leader of the Johannesburg Nazis who was already on the ship and scanning the passengers. Froelich was known to the Johannesburg Nazis as an anti-Fascist. When the Johannesburg leader saw Froelich he began to abuse him loudly, shouting insulting remarks at him. Just after that the First Officer of the *Ubena* came up to Froelich and told him to get off the boat.

Froelich said he was a passenger on the boat.

In that case, said the officer, we shall know how to deal with you effectively once we get on the high seas. The officer, becoming very menacing, warned Froelich that if he considered his own interests he had better not proceed.

In view of this threat, and having from the First Officer the very strong impression that if he sailed on that boat he was extraordinarily liable to slip overboard by accident during the voyage Froelich left without having time even to get his ticket from the purser before the boat sailed.

He was then stranded in Capetown, effectively as it seemed cut off from exercising his vote. However, refusing to accept this manoeuvre as final, Froelich got a lawyer to get the Deutsche Ost Afrika Linie to put through arrangements for him to reach the Saar in time for him to vote, pointing out that the line already had contracted to do this, that he had had other means of getting there which he would have used if he had not been promised a passage by the line, and that he had already given up his job and refused others because he was going to the Saar.

After some hesitation he secured from the line a passage on the *SS Watussi* which left Capetown on December 21st.

His friends in Capetown who knew that Froelich was known to the Nazis, and knew too the Nazi methods in these matters, begged and implored him not to sail.

He said he would sail and try to vote whatever happened. So his friends persuaded him to swear out an affidavit giving the facts and further to cable them immediately on his arrival at Southampton. This he did.

Week subscribers in South Africa arranged for the affidavit to be forwarded air mail to *The Week*. It reached us three days ago. (For the benefit of certain burglariously inclined Nazi gentlemen in London, we may mention that the document is not in this office, so they may spare themselves some trouble.)

Publication of this cliff-hanger story in *The Week* produced the desired effect. Even in stagnant waters it produced some turbulence. In its subsequent issue *The Week* was able to report some of the results. Under the heading "You Always Have Company" the paper said:

Amazing sidelight on how the British authorities estimate the terrorist methods of the Nazi organization was thrown by the action of the Home Office and Scotland Yard on the arrival of Hans Froelich, South African Jew on his way to vote in the Saar plebiscite.

The story of the previous attempt to intimidate Froelich and prevent him leaving South Africa for the Saar by broadly hinting that setting foot on the boat was about equivalent to jumping overboard in mid-ocean was told at length in the last issue of *The Week*.

That story was sufficient to give some indication of the exact truth of the statements by United Front supporters to "neutral" journalists today that the Saar vote was carried out under conditions of terror which virtually invalidated its claims to be a free vote.

As a result of *The Week*'s information regarding the perilous circumstances of Froelich's voyage to Germany via Southampton, half Fleet Street had its men on the dockside to see whether Froelich was alive or not.

Froelich was alive with a full story to tell of the extraordinary attempts to humiliate him by the passengers on board the boat.

From Froelich's account, however, it was evident that the Nazi authorities, already somewhat nervous of the fact that Froelich was known to have discussed his previous adventure on the *SS Ubena* with a number of friends in South Africa, had passed to the captain an extra special tip to see that nothing "happened" to Froelich aboard the boat, since the publicity attendant on his non-appearance was liable to be highly embarrassing.

So Froelich got to Southampton.

He was met by Home Office officials and by detectives. Detectives accompanied him to the train. He asked why. They answered "In case the Nazis are out for you."

He travelled from Southampton to London. On the station in London he noticed two men following him. He changed direction

and walked the other way. They changed direction too and followed him still. He tried once more, they still followed. Froelich
stopped and faced them. They explained that they were from
Scotland Yard and showed credentials. They added that for
safety's sake, they would accompany him to his hotel.

They did so. When they got there, the detectives refused to let
Froelich out of their sight until they had formally turned him over
to the care of the house detective of the hotel.

These facts were not, for some reason, reported in the local press.
They appear to be worth reporting as an indication of the real
atmosphere of Europe today, where a South African Jew who
happens to have distributed anti-Nazi leaflets in the streets of
Johannesburg, has to be protected by plain-clothes men in the
streets of London lest he be violently done away with by the
agents of the German Government.

A correspondent who has some experience of these matters comments that the situation here in London has got so that you never
know whether the grim-looking people who follow you about are
members of the political gang out to get you, or members of
another political gang out to protect you from the first gang, for
fear that a death on the premises or an unexplained disappearance
will prove politically embarrassing.

9 Abyssinian Road

IT would probably need a minute or two for more than one person in five today to answer the question "Just what was the Wal-Wal Incident and what did it mean?" The British press were reluctant to state in so many words that it meant that some time, sooner or later and probably sooner, Mussolini was going to attack Abyssinia. *The Week*, I take leave to suppose, was not deeply concerned with the welfare of Ras Tafari, Emperor of Abyssinia—another dictator, though a very small one. But, because he was so small and almost helpless compared with Mussolini, he instantly excited *The Week*'s political sympathy. It was upon Mussolini and his aggressive plans that the paper concentrated. As appears later, in a somewhat different connexion, *The Week* had a peculiarly well-placed "correspondent" actually occupying a responsible position in the Italian Embassy in London. With his often exaggerated view of the goodness of human nature, Claud said one must really be cheerful enough to assume that among any ten apparently full-blooded fascists, there must be at least one who was secretly anti-fascist. And of the others, there were likely to be two who would betray their cause for the sake of satisfying a private grudge or sordid ambition. I must say that this theory worked out rather better than could have been expected in relation not only to the Italian Fascists but the Nazis too.

What with *The Week* which was beginning to be quoted more and more extensively in the world press, and the *Daily Worker*, the Henry Luce enterprises, the Council for Civil Liberties, and a number of other activities undertaken under a proliferation of pseudonyms, by the middle of 1935 Claud, according to his friends, was beginning to show signs of strain. For a while he, as usual, took this kind of comment as an obscure way of suggesting that he should either work less or drink less. When he heard the word "nervous breakdown" he listened to it with interest; he knew it to be a disagreeable thing liable to happen to other people.

Then quite suddenly, at the beginning of August 1935 something or other persuaded him that they were right. He needed a holiday. Since he has always been exceedingly sensitive to changes in the weather, and above all to bad weather, I daresay the reason which convinced him was the arrival of a long cold spell. His conversion to the idea of a holiday was as sudden as his refusal to accept it had been prolonged. One morning he rang up Crystal at the office and announced that he was leaving that afternoon for the Mediterranean.

Presumably at a normally run newspaper or magazine such an event would have been of minor importance. Editors take holidays and there is someone ready to stand in for them. But things at *The Week* were not like that. With such rare exceptions as his absence on the hunger march, or brief trips abroad, Claud had always written every word that appeared in the paper. No contributed articles were ever permitted. Even when people sent, as they fairly often did, carefully written articles or reports, these were ruthlessly digested and re-written by the editor. "A little sheet like this," he said, "must be a closed fist. Other weeklies may perhaps be able to afford to have their fingers sprawling all over the place. Not us. There has to be one point of departure, and in consequence one style. That's what gives even our tiny fist a punch."

For rather more obvious reasons, nobody but himself was told, except in cases of direst necessity, of the names of correspondents and informants. "Ought not one to assume," Claud said, when people got bothered about this, "that at any time your flat may be searched, or someone will arrest you, turn you upside down, and shake you to see what falls out of your pockets?" Angry friends naturally replied that this was a typically high-faluting excuse for failing to answer letters, losing letters received, and forgetting dinner invitations. Whatever the truth about that, the practical results of the policy were that the state of affairs at *The Week* (never, I judge, very far from the brink of chaos) was apt to become entirely chaotic when the editor abruptly took off.

Crystal I am sure was reasonably philosophic. But others concerned were in a state of near panic. Who was to write *The Week*? Where was the information coming from? Claud had some pleasure no doubt in telling them that they had all been pestering him to take a holiday and now he was going to do it. He left behind enough material to fill, as he thought, about five-sixths of the paper. He promised to air-mail the remainder from Paris where he planned a couple of hard-working days.

He did so, and from Paris took a train for Port Bou, in those far-off days a tiny fishing village just on the Spanish side of the frontier. On the way something attracted him about the little coastal town of Sète. He decided to spend a day there. He had already made arrangements for the next issue but one of *The Week* to be put together by others in his absence. He had determined to have no contact with the office at all during his fortnight's holiday. However some nervous instinct or twitch caused him on his second day in Sète to ring up the office in London. The news was terrible. One of his recurrent nightmares had come true.

That is to say, by a string of unlucky accidents not just one but three of the principal stories he had left behind or sent from Paris, all from sources normally confidential and ex-clusive to *The Week*, had leaked in London and Paris. They had been published or, according to Fleet Street informants, were just about to be published in the London newspapers.

The stories were thus useless from *The Week*'s point of view.

A quick look at the time-tables showed him that if substitute material were to reach London in time it would have to be mailed from Sète that very evening.

Even years later he would recall this situation with a shudder. As a news source a small town at, so to speak, the wrong end of the south of France was about as arid a territory as could be imagined. Being overworked and overtired, to the point of near-exhaustion, it seemed to him that his mind had somehow blanked out everything he had heard during the previous fortnight or so in London which might have been used as the basis for a story.

Even the delicious Mediterranean sunshine which he normally found so stimulating failed to make any ideas sprout in the barren soil of his mind. Hoping that a couple of glasses of Pernod might do the trick, he sat down at the table of a pavement café. The drinks failed their purpose. He had found

in the past that sometimes the mere act of sitting at a typewriter with a blank sheet of copy paper in it was enough to set
a train of thought in motion. It was obviously worse than useless
to spend time wandering about Sète in the hope of borrowing a
typewriter. At that period it had the air of a town in which
nobody even possessed a typewriter, still less was likely to
lend it to a passing stranger. He had always maintained that to
write in long hand actually impeded the flow. He had hardly
used that method of writing since 1929.

Without much hope, therefore, he called for a pen, ink and
paper. He sat and looked at the paper and still nothing happened. Near despair, he went through his pockets. There
might just possibly be something scribbled on an old envelope
or stray leaf of a notebook in the last few days, from which he
could get some ideas. He drew another blank. Then while
fumbling for cigarettes he found a slit in the lining on one
pocket of his jacket. Putting his hand through the slit, he felt
between the lining and the cloth a crumpled piece of paper. It
proved to be one page of an obscure, poorly mimeographed
little financial tip-sheet issued intermittently in Zurich. It was
circulated, when it appeared at all, to a narrowly limited
number of bankers and other speculators in Switzerland and
Paris.

Claud could not remember ever having seen it before. Since
there were a couple of addresses and telephone numbers
scribbled in the margin it seemed that one of his Paris friends
in a hurry to give him these had found this piece of paper handy,
written the addresses and numbers on it and torn it off.

Sitting in Sète, Claud started gloomily and abstractedly to
glance at the dreary little pieces of financial information it
contained.

Suddenly his eye was caught by an item only four lines
long. It stated that a consortium registered in Switzerland had
been granted permission by the Abyssinian government to
construct a road through the country. The amount to be
invested by the consortium in the exploitation of this concession
was given as five million Swiss francs.

Claud candidly admitted to himself that according to strict
journalistic principles this information could hardly be used,
certainly could not be used at any length without exhaustive

checking. But it seemed to him that this was no time for the application of strict journalistic principles. And from there it was easy to reach the conclusion that if the thing was to be used at all it must be used boldly and extensively. In any case the alternative seemed to be the non-appearance of the next issue of *The Week* or its appearance with only a couple of pages. Pushing the rusty nib through the couples of flies which had drowned themselves in the ink-pot, he started to scribble.

He headed the piece "With or Without Geneva".

With just half an hour to spare it was in the mail to London, where three days later it appeared as follows:

With world attention hopefully centred on Geneva, news comes from Addis Ababa that the Abyssinian Government had granted permission for the construction of a road through that country to a consortium registered in Switzerland.

Oddly enough, the consortium, in addition to the discretion shown in getting itself registered in Switzerland, has successfully avoided any undue publicity in the British press, a fact exceedingly curious to reflect upon when it is considered that Abyssinia is—surely—news at the present moment and that the road in question is liable, if it ever gets built, very probably to alter the transport situation, in fact the whole international situation of the country.

Five million Swiss francs is the amount of money proposed by the consortium to be invested in the said road.

The road itself is to lead a matter of 350 miles from Addis Ababa, capital of Abyssinia, to Kurmurk, on the frontier of British Sudan.

Translated into terms of speed, what this means is that a journey which at present has to be undertaken by caravans, and lasts approximately three weeks, will suddenly become a trip capable of being carried out by motor lorries—military or otherwise—in the space of two days.

The consortium gets—together with its concessions—three highly important rights.

First it has not only the right but the obligation, *itself to carry out the transport arrangements along the road.*

In other words the controllers of the consortium at the moment well camouflaged behind a thick hedge of proxies will become the owners and controllers of a transport system throughout fitted to compete on equal footing with the present Addis Ababa–Djibouti railway. Or to complete the transport system represented by said railway.

The Addis Ababa–Djibouti railway is—as already reported in *The Week*—controlled by a French consortium on whose board of directors are prominently represented the Banque de Paris et des Pays-Bas and the de Wendel armament interests.

The second right which accompanies the concession is of the kind customary in such cases: that is to say, the Abyssinian Government pledges itself not to grant to any competing company any competing line of transport—apparently including rail as well as road transport—within forty miles of the Swiss consortium's road on either side.

A glance at the contour map of that section of Abyssinia shows immediately that what this amounts to is a monopoly of transport ways from the north to Addis Ababa.

The third right acquired by these interested "Swiss" is the most interesting perhaps of all.

It is the right to "first refusal" or prior claim on any and all mining rights for a distance of twenty miles on either side of the protected road.

At this point it is worthwhile to quote the little piece of press publicity discreetly released by the consortium.

"It is entirely within the bounds of possibility," declares this interesting effort, "that the road which is planned may in some possible districts lead conceivably through the alleged rich gold and platinum areas of Abyssinia."

Unacquainted as we are with the publicity man in question, we salute him without hesitation as a genius and master of his craft.

For the publicity material quoted was not distributed broadcast like the publicity matter of oil companies where it is dubious whether they have any oil or not. It was not even sent out indiscriminately to the financial editors of newspapers.

Quite simply it was allowed to reach the hands of a certain number of journalists selected, it appears, as being suitably placed to give publicity not as a financial come-on "it's your money we want" character to this concern, which is quite evidently in no need of this type of publicity.

On the contrary, what this consortium needs and what it is getting is an extremely efficient publicity whereof the general effect is that the consortium is on to a good thing: that it has the ear of the Abyssinian Government and that no one else need make any effort to tread on the pre-empted grass.

At this point the imagination of the writer in the Sète café was beginning to warm up. His story continued:

Of peculiar interest in this connection is the fact that the contract has quite obviously been framed with an eye to the possible redivision of Abyssinia among other powers.

The contract has been drawn up in such a way (or at least the lawyers of the consortium have tried hard to draw it up in such a way) that whether or not any power or group of powers can be given a mandate or sphere of influence over Abyssinia, this contract will still stand, or—if any power chooses to ignore it—it will still offer a magnificent "casus belli" to any interested power whose "rights" under this agreement are threatened by any political agreement reached at Geneva or elsewhere by the representatives of the "interested powers".

Considering the value of the gold and platinum mines possibly to be exploited in Abyssinia, it is indeed a matter of acute interest to learn that the northern concession in these mines has already been granted. The question now remains:

How many troops and whose troops will be sent to ensure that the perfect legality of the above-described concession is assured in fact?

Determined to forget all about London and *The Week*, Claud took the next train to Port Bou. Lying on the beach there a few days later he was casually reading the *Vanguardia*, Barcelona's popular and somewhat sensational daily paper. A particular set of heavy headlines caught his eye. They and the story from London which followed spoke of disclosures of international importance. Amazing news, said the story, had been received in London, and published in *The Week*, regarding the formation of a consortium which might well be the basis of a secret plan to partition Abyssinia. The story thereafter followed the main lines of what Claud had written for *The Week*. He was slightly shaken.

But he reflected that after all *Vanguardia* was not a particularly important newspaper. The fact that its London correspondent, possibly hard up for material, had passed on *The Week*'s story, which, as Claud frankly admitted to himself, was quite a load of bricks to have made out of one small straw, need not be considered alarming.

He continued to sun himself complacently at Port Bou. But later that evening news came of apparently revolutionary rioting in Toulon. Claud immediately decided to abandon his holiday and take the train for the great French naval base. On the platform at Marseilles in the early morning, he bought copies of the local newspapers. They too had headlines about the consortium. They too had sensational stories of the concession and its supposed consequences. At least one of the correspondents, obviously a man well used to reading between the lines of *The Week*, had taken the statement that the publicity material was not broadcast like the publicity matter of oil companies as a broad and sufficient hint that in reality not only the minerals mentioned in *The Week*'s story but oil too was in question. On this theme and its international and military implications, he dwelt at some length.

Claud confesses that reading these reports in the train between Marseilles and Toulon he felt aghast. He understood, he said, how Frankenstein must have felt when his monster really got into business. For most of the day at Toulon he was too busy observing the rioting in which several people were killed, and telephoning the reports to the *Daily Worker*, to read newspapers. But by evening the Paris papers had arrived. They too had lavish reports and commentaries on the subject of the consortium. These papers drew different conclusions, according to their differing political points of view. But they seemed to be at one in estimating the matter as of high significance.

Reading some of the papers one could have the impression that the consortium and the disclosure of its existence might trigger off an international war almost immediately. Relaxing on the Cannebière, Claud speculated as to what might happen were he to telephone some major news agency with a report describing exactly how what now seemed to him more and more like a mere figment of his own imagination had come into being at the café table in Sète. Would that perhaps be the prudent, as well as ethical, thing to do? Experience rather conveniently told him that the story, whatever its origins, was now moving briskly ahead under its own steam and was beyond his control. The only result of some sort of confession on his part would be that the agency to which he made it would assume that the confession, not the story, was some sort of practical joke. They would suppose that he was making it for some mysterious and possibly disreputable ulterior motive or, a far worse assumption, that he was either drunk or had gone mad.

Though still busy with the aftermath of the riot, Claud continued to be agitated by the results of the consortium story which itself was still agitating the local press. "The thing bothered me a good deal," he said later. But that particular bother ended quite suddenly.

One of the local newspapers carried a report from its Paris correspondent. This correspondent in turn quoted the *Echo de Paris*, which had just published a despatch from its London correspondent. The London correspondent, a highly responsible individual, was able to quote an official statement by the Foreign Office. It was to the effect that the reports of a consortium formed to exploit a concession in Abyssinia were correct. There was, however, the Foreign Office spokesman added, "no reason to attach political importance to the event".

The official confirmation by the Foreign Office did great good to the reputation of *The Week*. Claud on his return to London freely explained to one and all the circumstances under which he had "invented it". The only effect of this was to convince people that he had got the story from some particularly high and vulnerable source, and that the Sète episode had been made up in order to protect the source.

Even now it is not, I gather, quite clear to people who ought to know, whether this story in *The Week* was, in fact, a preview of the famous Rickett Concession in Abyssinia. The Rickett business was disclosed months later by Sir Percival Phillips, Special Correspondent of the *Daily Telegraph*. Sir Percival scored a notable journalistic victory over his fellow war correspondents. And his story certainly owed nothing whatever to *The Week*'s earlier, and far less explicit, account of a concession. Claud was of opinion that there was really very little connexion between the concession he wrote of and the Rickett Concession. One or two of the personalities involved seemed to be identical. But then, considering that any financier or group of financiers seeking concessions in Abyssinia was liable to use identical channels, this wasn't necessarily of much significance.

There was at one time an attempt to suggest that Phillips's scoop had been somehow "pre-scooped" by *The Week*. This was nonsense. The only common element was the fact that both the editor of *The Week* and the Special Correspondent of the *Daily Telegraph* were obviously aware that that kind of war, conducted by a heavily armed modern power against very unmodern-minded tribesmen and guerillas, is likely to be decided in the back-room of financiers rather than on the field of battle.

The scrap of paper at Sète would, one may suppose, have been more or less meaningless to anyone not accustomed to reading the political news backwards, as it were; that is, starting with the financial reports and working on from there. *The Week* had in fact on several occasions drawn attention to powerful Paris-based interests in the potentialities of Abyssinia, and thus to the Italian Fascist lobby in Paris.

The Week's continuous attention to Italian plans and actions in the Mediterranean was a fairly regular cause of annoyance to Mussolini's ludicrous Foreign Minister Ciano. It would be an insult to the young to describe Ciano as having been childish. During much of that period, the situation was made the more farcical by the fact that the Italian Ambassador to the Court of St. James's was Count Grandi. As was remarked of Grandi by one of Claud's friends who knew him well, was profoundly trusted by him, but who regarded him with treacherous derision, he looked like a man who had grown a beard in order to give himself time to make up his mind, while he talked with you, who he really was: whether indeed he existed at all.

There was an occasion when, in addition to general disclosures of facts supposed to be secret, *The Week* offered some detailed information regarding the exact nature of Italian armaments on, for example, the island of Pantelleria. The information included the position of gun emplacements and the calibre of the guns. It was not a disclosure pleasing to the Italian government. But since Count Grandi, through either illiteracy, laziness or arrogance, did not bother to catch the habit common among most of his colleagues in the Diplomatic

Corps of reading that small, squalid-looking anti-fascist sheet, nothing happened until the sheet in question reached Rome. Then indeed the telephone between Rome and the London Embassy started furiously to buzz. The fullest possible report must be made immediately. The unhappy Grandi naturally had to conceal as well as possible the fact that he had not the least notion of what the people in Rome were talking about. He had even less idea that one of the two men in the room with him while he conducted this extremely awkward conversation was, in point of fact, an active correspondent of *The Week*.

He told someone to rush out and buy a copy. It was explained to him that *The Week* was not available on bookstalls. It could be obtained by direct subscription only. He told them to get on to the offices of the publication right away and have the copy sent. Claud had anticipated a development of this sort, and he reminded Crystal of the supposedly very strict rule that only those who were already subscribers were entitled to receive back numbers if they ordered them. (This rule was made partly for economy reasons, partly to prevent the ever-active horde of libel-racketeering lawyers who did such good business in London from getting their paws on back copies and then inciting some fellow to take an action and split the profits.)

So when the Italian Embassy rang up, there was a longish pause while Crystal purported to be looking through the subscription lists.

To his great pleasure Claud could hear the outraged voice of the Embassy Secretary, not the crypto-correspondent of *The Week*, but an enthusiastic toad-eater for Grandi and Ciano, shouting "But this is the Italian Embassy on the line. Kindly be good enough to receive our messenger immediately when he calls for the issue in question. Payment will be made in cash."

This last, supposedly clinching promise from that particular source naturally gave everyone at the Victoria Street end special delight.

Crystal said that the editor was not present, but that she would seek advisement on the matter as soon as he returned. "But when? When?" screeched the Secretary. "It is a matter concerning the policy of our government." With immense dignity, Crystal replied in that near-parody of the Anglo-English accent she could sometimes adopt, that it was also a matter concerning the policy of the publication. They could ring back in an hour, she told them.

At this point a somewhat malign notion crossed Claud's mind. Many months before, *The Week* had conducted, successfully, an attack upon an official of the War Office. I myself, as a subscriber to *The Week*, felt that the attack was disagreeably personal. The allegation, a true one, was that the official in question, who had a good deal to do with the allotment of military contracts, was at the same time a considerable shareholder in an armaments firm. I thought then, and have always thought since, that the unfortunate official's financial investments were doubtless in the charge of some broker. He probably had no idea that he held any armament shares at all. So far as he was concerned, they might as well have been in the cheese-manufacturing business. It seemed to me unfair to pillory the man for what was, at worst, a careless indiscretion.

Claud denied then, and has always denied since, that anybody reading the story could possibly suppose that the integrity of the official in question was impugned. What was being impugned was a system, already denounced by a British official commission, under which people, however outstanding their honesty, might be held to have a certain duality of interest. He wrote that "while one knows what can happen abroad, and cannot possibly happen here, it is wrong that even British officials should be exposed to the obvious dangers of such a situation."

Friends of the official concerned made things rather more difficult by trying to prove that the official was a man of very modest means who could not possibly have had that number of shares in anything. *The Week* returned to the attack.

After a couple of weeks, Kingsley Martin was able to persuade his lawyers that even the *New Statesman* might now safely enter the ring. The paper, he wrote, had been waiting for the heavens, or the roof, to fall in on *The Week*. Nothing had happened. Therefore it was time, it seemed, for even a respectable organ such as the *New Statesman* to raise its voice and enquire why?

A question was put down in Parliament. The then Minister for War asked the questioner whether, if he heard just before question time that the official concerned had resigned from his position at the War Office, he would agree to withdraw his question. The questioner, a prominent member of the Labour party, agreed.

The immediate outcome was acceptable to all. *The Week* had established a principle. And the dismantled official was, after a decent interval, appointed to the post of Marshal of the Diplomatic Corps. But he had not only passionately resented *The Week*'s disclosures of his holdings in the armament firm. Some of his friends had circulated to members of the House of Lords a bitterly libellous letter about *The Week* and its editor.

It was with all this in mind that Claud conferred with Crystal as to what was to be said when the Italian Embassy rang again to try to get a back number.

The call came. Crystal, using voice to maximum, said there were still difficulties. A truly fearful noise then came over the line from some still higher official. "You people," it said, "do not seem to realize that it is on behalf of His Excellency, Count Grandi, Italian Ambassador, that I am speaking."

Crystal permitted a longish pause. Then she said that the editor was now present in the office and she would consult him on the matter. After all, she pointed out, it was a distinct breach of *The Week*'s protocol, and His Excellency would naturally appreciate the overriding importance of protocol in all things. A brief consultation would be necessary.

After a suitable interval, Crystal said, "The editor, though most unwilling to break with regular procedure, is prepared in this case to do his utmost to waive his rule against non-subscribers receiving copies of *The Week* previous to those of the current publication date. He is however anxious to do everything possible to offer any aid he can to the Ambassador of a friendly power and former ally. If His Excellency would be so good as to telephone the Marshal of the Diplomatic Corps, who is well known to *The Week*, the Marshal's approval will be treated by us as a justification."

Grandi did just that. *The Week*'s correspondent was present at the telephone call and Grandi's opening line was "Ah, good morning. I believe you are in touch with a paper called *The Week* . . ." It was a pity that, for its own security reasons, *The Week* had to give the story in somewhat diluted form.

10 Facts about Murder

"FACTS about a murder" was at least in England at that time not yet a cliché. It headed the main story of *The Week* of 11 September, 1935. The disclosure of the facts and the relating of those facts to a broader international situation were a vivid illustration of *The Week*'s theory. This theory, as I have said before, was that you can only get the British public to pay serious attention to a general situation by focussing on a particular one. It is not, Claud would assert, that the public is incapable of appreciating a general situation. But the public has been conditioned by the press to believe in what it supposed to be concrete facts rather than in theories. But even when concrete facts actually exist, they are constantly concealed. Therefore the most desirable objective is first to discover and disclose such facts and then seek to explain them in the light of a general situation and, putting it the other way round, throw light on the general situation by reporting the facts. The facts about the murder in this case were reported as follows:

Suppressed, for reasons which will become grimly apparent, by three governments, there reach us today from Pekin the real facts of the kidnapping and murder of the well-known British journalist Gareth Jones last month in the territory north of the Great Wall of China.

The truth is as significant as it is startling: for it throws an unmistakeably lurid light on the immediate plans of the Japanese in north-eastern Asia and on the attitude towards these plans of two of the other governments concerned—facts together composing a situation which may yet compete with Abyssinia for the headlines.

The Week recalled that Gareth Jones, and Dr. Mueller, the correspondent of the official German Deutsche Nachrichten Büro, had been kidnapped at the end of July when travelling from Dolonor to Kalgan, in eastern Chahar province, which lay between the western boundary of Manchukuo, the eastern boundary of Mongolia, and north of the Great Wall. It was a territory from which the Japanese had recently demanded the evacuation of Chinese troops.

> Mueller was subsequently released [*The Week* went on] and arrived at the beginning of August in Pekin. He held conversations with the British and German diplomatic authorities regarding steps to be taken for the release of Jones.
>
> It was announced that everyone, including the Japanese, was doing their best and that Jones's early release was expected.
>
> Then came the news that Jones had been murdered, which flared across the front pages of the British press for a day or so, accompanied by announcements that the British government was going to make a strong protest to the Chinese authorities: after which the affair dropped out of sight with a suddenness which attracted some attention in Fleet Street at the time, even in view of the competing crises which filled the front pages at the same period.
>
> So much for the facts given to the public.
>
> Here is the even uglier truth.

The Week noted that when Dr. Mueller arrived after his release, he gave an interview to a certain number of journalists, in which he fully described the real circumstances of the kidnapping. The same information was given by Dr. Mueller to the British and German authorities. His interview revealed that what he and Jones had really bumped into was nothing less than the early stages of a Japanese attempt to repeat in Chahar the coup which began to shake the world when Manchuria was invaded in 1931. *The Week* continued:

> It was on July 25 that they arrived at Dolonor. What was their astonishment to find the place beflagged with the flags of a Japanese-controlled "independent" government, supported by the presence of a full mechanized brigade of Japanese troops, composed of 4,000 men and 400 automobiles, among which were included a number of tanks.
>
> They observed, said Mueller, that the crews of the white tanks were in part made up of émigré White Guards.
>
> Astonished by these facts they visited the Japanese headquarters.

There they found an Indian gentleman who explained that he had once been a member of the Indian National Assembly, but was now head of the Pan Asiatic League—the Japanese organization for the extension of Japanese domination over Asia.

Mueller told those to whom he disclosed these facts, that when the Indian was questioned as to why the town of Dolonor was so stiff with Japanese troops the reply was that they had come "to protect the population".

It was after leaving the Japanese headquarters that the climax of their discoveries was reached. As they passed through the town they came upon a notice board, and upon the notice board was boldly written:

"Headquarters of the autonomous Government of East Chahar."

The significance of the notice board was unmistakeable. They had stumbled into the very middle of an event designed to alter the history of Asia.

They copied the wording on the notice board.

It was at this point that they were arrested.

Back at Japanese headquarters, the Indian of the Pan Asiatic League informed them that they were under arrest on suspicion of espionage. They had been seen taking notes, examining military transports, etc.

They were then grilled by a succession of Japanese officers, kept under arrest for several hours, and finally told that during the rest of their stay in Dolonor they must not leave the hotel where they were staying.

When they left Dolonor there were three roads they could take.

The Japanese, so Dr. Mueller told our informant in Pekin, strongly recommended "one of these roads".

They took that road and it was on that road that they were captured by the "bandits".

About the bandits one fact became singularly clear: they were total strangers to Chahar and were obviously not the "dangerous elements of the local population" which the Japanese officials had so often referred to. On the contrary, they had to ask their way about the area wherever they went.

This, just before they decided to release Mueller, they explained themselves. They said that they were not, in the technical sense of the word, bandits at all. They were Chinese nationalists from Jehol. They had there been recruited by the Japanese who retained their families "under control" as a form of hostage for the "good behaviour" of the hired "bandits".

They had then been brought over to Chahar and ordered to go about "making disturbances". This, they explained, they were doing despite their patriotic detestation of the Japanese.

Apparently—on this point Dr. Mueller was not clear—it was either because they had misunderstood their instructions or else because they wanted to double-cross the Japanese in a manner that would yet not get their families back in Jehol into trouble that they agreed to release Mueller.

That we repeat is the story told by Dr. Mueller to certain journalists and to the British and German officials on his release.

In the light of it the subsequent events take on a peculiarly sinister aspect.

According to *The Week*, Gareth Jones was kidnapped because he had run into the secret of the next Japanese "drive for Asia". He was sent by the Japanese along the road to his kidnapping. He was murdered in a Japanese sphere of influence, and no ransom was ever collected by those singular bandits, because he had found out the first facts about an attempt to repeat in Chahar the adventure of Manchukuo.

The British and German authorities concerned are both the agents of governments which for the same reason—the hope of securing useful allies against the influence of Soviet Russia—are strongly averse to doing or saying anything disagreeable to certain Japanese designs.

After Gareth Jones was murdered, the British announced they would protest to the *Chinese*.

But the fact is that *before* he was murdered, all these merry gentlemen who knew the facts of the story, and were nominally engaged in trying to save his life were in fact sitting round playing a neat little game of "murder".

They were all "doing their best". Except that they suppressed the essential facts to save the Japanese feelings and helped to conceal what was—and is—going on in Chahar. They sat by and kept mum while the Japanese authorities blandly announced that they too were "doing their best".

And while this amiable diplomatic game was in progress in Pekin, Gareth Jones was allowed to be murdered in Chahar, for fear of disturbing the "good relations" between the three "under-standing" governments of Tokyo, London and Berlin.

The murdered Gareth Jones had been for some time the secretary and, I think, to some extent confidant of Mr. Lloyd George. Lloyd George rang up the editor of *The Week* and asked for any further information he had. Claud gave him all such information, which naturally included some confidential material. This was material which could not be published without exposing informants of *The Week* to retaliation by Japanese agents. Lloyd George was, as the saying used to go, "neither to hold or to bind". He paid a personal visit to the Foreign Office. And even in 1935 a personal visit from Lloyd George was not something to be shrugged off. He was not a man you could sweep under the carpet.

In its subsequent issue *The Week* stated, "The latest on the Gareth Jones 'mystery' is that the Foreign Office, having been called upon by Lloyd George for an enquiry into the facts revealed by *The Week*, and having subsequently told various newspapermen that they had known nothing at all about the matter, has now consented to cable the Pekin Embassy for a report."

With perhaps justifiable smugness *The Week* added that "in this connection it is entertaining to recall that on the last occasion when the Foreign Office gave out a denial of a *Week* story to the newspapers they were subsequently confronted with an official document from Somerset House which rather pulled the pins from under the too hastily constructed dementi."

For exactly the same reasons which had occasioned the original murder and had delayed its proper investigation, it was a long time before anyone admitted that the facts as given in *The Week* were correct. The action of the Foreign Office in directing its protest to the Chinese rather than to the Japanese was, as Claud remarked at the time, a supreme example of "non-gunboat diplomacy".

11 The Marching Masseur

THE editor of *The Week* was always peculiarly sensitive to what might be called the *surréaliste* element in the conduct of great national and international affairs. His fondness for drawing attention to it got him into a fair amount of trouble. Pompous-minded subscribers, of whom there were a surprising number, felt themselves obscurely insulted. Earnest students of affairs thought it indicated an unduly frivolous attitude. A good many Communists were much bothered by it. Holding a somewhat primitive view of Marxism they supposed that this type of approach constituted some sort of deviation from the rigid principles of determinism.

"You can't win," Claud used to complain at the time. "If we tap the barometer and it jumps to storm they say we are undermining the public morale and probably spoiling people's weekends. If we tap it and get 'sunny' the denouncer says frivolous."

A particularly sunny interval occurred, improbably enough, on the occasion of the funeral of King George V. Of course, the event itself was sombre and sad. But as everyone who has attended a really pompous funeral knows, the danger of some farcical element disrupting the proceedings increases in direct ratio to the pomposity. In this case the element of farce was provided by what later came to be known as the affair of the "marching masseur". This affair was first launched, produced or created, whatever the correct word may be, by Claud, not in his capacity as editor of *The Week* but in his other recently assumed function as diplomatic editor of the *Daily Worker*.

Newsreels of the funeral procession showed, among the suitably mournful and gloomily dignified royalties and grandees taking part, a singularly inappropriate figure. This conspicuous odd man out, skipping nervously along immediately behind King Carol of Roumania, was dressed in a white coat. This fact in itself singled him out for notice as his coat gleamed in the midst of the darkly funereal garb of the Captains and Kings.

Also, while his fellow marchers marched with the stony-faced rigidity most of them had presumably learnt from attending many such functions in the past, the little fellow in the white coat seemed notably ill at ease. In fact he had all the air of a man who did not know where he was and in any case was wondering how he had got there.

All alert observers of the scene including, of course, Claud were fascinated by this phenomenon. They investigated various lines of enquiry. Sources included naturally the Roumanian legation and, as a result of information received there, the Turkish baths in Jermyn Street. The story which emerged was calculated at least to alleviate the gloom of a people mourning a dead king and, in many cases, well aware of heavy storm clouds gathering over the Rhine.

Claud, or rather Frank Pitcairn as he was when writing for the *Daily Worker*, broke the story in that newspaper.

It seemed that King Carol, a prominent roisterer of his day, had felt that it would be idiotically wasteful on this occasion not to combine business with pleasure. For various reasons, all of them obvious to anyone who knew anything of what was laughably described as King Carol's "private" life, he had not often been invited to London during the lifetime of George V. And although it was credibly reported that the atmosphere of the court would be less austere on the accession of Edward VIII, you could not absolutely bet that it would move so far towards permissiveness that even King Carol would be a welcome and frequent visitor. The royal funeral, to which it would have been quite impossible not to invite him, was for him in this sense a blink of sunshine, and he proposed to make hay in it.

The jollities of his trip came to a sort of climax on the eve of the funeral itself. For one thing, the funeral once over, King Carol would have to go home. And God alone knew when he would once again see the lights of London. Also the prospect of the funeral procession itself was daunting. King Carol was not a man to face without queasiness the prospect of marching erect and in slow motion through the streets in a London January and thereafter having to stand about in a properly dignified manner in some hideously draughty building in Westminster. With these thoughts in mind, he went out on the tiles even more vigorously than usual.

The dawn came, but it was no bright dawn for King Carol. The prospect of his reaching the funeral parade at all seemed bleak indeed. However, one of his aides suggested that there was just a chance that a Turkish bath might pull him together sufficiently for him to attend the ceremony without visible disaster. This advice the King followed. The bathing process took quite a long time. So did the subsequent massage, which the King found extremely beneficial.

He would have liked the massage to have gone on and on. But the moment when the kings and other dignitaries had to assemble in front of Buckingham Palace was getting awfully near. By this time the King had come naturally enough to look upon the masseur who was doing him so much good if not as a father figure at least as some sort of guardian angel sent by the mercy of Providence to rescue him from an otherwise disastrous situation.

When the aide rushed in to say that the King simply must get off the couch immediately, pull on his gala uniform and make for the Palace, the King felt that he might just do it but he was damned if he was going to leave the care of his guardian angel. Groggy but with all the determination of near despair, he explained to the masseur that his beneficient duties were not yet over. Money was no object. Roumania was a rich country. The masseur could charge what he liked. But he absolutely must not, the King shouted as he moved towards the door of the baths, leave his royal client now. He must jump along with the King and the aide into the waiting car. There would be a minute or two in which, however cramped the conditions, the massage might usefully continue.

The masseur obeyed the royal command. In a few minutes the car arrived at the edge of the cordoned-off space in front of the Palace reserved for closest relatives as well as that distinguished company which was to head the procession behind the coffin. From this point on King Carol was supposed to be on his own. His aide could not accompany him through the cordon. The entire enterprise seemed to the King more daunting than ever. He felt that now or perhaps half-way down the Mall he might easily fall down. And unlike other men who have faced similar situations he was not only personally tottering but knew that with him was tottering also the fate of the Roumanian monarchy. In a few brusque words he instructed the masseur to follow him and spoke with royal *hauteur* to the officer who was saying that he had instructions only to admit one. In the last words which it was possible to utter before the obligatory hush fell upon all, the King admonished the masseur that he must at all costs march closely behind him. He must be ready at any moment, at any sign of totter or sway, to jump forward and support as unobtrusively as possible the flagging monarch.

Once again the masseur obeyed. And in this manner, bewildered but loyal to the last he marched in the sight of the assembled public and the newsreel cameras all the way from the Palace to Westminster.

Within a few hours of its appearance in the *Daily Worker* the story was of course being cabled to every country in the world, in particular to the United States. It was read with hilarity by many millions the world over, a reaction not shared, at least not publicly, by the representatives of the Roumanian government in the various capitals. Naturally all their ambassadors and ministers immediately rung up for comment on the episode. Paralysed with horror and uncertain just how far the facts could be absolutely proved, they allowed fatal minutes and in some cases even hours to pass while they telephoned or telegraphed Bucharest asking for information and instruction. At the royal headquarters in Bucharest the story was viewed as a about the most unfunny thing that had ever hit them. It was obviously going to be used either publicly or, if censored, as part of a whispering campaign by everyone from members of the Royal Family hostile to King Carol and his mistress, Mme Lupescu, to dissident Liberals, Republicans, and outright Reds.

Official denials and denunciations, issued with especial vigour from the Roumanian Legation in London, were turned on like water out of a fireman's hose.

But too late.

For by this time scores of people all over the world were busy following up the story, interviewing eyewitnesses of the scene in London, embroidering the tale, writing jokes and even little poems about the King's adventure, and of course drawing cartoons. Roumanian officials kept insisting that all of this was in the worst possible taste. They were, of course, quoted with delight. Among the least happy of those concerned was the official of the Roumanian Legation who, in the belief of a great many people, was responsible for disclosing the original story to Claud.

Various other people got in on the act. One of them was a distinguished elderly London journalist, a friend of Claud, who with the idea of confusing further an already confused situation said that he had seen the whole masseur episode in a dream three nights before Claud had even begun to investigate the story, and that what Claud had actually written about must have been this dream. In the general mirth the dream story itself appeared in various distorted forms. And, of course, the original story continued to be quoted and written around. The *Daily Worker* reported the denials and also excerpts from the world's press under the heading "The Masseur Goes Marching On".

A little later *The Week* found a somewhat more serious side of the affair:

> In case any subscriber has not seen news of it elsewhere, and because censorship is a subject of particular interest to us, we draw attention to the censorship—with violent ink and razors—of the last copy of the American news magazine *Time* to reach this country.

> *Time* had run a story from the British *Daily Worker* giving the facts about the masseur who marched in the train of King Carol in the royal funeral parade. It had also mentioned the fact that Prince Starhemberg drank too much while he was here which everyone who ran across the Prince at that time knew already.

> People who get their copies of *Time* direct by post, were privileged to read the complete magazine. People who buy their copies off British bookstalls found them deliberately and elaborately mutilated by the censors.

> The facts aroused considerable comment, (a) on the censorship, (b) on the clear notion of business ethics displayed by the London distributors of the paper who offered for sale at full price and without warning of the mutilation, a very much more than shop-soiled article. Maybe these gentlemen will presently start cutting pages

out of books and then trying to sell the books full price. In response to many queries, we regret to state that all these exceedingly nasty goings-on are, so far as we can find out, in this country perfectly legal.

Later in the same year the practice of mutilating American magazines carrying stories considered unseemly for British readers was carried a good deal further. This was during the period when the affair between Edward VIII and Mrs. Simpson was being so lavishly reported in the American press. The London distributors of *Time* magazine in particular were kept extraordinarily busy with their scissors, literally chopping out columns or half-columns, and pictures with captions, which referred to the matter. A good many subscribers to *The Week* accused the distributors of a breach of business ethics identical with that referred to by *The Week* on the occasion of the Masseur's March. The people who seemed to be responsible said that, in fact, they were not responsible. The explanation appeared to be that, supposing either the King or Mrs. Simpson were to take libel action against an American magazine such as *Time*—a more than unlikely proceeding—the likelihood was that the magazine itself, being based in the United States, would get off scot-free. But the British distributors and the owners of all bookstalls on which the magazine was sold would be liable for heavy damages.

The explanation, though legally sound, did not seem to reduce the absurdity of the position. The libel laws, then as now, had many absurd features, among them the one spotlighted by the cases of Carol II of Roumania and Edward VIII. In neither case was there the slightest possibility of the principal concerned taking legal action. It followed that the question of how much the public was to be allowed to read on any given subject was not to be decided directly by the libel laws. The answer to the question depended in fact upon the state of nerves of this set of newspaper distributors. Such people are not, at least in England, usually notable for anything in the way of a crusading spirit. If the choice were to lie between the outside possibility of losing say, £50,000, or pushing a piece of news down the drain, no one would have much doubt as to which way the choice would go.

III

12 Turning Point

IF one were looking for the year that represents the turning point of the 1930s, the obvious candidate would be 1936. That year is perhaps better described as the decade's point of no return.

The Germans successfully invaded the Rhineland. It was Hitler's first open act of external agression. There were, of course, there still are, plenty of people to deny that it was a genuine aggression at all. He was, after all, simply occupying territory which was German anyway. But that was not the way it looked to those who all along had been proclaiming the aggressive designs of the Nazi government. More importantly, it was not the way it looked to Hitler. For him it was a test case. It was a clear breach of the Locarno Treaty. Therefore, if it could be done without counteraction by Britain and France, it would prove that those two countries were too weak, or too divided to act. In particular, it would disclose, like lightning in the dark, the relative strength of forces within the two Western powers. And from the way it turned out Hitler would be able to draw his own conclusions.

The Week, sharply conscious of these facts, regarded the reactions of London and Paris as of much more than passing importance. It believed that their surrender on this point would really constitute a decisive event in the history of the decade.

Four weeks before, *The Week* had reported from its peculiar sources the existence of an explosive situation inside Germany. Summarized and a good deal oversimplified, the situation, *The Week* learned, was one in which the German governmental chiefs ranging from Hitler to the banker Schacht and the generals had reached a kind of *impasse*. The consensus was that there either had to be a new "June 30th" (that is to say a killing off of radical elements among the Brown Shirts) or, if that were to be averted, a major demonstration on the foreign front.

The generals were naturally in favour of killing off Brown Shirts. At the same time they were extremely nervous of external action because they believed that counteraction by the French, probably supported later by British military action, would cook their goose. However, the issue was decided in favour of the foreign adventure, and German troops re-occupied the Rhineland.

Amid all the argument about who should have done what, and whether anyone could have done what seemed the necessary thing to do, one fact seems certain. The crisis really was a turning point in the history of international relations in the Thirties. *The Week* had this to say:

Outstanding factors in the situation up to the early hours of the morning of Wednesday March 11 are as follows:

The advance of the German troops into the Rhineland was a direct result of the situation within Germany described in *The Week* Number 149.

This situation continues, in a modified form, to exist. The "new June 30th" promised by Dr. Schacht to the British bankers was actually within a few days of accomplishment when the decision to call the Reichstag and announce the invasion of the de-militarized zone was reached. It will be recalled that the first reports leaked out of Berlin on the afternoon of Friday March 6th hinted at the possibility of a new "purge" being about to be carried out.

The reports were correct in the sense that the alternative presented to the various sections of the German authorities during that week was between a purge of a drastic character, and an external explosion. The week leading up to the calling of the Reichstag was filled with almost hourly discussions which were frequently extremely acrimonious, between the army leadership, Dr. Schacht, Goebbels, and an assortment of Nazi bosses, and Hitler.

The report that the Reichswehr generals wanted a denunciation of Locarno (a treaty which included the continued de-militariza-tion of the Rhineland) but no actual occupation of the Rhineland zone is correct. The ground given by them was that they, like all generals, were not quite ready for war, and needed a few more months at least before being pushed into it.

They and Schacht were overridden by the Nazi bosses, who claimed that nothing short of actual occupation would suffice to affect in the sense of "rallying the boys around the party" the internal political situation. Adding impetus to this pressure was the knowledge that unless they could win on this issue the internal killing was liable to start at almost any moment and—in a lesser degree—the demands of the Rhineland zone building contractors for fortification contracts similar to those already filling the pockets of their colleagues outside the zone.

As a result of the unwilling attitude of the generals two things happened: the first was that Hitler informed the ambassadors that the occupation would be of a "purely symbolical character". The second was that the 40,000 men who were actually sent in moved in not simply as though on a ceremonial parade but in full military order with all the preparations for actual fighting taken.

The idea was that the statement to the ambassadors would at least delay any possible resistance that—in the opinion of the German generals—might be contemplated, and that in any case the very large force complete with artillery and bombing squadrons which was actually sent would be in a position to deal with any military resistance, particularly in case the ambassadors had really believed the story told them by the chancellor to the effect that "only a couple of battalions" were being moved in.

Simultaneously with the invasion of the zone, very large Japanese troop movements began on the border of the Republic of Outer Mongolia, virtually the whole of the existing forces within reach being pushed up to the Manchurian side of the frontier. Despite these precautions, acute nervousness reigned among the German generals during the whole of Saturday, their chief fear being that the British Government despite various undercover assurances conveyed in oblique fashion through Lord Londonderry, might after all stand by its signature to the Locarno Treaty. It was known that—as reported in *The Week*—there were increasingly large elements in the Conservative Party opposed to the pro-Hitler policy of Mr. Baldwin's group, and it was feared in Berlin that they might be strong enough to carry the day.

The Week noted with amusement in connexion with the threatened purge that three days after it had reported the news, certain German government sources had sent for subscriptions to *The Week* and the reports of "the couple of gentlemen from Germany who busy themselves with our goings and comings" had been "positively voluminous". The story continued:

It was at this point that the factor which probably nobody had correctly estimated came suddenly and powerfully into play. This was the attitude of the British press. Although some of the manifestations of what went on have been obvious to everyone who reads newspapers, it is worth reporting here one or two of the significant features in the background of an event which may be said to have played a major part in the developments in the past four days.

First indications of the kind of thing that was going to happen occurred when a supposedly responsible Sunday newspaper published a falsified version of an article of Pertinax of *Echo de Paris*, the falsification giving the impression that "even" Pertinax was prepared to regard the invasion of the Zone as a not too serious affair, which should not preclude amicable consideration of the accompanying German conditions and demands.

That night in London newspaper offices was probably the most remarkable in a quiet way, that had been seen since the Great War and Crew House. (Crew House was during World War I the headquarters of British propaganda under Northcliffe.)

Innocent old hands of no very strong political opinions found their straightforward "write-ups" of the invasion of the Zone seized from their hands and rapidly divested of anything which might suggest to the British public a serious picture of what it meant when 40,000 armed men of the most highly mechanized army in the world suddenly moved forward to a new strategic position on the map of Europe.

Certain correspondents in Paris were astonished at the "suggestions" reaching them from London as to what they should look for and write about: some were even more astonished when, in the great blaze of indignation that was Paris they read the London-edited version of their stories wherein they were made to state that Paris was "calm" and to suggest that Paris was not seriously opposed to negotiation on the basis of the broken treaty and the new German demands.

The fact which threw out of gear the calculations of all but the

most astute brains in the Foreign Offices and embassies was the
sudden alignment of the *News Chronicle* and *Daily Herald* with
the policy of the Rothermere Press. All alike declared the aggression "deplorable". All alike hurried on to urge that there should
be as little delay as possible in agreeing to the demands of the
aggressor.

The Week regarded the "lightning switch-around" of the
News Chronicle and *Herald,* which almost on the eve of the
invasion of the Zone had been maintaining an apparently
anti-Fascist and anti-aggression policy, and had been tending
to support the Eden group as against the Baldwin group in
the Cabinet, as one of the most interesting and, in its effects,
most important domestic political phenomena of the previous
few years. According to *The Week,* the immediate effects of the
switch-around were:

(1) Extremely important effect of, for the first time, breaking
down the solidity of the "peace ballot vote" the existence of which
had been a dominant factor in British politics ever since the ballot
of the 11 million. It is of course quite impossible to calculate just
what proportion of the peace balloters were actively opposed to
Hitler and Hitlerism, but our reports indicate that the number
was very large indeed. When therefore a newspaper which circulated widely among precisely the "peace balloters" and had but
recently played a leading part in the campaign against "rewarding
violence and aggression" suddenly appeared in vehement support
of the Hitler government policy and proceeded—by identical
methods—to run a campaign in favour of rewarding the aggressor
by immediate agreement with his political proposals, the confusion in the minds of the peace balloters was huge. It is too early
to estimate the full effect of this change but is worth noting that
it will be very great.

(2) The effects on the position inside the Cabinet were no less
drastic. The weakness of Mr. Baldwin's position since the elections,
and particularly since the scandal of the Hoare-Laval Pact had lain
precisely in the fact (a) that he was known not seriously to support
the League of Nations, (b) that he was an advocate of an Anglo-
German alliance with the French tacked on as a substitute for the
League, (c) that he had opposed to him most of the younger men

in the Cabinet and that they in turn had, or thought they had, the support of the Liberal press.

The *Chronicle*'s advocacy of the proposals outlined in Berlin to Mr. Baldwin's emissary Lord Londonderry, had upon the conformation of the Cabinet the effect of an earthquake: an immediate result being that Eden's possibility of holding out on any line in opposition to Baldwin has been reduced for the time being to a very low level indeed.

(3) The effect on the domestic situation in Germany has also according to two preliminary reports reaching us been considerable though it is of course too early to estimate it fully. A fair idea may be gained from the letter reaching us this morning from a prominent German civil servant who is also a pillar of the German Protestant Church and has for long by devious ways contrived to remain a subscriber to this service.

This man who has sometimes sent us information from Germany before sent us a clipping from a German paper as an example of the really laughable extent to which the Hitler newspapers misrepresent British Liberal opinion. The quotation purported to be a statement from the *News Chronicle*. "Can you imagine," our informant wrote, "anyone believing such a paper would write such stuff?"

The grim cream of the jest is that the quotation is entirely accurate.

The Week took it for granted that the support won by Hitler's invasion of the Rhineland for his foreign-political aims in very unexpected quarters in England would have for a time a weakening effect on the middle-class "liberal" opposition in Germany and a corresponding strengthening of the attack of the Nazi party on the Churches and the Jews. It continued:

Noteworthy among vital facts of the situation more or less successfully concealed by the British press chorus were (1) that the Franco-Soviet Pact cannot conceivably be regarded as an encirclement of Germany since Germany has been persistently invited to join it and as persistently refused to do so; (2) that the refusal of any Mutual Assistance Pact in the East is an admission of the intention to aggress, for why otherwise should a government be nervous of mutual assistance against an aggressor and prefer instead "non-aggression" pacts in which no third party is bound to assist a power which is the victim of aggression.

(A partial but not complete explanation for this sudden move of the *News Chronicle* is to be found in the fact that following the almighty shake-up recently occurring there, Sir Walter Layton, whose sympathies are with Lord Lothian and his policy of support for Hitler, has been exercising a very close control of the editorial policy of the paper.)

News of the actual events of Europe during the past few days has been allowed to reach the public in Britain only in singularly distorted form, and is still being liberally distorted to suit the British Government and press viewpoint of certain agencies.

On the night of Saturday the French government discussed immediate full mobilization.

On the same evening the French government received assurances of support from the Little Entente and the Soviet Union.

On Monday the Polish government created a profound sensation by delivering to the French government at once an assurance and a threat. The assurance was to the effect that Poland would support to the full any measures taken against the German government's immediate aggression and future war aims by the French. And the threat was to the effect that unless the French did take such action, then the Poles would consider the Franco-Polish alliance as terminated, since it would clearly be futile to consider an alliance with a power that was unable to resist even so flagrant an attack.

The British Ambassador in Warsaw on Monday hurried to see the Polish Foreign Office in the hope of dissuading the Poles from taking so strong a line against Hitler. He was rebuffed.

The French government being unaware of what the British press might do had gathered that the Foreign Office was in favour of honouring the Locarno Treaty and of taking a firm stand against the aggressor. The French information was correct in the sense that the majority of the Foreign Office was bitterly opposed to the acceptance and recognition of another step on the way to the Nazi hegemony of Europe.

Fleet Street and the Baldwin group together howled them down.

The position on Tuesday was that following Eden's speech in the House of Commons the French government took up its stand as follows: if the British Government would shift from its position of support for Hitler and stand in with all Europe against the aggression then it would be easy to conduct fairly mild and slow-going methods of sanctions against the Nazis, since the risk of actual attack would be virtually eliminated by the comprehensiveness of Europe's "peace front". If, however, the British Government should refuse to stand by Locarno to the full then it will be necessary to consider much sharper methods including military action.

In the light of French diplomatic documents disclosed fairly recently and referred to by A. J. P. Taylor in his *English History 1914–1945*, this passage in *The Week*, though factually accurate, was in a sense misleading. For it is probably correct to interpret the documents concerned as meaning that the French General Staff was in fact already committed to an entirely defensive policy. It would not, because according to its own calculations it could not, advance the French Army a yard over the French frontier. It would not and could not therefore move into the demilitarized Rhineland Zone. This, assuming it to be an exact picture of the attitude of the French War Office, was naturally a very powerful factor in Paris. And to that extent French talk of direct military action could be regarded as bluff.

On the other hand it has to be remembered that even the French General Staff was not at the time all-powerful. Naturally like all General Staffs it had a plan which it had been working on for years, in this case a totally defensive plan, and it hated to have to change it. Nevertheless it could have been changed. There were numerous young yet influential officers of the French Army who were alert to the dangers of the purely defensive policy and to the possibilities of a new type of military flexibility. In the years that followed and the final disaster, most of them disappeared without trace. Only Charles de Gaulle remained to remind people that they had once existed and been a potentially effective force.

With the situation in Germany [*The Week* continued] going from bad to worse, it is clear that another attack of the kind just experienced cannot be long delayed if nothing is done in the present instance; and the attack will of course be the more drastic in view of the proofs now given of British government and press support. The Reichswehr, in view of the situation, must of course accelerate its preparations: with the invaluable assistance of the new positions now taken on the Rhine. Added to this is the fact that if nothing is done, the Polish alliance will collapse and the Little Entente, left to the tender mercies of Hitler, will be in danger of doing likewise. With war a certainty in the near future if the Hitler advance is permitted, the French are prepared to risk conflict now rather than later in the year when the Germans will be for the above reasons stronger.

The new factor in the situation which most affected Mr. Eden and Lord "Nanny" Halifax on their arrival yesterday was the confirmation of the failure of the British Minister in Warsaw to prevent the Poles sending not merely their assurance of support, but the rest of their message as disclosed above.

They also had an opportunity to gauge at first hand the real French opinion which had been so studiously concealed by the British press.

(Here again the phrase "real French opinion" has probably to be considerably qualified in the light of later revelation. On the other hand it is true that opinion of the kind referred to was deep and widespread in France and it is true too that its existence was largely concealed from the British public.)

Conversations with journalists in various parts of the French provinces conducted by telephone from this office last night confirmed in the last-minute check-up the depth and extent of French opinion on the question.

The "calmer atmosphere" of London, as a ground for the decision to remove the proceedings to England must frankly be described as poppycock. This is not a tea party which may depend for success on the character of its surroundings; nor will subjection of the Continental delegates to the direct impact of Fleet Street's loudspeakers be likely to do much to change the situation.

The possibility of inviting a representative of Herr Hitler's régime to attend is of course the more concrete reason for the change and is not unconnected with the arrival three days ago in this country of the Duke of Saxe-Coburg Gotha, cousin to Edward VIII and the first German royalty to become a Nazi. It is noteworthy that even before the suggestion of the move to London was conveyed to the powers at Locarno, Dr. "Putzi"

Hanfstängel, Nazi press chief, had thought it worthwhile to follow the duke to London.

If British refuse to act on breach of present Locarno, the French will find it hard to take seriously the British any more than the German signature on any new pact. Nor will the French easily consent to break up the whole "peace front" organized with Russia and Little Entente for the sake of being number three in a temporary Western lineup.

Remains faint possibility of the British—by financial pressure—breaking down the French stand and accepting Hitler's terms. In that case the next German attack is likely to be Austria.

In point of fact, German intervention in Spain constituted the next attack. Austria came after that. It seems to me that the fact that things turned out one way is no proof that they might not have turned out another. For me at least part of the fascination of *The Week* is its close-up of a whole series of battles at a moment when their outcome was still undecided. For after all if any of these battles had resulted, either in Germany or in Britain, in the victory of individuals or groups who were in fact defeated, the whole course of things would have been different.

Pursuing its analysis of the Rhineland occupation, *The Week* in its issue of 14 March 1936 dealt not only with the direct clash of policies between nation and nation but the tussles and tensions within each nation itself.

The policy split in the British Cabinet [it noted] was last night closely following age lines: most of the older men still for acceptance of Hitler's terms to Europe, most of the younger for honouring the British signature on the Locarno Treaty or at least making a show of so doing.

Chief advocates of acceptance of the Hitler terms are Monsell, Hailsham, Runciman and Collins.

Despite the recent swing of support by the Liberal press from Eden to the pro-Hitler group, Eden, Duff Cooper and the majority of the younger men are putting up a considerable fight. The swing back of the Liberal press during the past couple of days is belated and so far unhelpful.

Baldwin, disinclined by character to prolonged exertion of

mind, was last night confused, asking one person after another what on earth anyone could do next.

Monsell appears as leader of the acceptance group. Pushing him are the same forces which pushed through the Anglo-German Naval Treaty and operated powerfully to delay sanctions against Mussolini, namely the Lords of the Admiralty who proclaim their profound conviction of the utter vulnerability of the British fleet even to the Germans. Liberal and Labour support for the Hitler terms has on this occasion considerably strengthened the Admiralty position.

The circumstances of the meeting at the House of the Foreign Affairs Committee of the Conservative Party are that a message was sent down to them from Downing Street virtually abdicating Cabinet authority, begging them to figure out what to do.

Faced with certainty of (a) collapse of the League of Nations (b) an early repetition of aggression by Hitler in the event the present manoeuvre is successful, opinion was in favour of a fairly definite stand in favour of the collective security system but entirely divided as to ways and means.

Worth reporting for the light it throws on the trend of the discussion is the fact that one leading Conservative stated that if it came to a choice between the Nazis and the Bolsheviks, as for him he preferred the Bolsheviks who at least possessed a coherent, progressive and intelligible plan of living which seemed to be getting somewhere, compared with the dreary vista of terrorism, internal and external, offered by the Nazi régime.

At midweek there were indications of a stirring among financial interests in London favourable to Hitler towards a possible attempt to stage a bear attack and withdraw all our Paris balances. Paris immediately let it be known any such attack will be met with almost instant embargo. Collapse of attack with possibility of attempted renewal today or Monday, prospects of success being meagre.

The first full eye-witness account we have heard—or seen printed —of the scene in the German Reichstag when Hitler announced the occupation of the Rhineland twelve days ago states that: (a) the tension was precisely similar to that existing when Hitler made his apologia for the shootings of June 30th, 1934. (b) There was not a clap or a sound of applause when Hitler appeared to make his speech. (c) Hitler himself was so nervous that he twice got tangled up in his words—an exceedingly unusual event with him (d) Goebbels and the other Nazi lieutenants were actually dead white with nervousness.

In general this account, received from an informant who was in Berlin until yesterday, confirms the report of *The Times* correspondent to the effect that the German government was by no means certain that the French would not reply to the advance by exercising to the full their right under the Locarno Treaty and throwing out the invaders by armed force. It was only the conviction of the appalling gravity of the internal situation which decided the government, against the advice of the Army High Command.

It is worth reporting that on the day of the advance it was fairly generally rumoured and alleged in Berlin that the troops were needed to overawe and if necessary to support the police against the people in the Rhineland Zone, those being predominantly Catholic working-class people forming one of the vanguards against the Nazi régime in Germany. We believe that the allegation is somewhat exaggerated. There is considerable significance that it was on that day so commonly made and believed in Berlin.

In the event of course, it has turned out that with the active assistance of the Liberal and Labour press the Hitler régime has in all probability been in fact permitted to get away with precisely what the German opposition told it it could never get away with and have been correspondingly strengthened as a result.

The final phase of the Rhineland crisis was reached with the convening of the League of Nations Council at St. James's Palace, London. *The Week* remarked:

With the success of the British government in getting the Nazi representatives to the League Council a new phase in the operation of the League of Nations has begun. It is indeed possible that the League of Nations as it has existed during the past couple of years has already ceased to exist.

The next two days will tell whether the League in face of the open wrecking efforts from Berlin, the hostility of the majority of the London government, and the complacent approval of these phenomena by the former League champions in the British press is indeed capable of survival as a force for peace and security in Europe.

Indications at the moment are that the League will either cease to exist at all as a result of the doings in London in the past few days or will develop into an agency of Germany and its supporters here.

This will mark the third phase in the evolution of the League which during the Twenties was in the main an instrument of the allied powers victorious in the late war, and which became for a while an instrument useful to those powers temporarily favouring peace against aggression, and is now on the way to becoming the instrument of precisely the opposite group.

Whether it does so or not—and that it is certainly not possible at the moment proclaims that the League is quite dead in that sense—depends now upon the activity and vigour of the Labour organizations and particularly of the British Labour organizations in relation to the League and to the governments concerned.

The evolution of opinion within the British Labour Party therefore becomes a factor of extreme importance in the total situation.

Checking round Labour leaders and rank and file, we find this week that the genuinely pro-Hitler elements there are composed roughly of three groups: there are those somewhat misinformed elements who base their attitude on the undoubted fact that "Germany has had a raw deal" in the past and that anyway the French made the British pay rent for the trenches during the 1914–1918 war.

There are the pure pacifists who in the mistaken notion that to resist aggression involves war but the correct notion that to resist aggression involves the risk of war, are prepared to face the certainty of war in Europe soon rather than the risk of war in Europe now.

There are finally those who reckon that the "removal of the cause of irritation" for the German people will deprive the Nazi government of one of its strong powers, thus weakening the Nazi government and tending towards a more peaceful evolution of its policy.

This attitude of course assumes that the Nazi government which is admittedly dependent on outside irritation and a series of exterior explosions as an alternative to an interior explosion which will blow it from power, will childishly permit the strongest card it has to be taken away: it will in fact set the first example in history of a régime willingly committing suicide.

Indications are that none of these views will for long predominate in the Labour Party, and that there will form itself within the Labour Party an opposition to the sort of policy that has been carried on during the past two weeks of a more formidable character than has yet been seen.

It is already clear that the defeat of the League—if it is finally accomplished—by Berlin and part of the London government will be used as a very powerful argument by the London government on behalf of the Armament White Paper which has already roused a very considerable storm in the industrial sections of the Labour movement. It appears probable that at the moment of the defeat of the League, there will be seen also the important birth of a movement directly against equally the threats of aggression by Fascist governments and the war preparations of the local government. Such a movement of course already exists; its birth will take place simply in the sense that it is likely to affect very much wider strata of society and to be more concrete and resolute in its plans as the result of the experiences of the last ten days.

This was a fairly characteristic mixture of informed political reportage and over-eager prophecy. That is to say, the analysis of opinion among what *The Week* so rudely called the "genuinely pro-Hitler elements" in the Labour party was accurate enough. Naturally the phrase itself was exceedingly offensive to loyal Labour party supporters among the subscribers of *The Week*. Quite a number of them did in fact take one or other of the three lines indicated, and did so more or less in accordance with the reasoning attributed to them by the paper.

Since no other paper was analysing the Labour party in this particular way the report had a certain impact and resulted in considerable discussion in Labour party circles.

The final paragraph of that report, however, raises far more controversial issues. In fact they were issues which preoccupied and to a considerable extent bedevilled the Labour party throughout almost the whole of the remainder of the 1930s.

The prophecy contained in the last sentence of the report regarding the speedy strengthening of opposition to war preparations was simply not fulfilled.

More significant perhaps is the fact that in making that prophecy *The Week* seems to have been happily unaware of the paralysing contradictions which were going to arise on this issue. Dozens of historians and political polemicists have in years since then worried the matter to rags. I myself suspected then and believe now that those people were right who felt that there was an insoluble contradiction in the attitude of at least the Labour leaders. Surely it was quite impossible to demand sanctions, to call for action which certainly risked war, and at the same time violently opposed the Conservative government's rearmament plans. To me it seems that the Labour leaders would have been in an impregnable political position if they had not only demanded collective action for peace, but had gone on from there to admit that such action could involve war, and from there again to support a maximum rearmament of Britain.

After all there was certainly the possibility that in the general election in which both parties were demanding rearmament, Labour might actually win. Each party would of course claim to be more patriotic than the other. But it would have been a great deal easier for the Labour party than for the Conservatives to represent themselves as having so to speak patriotism plus. The plus would consist in love of democracy and hatred of fascism. They would be rearming to help save the democrats and working-class of Europe from Fascist tyranny. They would thus have been in a position to exploit ruthlessly the Conservative record of cynicism in regard to the League of Nations and, in many cases, evident connivance with the Fascist leaders.

Claud took and has always taken a quite different view of the situation as it existed then. When pressed he would admit that naturally if the Labour leaders were to act genuinely and vigorously along those lines some good results might be achieved. But, he argued, to suppose that they would do any such thing was to indulge oneself in daydreams. First, the existence of the above-mentioned "genuinely pro-Hitler element" in the Labour party was quite enough to hamstring any action of this kind. They would always be strong enough to prevent the Labour party ever openly and honestly admitting that any serious and credible collective action to save the peace must necessarily involve the risk of producing a war.

The record of the Labour party during the latter part of the

Thirties proved this estimate to be more or less correct. But that still did not conclude the argument. Let us assume that the policy of the Labour leadership was fatally flawed by this type of political dishonesty or cowardice. Was that any reason why people to the left of the Labour leadership should also oppose rearmament by the British government?

To this Claud gave two answers. One of them I think may have been correct. The other was certainly mistaken.

The first was to the effect that given the known character, policies and aims of the Conservative leadership, rearmament under that leadership could not be considered a strengthening of collective security. Nor since that leadership was constantly ogling either Hitler or Mussolini or both, could it possibly be represented as any sort of reinforcement of anti-Fascist forces. Rather, in fact, the contrary. The next step more likely than not, would be a mutual understanding between a strong Germany and Britain. Then two things were likely to happen. At home the Conservative government would move further and further to the right. It would, although this would not be the most important factor in such a move, be increasingly anxious to do nothing which might exacerbate its relations with the German government. It would also quite naturally be anxious to demonstrate to all whom it might concern, and particularly to the Nazis, that the existing British Establishment was perfectly capable of defeating anything in the way of subversion, radical socialism, or unduly aggressive action by the trade unions. (It is certainly a fact that at that time this particular topic was a favourite in conversations between representatives of the German and Italian authorities and spokesmen of the British government. And the British government spokesmen did in fact quite often point to numerous domestic measures, as for instance the Sedition Bill, as evidence that there was a strong and if necessary harsh hand at the helm.)

It was not to be supposed that these considerations alone would move the government to the right. They would simply play an important part in accelerating a movement which seemed at least to observers on the far left to be not only natural, but already visibly on the way.

I must say here that although a crusade to the East was

visibly desired by a considerable section of the Conservative leadership, there were other Conservatives who argued tenaciously against it on what seemed to me very realistic grounds. The gist of their argument was that in that case either the Germans would defeat the Russians, whereupon within quite foreseeable time and with the vast resources of Russia at their disposal, they would turn and mangle the Western powers. Or, which Conservative observers thought a good deal less likely, the Russians would smash up the Germans and we should then have the very result which the policy had been designed to prevent. The Bolsheviks would reach the Rhine.

The Left certainly thought the most probable outcome of a strengthened British armament under Conservative leadership would be precisely the driving of Germany to the East. It was a belief which in certain British Left circles amounted almost to a dogma. Rather surprisingly it was not, so far as I know, treated as a dogma in Moscow. It was certainly regarded as a high probability. But equally the Soviet leaders I think were of the opinion that ultimately a war between the "imperialist states" was just as likely. Indeed somewhere along the line Stalin astonished some British leftists by stating something of the kind in a public speech.

As between war in the West or war spearheaded by Germany against Russia, Claud thought the odds were not more than about three to one in favour of the latter possibility. In this he differed from most of his friends. But he thought too that a war of that kind under the political and social conditions of Britain in the early and mid-Thirties could be nothing but a repetition of the 1914–1918 war. It would be simply a clash of predatory interests in which the mass of the people of both countries would suffer miserably.

Therefore from his point of view rearmament or the encouragement of rearmament under a Conservative government could produce only this kind of predatory conflict, or else an attack upon the Soviet Union which would be disastrous whatever happened for the reasons which I have mentioned above as adduced by a good many Conservatives.

"Of course," Claud remarked at the time, "we must remember one bit of gilt on the gingerbread. These ruffians in the government are at least at sixes and sevens among themselves. Think how bloody awful it would be if they were united. They could tie us up and sell us to the Germans in jigtime."

By way of "encouragement" to "men of good will" he wrote early in May 1936 a general appraisal of the situation within the Cabinet—plus a further side-swipe at the pusillanimity of the respectable Labour opposition.

That there really is no coherent British foreign policy [wrote *The Week*] because there is no coherent British Cabinet, is the simple truth behind the great parade of foreign political motions currently being gone through all the way from Downing Street and the Foreign Office to Chequers and Leamington, and the anxious speculations of the Foreign Press.

Jules Romains attributes to M. Caillaux the observation that "domestic politics are like love-making: while you are at it you are unable to pay attention to anything else." The British Cabinet, at the moment of—and largely on account of—the gravest possible international crisis, cannot pay attention to the international crisis because all its members are engaged in one form or another in figuring angles and laying political bets on the internal political situation which the international crisis makes worse and worse.

In this sense the Cabinet crisis in general and the Budget leak in particular really got more acute the more people—afraid of the consequences of an explosion—tried to prevent them becoming more acute.

It is a significant fact that the Labour Opposition at the end of last week was refusing to respond to the urgings of outsiders to throw its hat in the ring and publicly name the minister whom so many people are privately either exposing or maligning as the case may be, on the ground that any attack might give the gentleman in question an opportunity to counter-attack.

This is the position of the internal opposition to Mr. Baldwin in the Cabinet itself: fearing that Mr. Baldwin will make a damaging allegation that his opponents are clever, the Conservative Opposition—declaring damagingly that Mr. Baldwin is clever—are busy seeing how stupid they can look by way of increasing confidence in themselves. This form of competition in the appearance of stupidity, however high a standard of achievement may be reached, is not of course a sound background for a vigorous foreign policy....

The Prime Minister refuses to take an attitude about anything because if you take an attitude it can be criticised and he quite rightly thinks it dangerous to expose himself to criticism at such a moment:

The Foreign Secretary is in a state of confusion because he feels himself genuinely to be a very young man and would like some guidance, but can only get it from people theoretically inferior in political position to himself:

The First Lord of the Admiralty's domestic affairs point to an early resignation, so that he knows it does not matter very much what he says or does:

The Home Secretary is in the position of realizing that the government as it stands is heading for a smash in which he will lose his job and that the only solution is a reorganization in which he will very likely lose his job too:

The Dominions Secretary has got his job mainly because of a pledge which his politically deceased father thinks he got from the late King in the year 1931, and is likely to hold it only just so long as anyone continues to think it worth while to try to keep up the pretence that "Labour" have a couple of seats in the Cabinet:

The Minister for War has ruined his prestige with the party bosses by getting himself involved in a politically dangerous row with the Church vote:

The Lord Chancellor is paralysed by his mingled fear of the German menace, distrust of the League of Nations and inability to make up his mind to take the plunge in precipitating a drastic solution of the crisis which hamstrings any possibility of effective action against the policy of Berlin:

The Minister for Air sits holding the disastrous legacy of Lord Londonderry's affection for General Goering, and in any case carries so little political weight that he cannot move in any direction unless he is sure that at least two or three people whose names the public can remember from one day to the next are moving the same way:

The Chancellor of the Exchequer has produced an unpopular budget and still cannot make up his mind when to make a real thrust to upset the Prime Minister.

This situation, no single feature of which is abnormal in itself, is serious because it exists under the terrible splitting pressure of an international crisis. It is important too because it in part accounts for the series of mostly mistaken conclusions that have been drawn about British policy in Paris, Berlin, Rome, Vienna, Warsaw, Prague, Belgrade, Sofia, Bucharest, Athens and Angora.

This was followed, a couple of weeks later, by a less light-hearted report.

Behind the confusion in the press, partly deliberate and partly accidental, British government policy moved this week nearer towards a crisis very different in character from the simple, public "sanction" and "anti-sanctions" row which has held the headlines long after, so far as the government was concerned, the thing was settled.

It is a crisis of which the outcome will sooner or later—and probably sooner—profoundly affect all people. In view of the attitude of the local press it is necessary to report in some detail upon some decisions, factors and personalities which for some reason or other scarcely get reported elsewhere. . . .

Into the centre of the present picture has moved the London *Times*. The influence of the London *Times*—sometimes exaggerated, sometimes underestimated—is one of the features of British politics most misunderstood by foreign observers . . .

Half the statesmen in Europe pored anxiously this week over the increasingly peculiar editorials of *The Times*, culminating on Tuesday in the plea for secret negotiations between Hitler and the London government. They studied, too, the strange story of *The Times* parliamentary correspondent who put himself unenviably on record with the profound thought that the Chamberlain speech (on foreign policy) was to be "explained" by the fact that Mr. Chamberlain had not had time to think much about what he was going to say.

To help its readers to understand the significance of what had happened, *The Week* went on to describe the "apparently trivial and often pitiable circumstances" of *The Times* as it stood then.

The Times is a great newspaper. It treats its staff so well that it is full of men who for years have been proclaiming every six months that they are going to get out before it is too late and are still there working for it.

Its editor, Mr. Geoffrey Dawson, has never, so far as we know, had any such desire. An able and charming man, he is the unfortunate victim of a form of society—or rather of a section of British society—which impresses deeply upon the consciousness and the subconsciousness of its youthful authors a feeling amounting almost to awe in the presence of inherited wealth, inherited security.

The Geoffrey Robinson (as he then was) who went to Eton fifty years ago, went there as a scholar with money earned by his own abilities. It is alleged by people who ought to know that in the Eton of that period it was possible for a scholar to acquire a very vivid impression of the nice superiority-attaching disposition of people who were at Eton for no good reason beyond their birth and inherited money.

However that may be the career of Mr. Robinson (since 1917 of Mr. Dawson) from the days when he was one of "Lord Milner's young men" to his present eminence among the Astors, has been of a kind to impress upon him with increasing emphasis the importance in upper English society of the right people, and has accustomed him to find rank a balm for the suffering he certainly undergoes not very gladly in the presence of fools . . .

The Declaration of Editorial Independence which he secured from Astor when they became respectively editor and controlling owner of *The Times*—at a moment when the new controllers were searching, in their own words, for a "not too strong personality" to put in the editorial chair about to be vacated by Mr. Wickham Steed—did not, as things turned out, amount to a great deal.

The social influences to be brought to bear upon the new editor were considerably more subtle than the open dictation of the deceased Northcliffe which was the sort of thing Mr. Dawson had in mind to guard against.

It is not from Major Astor as an individual that the principal influence of *The Times* emanates, but rather from the Astor family as such: a family which in these 1930s shares, and disputes, with the Cecils, an extraordinary position of concentrated political power. Possibly any family which had the money, the position, the numbers and the political interest of the Astors could exercise a similar influence on *The Times* even without owning it. It just happens to be the Astors that do it, and in any list comparable to that of what French election slogans called the "200 families who are ruining France" the Astors will have a prominent place.

Major Astor (Eton and New College), is as determinedly English and aristocratic as only a Philadelphia origin can make a man. A gallant and fairly successful officer in the war and provided by the Conservative party with one of the safest seats in its possession (Dover), he cannot be said to have cut a particularly brilliant figure in the House of Commons. He bought *The Times* with very little notion of ever making any money out of it, but rather with the idea that from the point of view of an earnest Philadelphian it seemed in a general sort of way a good idea at the time.

Lacking any very deep or clear notion of where to go or how to get there, he in fact is reduced to a somewhat negative position which really is not very much more than that of a funnel for the influence of other members of the Astor family.

In these circumstances it is not surprising that the vigorous—if not very profound—personality of Lady Astor should at this critical moment be expressing itself with an effect which would be incredible if it were not for precisely the situation we have just described.

The Week saw it as one of those situations which occasionally occur at critical and even catastrophic moments in history, "when society produces a condition wherein the personal whims, prejudices and well- or ill-conceived notions of a single individual, play a role of absurdly disproportionate importance".

Lady Astor for instance is obsessed with a vivid personal dislike of the French, a sort of antipathy which some people have tried to explain by attributing it to the hostility between the extremities of Anglo-American Puritanism and traditional French Catholicism . . . she has maintained, too, a basic belief that Bolshevism is an affair of bombs and knives between the teeth—possibly not too clearly distinguished in her nimble mind from anarchism.

With this sort of idea latent in their minds—and not counteracted by any more thorough understanding of the situation and its terrible dangers—the Astors have been the easy and obvious target for German propaganda and German diplomatic activity during the past two months. There is no doubt that at the beginning of the Nazi régime they shared—and *The Times* certainly reflected—the general disgust at its methods.

But what with dislike of the French, what with fear of the "Red menace", what with the barrage of suggestion from Berlin to the effect that the French and the "Red menace" are now virtually fused into one and the same force, the Astor influence has today become one of the most important supports of German influence here, and *The Times* after so recently denouncing a foreign policy which included the murder of Dollfuss, today urges upon a recalcitrant Foreign Office that to avoid secret bilateral conversations with Berlin if Berlin wants them is "mere pedantry".

If everyone treated the policy of the Astors and of *The Times* with no more than the deference due to this queer concatenation of social accidents and psychological foibles the matter would be unimportant. When Mr. Ward Price—following the lines forecast a couple of weeks ago in *The Week*—writes a piece in Lord Rothermere's *Daily Mail* this Tuesday morning urging an Anglo-German-Italian line up to defend the world against bolshevism from Moscow to Paris, the political results are minimal.

When the Astors and *The Times* pursue a similar policy on a similar level of political and strategical thought and knowledge that has results.

For one must recall the awe with which many politicians still regard *The Times* and also the fact that from the point of view of numbers of what hoped to be "rising young politicians", invitations to Cliveden are more important than the fact that the end of all these lovely editorials, dinners and garden parties will be war.

13 Leak

COMPARED with events in the Rhineland, the Budget Leak scandal of 1936 could be regarded as a very minor episode. Indeed, it was the open desire of the authorities that it should be so regarded. To *The Week* this appeared the maximum of hypocrisy. For it considered the leak scandal as the unsubmerged tip of the iceberg. In fact, it was only because of violent differences of interest between the highest political and financial powers that even that tip had been allowed to emerge.

Its City contacts gave the paper a close-up view. Naturally this was no closer a view than that available to a dozen financial editors. The difference was that *The Week* was interested in giving the affair maximum importance. Everyone else was more interested in playing it down, in preventing a "deterioration of the atmosphere".

The Week opened up with an attack upon the Libel Laws. It also described the personality who was being currently spoken of by every reasonably informed person in London as the author of the leak, in terms which made it perfectly clear who was being talked about.

Everyone who knew that the man being talked about was Mr. J. H. Thomas at once recognized the figure, and the people who had not known before began to deduce the man from the adjectives.

Just before the Budget scandal finally broke, *The Week* reported:

> We are advised that the British Libel Laws, which seem designed to prevent a man being kicked until he is down, prohibit us from mentioning the name of the Cabinet Minister who is stated by people in the City and in the House of Commons, who ought to be in a position to know the facts, to be responsible for the Budget leakage.

The Week suggested that

Under the stifling censorship which the Libel Laws impose upon England, a man who ought long ago to have been investigated, and either cleared of the charges made against him, or, if he could not be cleared, publicly chased from the Cabinet to pursue elsewhere that career of boozy racketeering and financial jerrymandering of which his enemies do not hesitate to accuse him, continues to this day to display his squalid pawkiness on the government bench.

It was not only the Libel Law, *The Week* suggested, which reduced the British press to emitting a series of more or less well-muffled belches, as the rumours about the Budget leakage spread. There seemed at that time to be a kind of unwritten, unspoken understanding among the gentlemen of the press that certain facts of life were not suitable for display to the general public. They were kept apparently on some special shelf, like medical books in an old-time provincial library. To loan them might corrupt the readers.

First there were the muffled rumours. Then the establishment of a judicial Tribunal, and finally the resignation of Mr. Thomas on the ground that his name had been "bandied about", removed at least from those immediately concerned the protection of the Libel Laws.

The press, of course, reported the proceedings of the Tribunal. They were squalid enough. And anyone possessing even the weakest magnifying glass to help in reading between the lines, could see that that particular thing could hardly have happened if a lot of other things had not been happening at the same time. These, of course, were things which were not mentioned before the Tribunal.

At the time, a number of subscribers wrote to *The Week* about the matter. They said that hitherto they had been sceptical about the picture of the "atmosphere" in high places which *The Week* had seemed to think existed. Some of these subscribers now said that they realized that the Budget scandal could hardly have occurred if the atmosphere had been even one half so pure as they had supposed.

The moment that the Tribunal was over, the British press followed the practice customary at the time. That is to say, it rang down the curtain. It announced that this unsavoury

episode had been nothing but an episode. "They are implying," Claud said, "the existence of a really extraordinary
phenomenon. They claim that what we had here was a symptom
without a disease." Many people were irritated when the
press, having given great space to some affair and thereby
indicated its importance, suddenly shut off all further news.
(The same thing still happens, of course.) It seemed on such
occasions that there was a volcano, that it erupted, that all
was then over and that the geologists could go home without
studying the underground facts which led to the eruption.

Intelligent people naturally find it annoying to be treated
as children. And intelligent people in Britain at that time
were being treated as children more regularly than was
tolerable to many of them. That was one of the reasons why
those who knew about *The Week* read *The Week*.

It was the only paper which sought to explain that the
explosion of the Budget scandal was not automatic. There had
been moments when powerful elements in the Cabinet had
nearly succeeded in suppressing it altogether. There had been
fierce conflicts of opinion.

Despite these dangerous differences [*The Week* reported] agreement was reached in fact on the need for cutting, with as good a
grace as possible, any losses there might have been as a result of
the "bandying" of names and affairs, etc. etc.

It is important to note that the factor which played the biggest
role in getting the Government together on this line, was just the
ascertainment—after a swift and thorough check-up—that the
name of no other Cabinet Minister was liable to be bandied in
the same way, and then the relief felt by the other Members at
the discovery that the only man in trouble as a result of the
bandying was "not after all, one of ourselves".

It is the belief in Conservative circles, that with a little adroitness
and ingenuity the fall of Mr. Thomas can be turned into a positive
asset to the government, with no harm done whatever to the
prestige of Mr. Baldwin and his friends, or Mr. Chamberlain and
his friends.

There are even people going about the House of Commons this
week quite openly pointing out that Mr. Thomas was really what
they describe as a legacy from the Labour movement, so that any

bandying which may go on about him ought not to be allowed in any way to reflect upon the wisdom, discretion and honesty of the National Government as such.

The promptitude and vigour of the Tribunal itself, the swift resignation of Mr. Thomas on the bandying issue have all contributed to the lightening of the Government boat in what looked to be heavy weather.

There may be serious breakers ahead but that depends in the main on the attitude of the Labour party. And the leadership of the Labour party, with that almost morbid defensiveness which has become one of its most paralysing characteristics, is inclined, we are given to understand, to "avoid trying to make party capital out of the affair".

Behind this attitude is the fear that somebody will say "well after all, Thomas was one of you, wasn't he?" And someone else will say "don't kick a man when he's down", and so on, and there is an odd timidity in the Labour party leadership, which causes some of its members to hold the belief that if you cannot win in the best possible taste, it is better not to win at all.

What *The Week* described as the "morbid defensiveness" of the Labour party leadership was spotlighted by the Thomas affair. But the Thomas affair simply brought to the surface a phenomenon which had been a major factor for many years. This same defensiveness amounted to a Labour party neurosis. It had been powerfully at work during the terms of both the first two Labour governments. It had conditioned MacDonald. And later in the Thirties it remained dominant. It was the motive force of what became known as "Morrisonism". It was, that is to say, the motive force of the policy which considered that the main and indeed essential objective of the Labour party must be to capture what was described at the time as the middle-class vote. Then, as earlier, the main objective of many Labour leaders seemed to be to convince some nebulous entity known as "the country," that despite their humble origins and/or radical ideas, the Labour men were "fit to govern." It was a concession to snobbery, unparalleled I think in any other country.

Whether it was by wishfully thinking or under-informed, I do not know, but *The Week* certainly underestimated the strength of this attitude in the Labour party of the period. It seems to have believed that at any moment there was a possibility that the opposite, radical tendency in the Labour party would, after all, prevail. It saw and reported evidence of tendencies favouring the United Front and, later, the Popular Front.

These tendencies certainly existed.

Equally, they were certainly underestimated by the press. *The Week* was no doubt correct in occasionally drawing attention to their existence. But it did suggest that they were a great deal stronger than was in fact the case. To this the editor would reply that the game was not over, the whistle had not blown. Therefore, it was both mistaken and defeatist to assume that for instance "Morrisonism" had really won the game. The radicals might shoot a winning goal yet. The optimism of *The Week* was, in fact, very nearly unquenchable. It brought considerable ridicule upon the head of the editor. Knowledgeable friends said that at least so far as Labour politics was concerned he was a babe in the woods.

His conclusions on the Budget leak Tribunal were, however, far from optimistic.

Informants suggest that a certain amount of refined finger-wagging and eyebrow-lifting about the evils inseparable from the capitalist system is likely to be the extent of the Labour party attack arising out of the Budget Bandy situation.

Naturally, there is strong opposition to this attitude within the Labour party, and naturally a good deal depends upon the reception by the public of the exact terms of the Tribunal's report when it comes to be published.

For the moment it is a remarkable, but unquestionable fact, that Mr. Baldwin's position has on the whole been very slightly but perceptibly improved by the events of the past weeks: the duration of the improvement is a matter of pure speculation.

A week later, just when all official circles and most of Fleet Street were heaving sighs of relief that the Budget scandal was over and Britain was back on an even keel, *The Week* returned to the subject. It decided to go "behind the Budget scandal".

Despite the brilliance which has been the subject of so much praise in the newspapers, the Budget Tribunal did not—and

therefore presumably could not—do more than touch the fringes
of the situation out of which the Budget scandal arose.

People who have for long been expertly watching and investigating the development of that situation, and who played a major
role in the explosion of the Budget scandal itself, claim that behind
—and to some extent apart from—the disclosures of the Budget
Tribunal, there exists a wider and graver state of affairs than the
Budget Tribunal was able to hint at.

Those people, and there were quite a number of them, who
had at least a hazy idea of *The Week*'s City contacts, naturally
had an idea who those people who had played a major role in
the explosion of the Budget scandal really were and they knew
that these people had close if intermittent connections with
The Week.

Some of those who were aware of these facts were delighted.
Others were dismayed.

The fact is [*The Week* continued] that among those interested in
the affair are members of a gang of financial racketeers whose
activities—particularly in the provinces—would appear to make
Chicago look like child's play.

The gang in question seems to have specialized in the buying of
municipal councillors and others in various similar positions, who
were strategically well-placed to provide, first, information of the
greatest value to the companies whose chances of making money
depend on the actions of municipal councils, and secondly, to
"arrange" for the councils in question to vote in the right direction
on matters affecting the companies wherewith the racketeers are
directly or indirectly concerned.

This was one of the few occasions on which the notorious
corruption of public life at the municipal level was publicly
drawn attention to in a British publication. It was one of those
things that everyone in pubs and clubs talked about up and
down the country but which nobody expected to see committed
to cold print, or even to a mimeograph. It was another instance
of the gap existing between what everyone knew and what the
press chose to print.

The Week went on to describe in somewhat alarming detail

the activities of the gang in question. Of course, in terms of *The Week* the word "gang" could include in its application prominent City figures and members of the government. Narrowing the area, *The Week* continued:

Several Northern cities provided a hunting ground for the gang, and owing to the happy combination of the British Libel Laws which compel everyone to write and talk as though they had a plum in their mouths, the advertising situation which ensures that there are hardly any newspapers prepared to expose anything which involves the rich men of the locality, and the blessed, carefully inculcated innocence of about 75% of the British public, which believes that by some miracle British public life is cleaner than public life in France or the United States, the gang got away with it with very little trouble indeed.

Apparently—though not certainly—because they repeatedly insured themselves against the passage of certain local measures which went through with monotonous regularity, the gang aroused the suspicion of at least one important insurance broker, who was, it seems, hot on their trail before the gang happened in on the budget insurances, which were in fact a mere sideline so far as they were concerned.

Naturally, in the carrying out of their business, the gangsters in question established close financial and social relations with many of the most influential political persons in the country.

There was therefore very widespread activity—and in the end relief—among many highly placed persons, when the Budget Tribunal failed to disclose anything whatever beyond the fact that Mr. Thomas had disclosed certain Budget secrets to Mr. Bates and Sir Alfred Butt—neither of whom are connected at all with the gang we have been describing.

It is in this sense Mr. Thomas may be said to be the victim of political and financial interests who have found it exceedingly convenient to make of him an easy lightning conductor for crimes whose authors are a great deal more numerous in governing circles up and down the country than the Budget Tribunal was able to suggest . . . So far from the Thomas leak being a mere episode or interlude in British public life, it had chanced to be the only one to get itself more or less forcibly disclosed.

The successful Budget insurances taken out in the year 1934, did in point of fact bring more money to certain individuals than those taken out this year. The schedule of these insurances was, we understand, presented by Lloyds to the Budget Tribunal.

We understand that experts regarded as exceedingly improbable that the £30,000 worth of insurances taken out this year and still unclaimed were taken out by people connected with Mr. J. H. Thomas, since Mr. Crocker has thoroughly investigated all his connections. [The unclaimed insurances were of course only a fraction of the total.]

Since the people to whom these insurance payments are due made their bets by telephone, and have not claimed the winnings, it is correctly assumed by people who do not pay too much attention to *banzais* of the newspapers over the "thoroughness" of the investigation, that other important political personalities were involved.

As Ben had often remarked, the editor of *The Week* regarded all times as crucial. He believed, according to Ben, that "practically every month is a crucial one in the history of the human race." And, Ben would say rather ruefully, "Do you know, he seems to be able to prove it."

Furthermore, Claud thought that there was no real division between the domestic situation in Britain and the international state of affairs. The national press tended to make that division. In *The Week*'s view, to do so was false and misleading. Having therefore deliberately drawn attention in the story about the Budget leak and the activities of "the gang" on municipal level, *The Week* in the same issue turned immediately to what was thought of quite distinctly as *la haute politique*. It was Claud's view that if the British domestic situation was in a mess, then the consequences were certainly going to be felt on the international front. In particular, international observers and, more particularly still, hostile international observers, were going to know about what was going on in Britain and particularly in the Cabinet and use it for their own advantages.

Following the collapse in face of Hitler's action in the Rhineland, there had been signs of some pulling together of the anti-Nazi forces in London and Paris. And that in turn had provoked what was called at the Foreign Office "the German counter-attack" on the London propaganda front, with, as *The Week* repeatedly asserted, its headquarters at Cliveden.

Moving round and about London, the editor found to his dismay that the violence of the "counter-attack", the apparent pervasiveness of Nazi propaganda, had convinced a good many of those who had tried to pull themselves together that the whole thing was hopeless. The creation of just such an impression was, naturally, an essential part of the propaganda itself. The good propagandist must always seek to convince the enemy in advance that his cause is hopeless, that he is swimming against the tide of history, etc.

The Week reported that, on the contrary, it would be dangerously mistaken to suppose that the Nazi influences were winning hands down.

The British government had addressed a questionnaire to the German government, seeking to get the latter to define its aims.

> While the German propagandists are working to split the French and the British and in particular to prevent an extension, fatal to their plans, of the security system represented by the Franco-Soviet Pact, the Foreign Office not only does not believe that there is the slightest prospect of a "satisfactory" reply to the British questionnaire, but does not believe that there was really any point in sending the questionnaire at all since German aims are already perfectly familiar and there is nothing to suggest that any reply that may be made from Berlin will offer any assurance more binding than the assurances publicly made by Hitler of his "peaceful" intentions, which culminated in the invasion of the Rhineland.

> Owing to the utterly confused and divided state of the British political forces, which prevent the firm formation of anything which will even look like a consistent British foreign policy, the German propagandists find it well worth while to continue their efforts behind the scenes in London for the reason that even though, for the time being, they do not succeed in drawing the British in the direction they and their friends want them to go, they do at least have an important effect in paralysing British activity and preventing—or at any rate delaying—a British move in the direction of the reorganization and reintegration of the collective security system.

Strange as it seems now, that issue of *The Week* ended instead of beginning with a brief and ominous note on Spain. The note was certainly prophetic. But in view of what happened within a matter of six or seven weeks, it might appear curious that it should have appeared practically as a footnote.

Headed "Spain", it said:

> Intensive underground activity suggests that the long-delayed attempt at a Fascist putsch by the higher ranks of the army officers is not likely to be delayed much longer. [It was in fact delayed only until 17 July.] The reorganization of the army which will, in fact, amount to a certain democratization of the army, is due this month. The disorderly elements of the Right are believed determined to try to get in their blow before the reorganization can be carried out.

The Week's information from Spain was, as everyone soon knew, correct. It would have been a very bad mark for *The Week* had it been otherwise. But a few months later Claud was suffering pangs of guilt for not having given the information he had about Spain greater prominence.

"The fact that we smuggled in that little item of information at the foot of the last page," he said, "proves that we were well informed but stupid. We were, I think, in the same boat with those people in ancient Athens who, as we all recall, voted against Aristides, a good man, simply on the ground that they were 'tired' of hearing Aristides called the 'good'. Of course we had plenty of information about the coming military putsch in Spain. We also had a great deal of information to the effect that this was not just a putsch being organized in the officers' barracks and the Right Wing political clubs in Madrid. We were told over and over again that the putsch was simply the first move in a big international act by first the Italian and then the German governments. We had, of course, drawn attention over and over again to the aggressive intentions of those two governments. We had written at length about the Italian aggressive aims in the Mediterranean. All the same, we underestimated grossly the international significance of the coming putsch in Spain.

"Perhaps it is one of the advantages of villains that in the end one becomes bored with reporting on their villainous activities. I think we were a little bored with the reports we kept giving of the goings-on of the Nazis and the Italian Fascists. And I suppose one ought to admit to some sort of sordid fear that we might, by giving too many of them, start to bore and thus lose our subscribers."

Although he admittedly failed to estimate properly what the impending revolt in Spain was going to mean, Claud, according to friends, kept boring them all during the month of June and the first week or so of July that year, by repeatedly bringing discussion around to the question of Spain.

When asked why he did so, he said he really had no evidence to go on but had a feeling in his bones. His friends told him to keep his feeling to himself until he could explain how it was supposed to be of interest to other people. However, his bones throbbed more than ever when, at some kind of international trade union meeting in London, he met M. del Vayo. Del Vayo was there with the Spanish delegation. He had been a foreign correspondent in Berlin and he and Claud had many mutual friends. Del Vayo later became Foreign Minister in the Republican government of Spain. Sitting in a bar in Blooms-bury, he told Claud, spelling it out in terms which even Claud thought lurid at the time, what he thought was going to happen in Spain and why it was going to happen.

14 Reporter in Spain

AFTER talking for several hours on different occasions with del Vayo, Claud still failed to appreciate the importance of what del Vayo was telling him. He still didn't grasp that the impending affair in Spain was far more than a merely Spanish affair. Much later, when the archives of the old Foreign Office were opened, the truth of what del Vayo had said was revealed for all to see. The old Spanish Foreign Office had known all along that the Italians and Germans—particularly the Germans—were engaged in a long-term plan for a right-wing putsch in Spain. Its object was to destroy the incipient Spanish democracy and this would result in a situation in which Spain's position in modern Europe would be shifted in a direction favourable to the central powers. It was not, apparently, their aim to occupy Spain in their general attack upon Western Europe. The right-wing generals would, they thought, do that on their behalf. What was wanted, in Rome and Berlin, was simply that Spain should be "neutrally hostile" to France.

It is often suggested that after the occupation of France by Germany, Hitler wanted Franco to allow the German forces to advance through Spain to Gibraltar. Franco is supposed to have refused them passage. Given the way things fell out at the end of the war, Franco never denied that he did that thing. Since the German Army at that time could have gone through Spain like a knife through butter had it so desired, the picture of Franco in the posture of Horatius at the bridge has always seemed a little improbable. And those Spanish archives certainly suggest that Hitler at no time had anything of the kind in mind. The isolation of France was the objective. And that objective was, as everyone knows, achieved in the course of the Spanish War.

As I have said, it was surprising that the editor of *The Week* should have entirely missed the significance of what del Vayo was trying to explain to him. The second surprise event was that Claud suddenly chose this moment to take another holiday. As usual this decision came suddenly. As usual it was dismaying to the staff of *The Week*. And as usual the editor, having decided to go, decided to go at once. He intended to go to Villefranche in the south of France. In Paris he got on the wrong train. He found himself, in fact, on the same line which in the previous year had taken him via Sète to Port Bou just across the Spanish frontier. Remembering that his previous holiday in Spain had been abruptly cut short by the riots in Toulon, he thought there was after all no need to take all the trouble involved in changing trains and somehow trekking back to Villefranche. He would see Spain after all.

He fetched up on a beach south of Tarragona. At that time this section of the now over-populated Costa Brava was entirely undiscovered by foreign tourists. This particular section of it was normally used as a watering-place by a small number of Spanish grandees from the baking interior. That year of 1936 even they were absent. The hotel was empty. Remarking on this to the staff, Claud was told that the normal clientèle was unlikely to come that year. Why? Because people of that kind knew that "something was going to happen". They were staying at home, ready for it. On 17 July it happened. The Fascist rising began. The "holiday" lasted not for a couple of weeks but for months. By September the editor of *The Week* had enlisted in the Spanish Militia, the first, I think, of his countrymen to do so, and was encamped on a mountain top in the Sierras north of Madrid firing at Moors with an old-fashioned Spanish rifle.

Claud had certainly engaged in a good many conspiracies in his life. So that on this occasion nobody in his senses believed for a second that his alleged holiday in Spain had not been carefully planned. It was perfectly useless for him to explain that his arrival there had been the result of a mere accident. He had got into the wrong train in Paris. People thought that sort of explanation from that sort of man amounted to an insult to their intelligence. Obviously he had in fact been acting on information received from the Comintern or other international organization. He had gone there as a secret agent. The notion fitted perfectly their image of *The Week* and its editor. Being, like many fictions, more satisfactory than the truth, belief in it was unshakeable. A friend who had even witnessed the episode at the Paris station, and had seen with his own eyes that Claud, with a ticket to Villefranche, had got into the wrong train, was later convinced that the whole affair had been a deliberate ruse.

With the outbreak of civil war the editor of *The Week* had immediately become also the war correspondent of the *Daily Worker*. So far so good. But both publications were grievously disconcerted when the editor of one and the war correspondent of the other suddenly disappeared into the ranks of the Spanish Militia. For a man with so high an opinion of his own abilities it was odd that Claud should also take, as he did, the view that really the whole business of journalism was a knack, and that anyone could acquire it who took the trouble. He was therefore, he considered, by no means indispensable. He was tired, he said, of sitting there in Madrid exhorting other people to fight like tigers and if necessary lay down their lives for the Cause. He was sick of writing stories praising other people's sacrifices.

"I began to feel," he said "like the man in the story about World War I. In the days before conscription came to Britain he was asked why he did not volunteer for service in the war to save civilization. He said, 'But I am the civilization all you other fellows are fighting for.' "

The staff of *The Week* gallantly did their best to fill the gaps left by the editor's abrupt departure.

In the autumn he returned briefly to London to throw any weight he might have into the balance at a meeting there of trade union leaders from the West European countries. The Spanish trade unions had sent a messenger up to the Sierra to tell him that, objectively speaking, his presence in London could be more important than his presence as a platoon commander on the mountains north of Madrid. Lying in a dugout on the mountainside with this trade union representative, and another man who really was an agent of the Comintern, Claud argued that they had the whole thing upside down. It was true, he said, that he was by no means a good platoon commander. In fact his entire military experience consisted of a spell as an officer in his school corps. On the other hand even this experience was considerably superior to that of the men under his temporary command. They were peasants from the district of Almanza. They knew even less about military tactics than he did; even he could give them a tip or two.

On the other hand there were hundreds of people in London, he asserted, who would do the required job at least as effectively as himself. He told them that they were under an entire misapprehension. They believed that he really carried some weight in London. Anxious to get back to his platoon he depicted in exaggerated terms the lack of influence of *The Week* and the *Daily Worker*. The Spanish trade union man and the Comintern agent were unmoved. They insisted that he return immediately. He went on arguing all the way down the path thick with pine needles, leading from the dugout over the mountainside to the main road where the agent's car was waiting. He admitted afterwards that his arguments were partly specious and not what the Comintern agent would have called strictly objective. He just wanted to stay in Spain, and stay right there on that particular mountainside.

The arguments were useless, however. He returned briefly to London. Naturally since he was a delegate of no organization there was no possibility of his attending in any official capacity the strictly secret meeting of the international trade union leaders. On the other hand the Spaniards considered it very important that he should be personally present and be able to see with his own eyes precisely what went on at this secret mission. They therefore arranged for him to be present in the capacity of a humble interpreter on behalf of the Spanish delegation. Since a good many of those who were going to be present might have seen the editor of *The Week*, or the Diplomatic Editor of the *Daily Worker* somewhere, sometime, it was agreed that he should be faintly disguised. The Spanish idea of a faint disguise was an enormous wig and preferably some form of moustache. Claud thought this was going too far. People would notice. He settled for some minor changes in his facial appearance, and wore noticeably Spanish clothes. Even so he was made extremely uncomfortable during one of the secret sessions by glances shot at him from time to time from the eyes of the astute Ernest Bevin, the head of the British trade union delegation.

He had recently rather often had occasion to denounce

Bevin as a reactionary. Worse still, in the circumstances, he had on several occasions had drinks with Mr. Bevin in one bar or another, and despite his disguise, Claud had an uncomfortable feeling that from time to time Bevin was looking at him from behind the top table at this secret conference of the great trade union powers with the air of a man who thinks he has seen that fellow somewhere before.

The secret conference reached decisions which from the point of view of the Spanish Republicans and indeed of anti-Fascists in general were disastrous. Particularly bad was the rôle played by Bevin.

The secret proceedings were of course reported in full in the *Daily Worker* and were the subject of considerable comment in *The Week*. Bevin's acute suspicion that there had been more to the Spanish interpreter than met the eye was confirmed. But by this time it was too late.

To the dismay of the staff of *The Week* Claud took it for granted that he would immediately return to Spain. It was argued against this move that his presence in London was more "needed" than his presence in Madrid. At first he tried to argue that this was untrue in the sense that anyone could pick up the threads of the work in London whereas the job in Madrid was more difficult. Finding that nobody believed this statement, he fell back on a more clinching argument. He said, truthfully enough, that he had temporarily lost all interest in anything that might be happening in London. The place appeared to him a mere blur. He was entirely obsessed by the struggle centring on Madrid. If he remained in London he would be perfectly useless as an editor. His attitude convinced people that in this he was absolutely sincere and probably correct.

But there were still some snags in the way. The French government under the premiership of the Socialist Léon Blum was leaning over backwards demonstrating its fidelity to the policy of non-intervention in Spain. In close collaboration with the British Labour leaders the Blum government had agreed to demonstrate its loyalty to this policy by taking the strictest measures to prevent the infiltration of volunteers from outside Spain to fight on behalf of the Spanish Republic. It would refuse exit from France into Spain to, for instance, any holder of a British passport who had not got from the British Foreign Office a special visa for Spain. Anyone who attempted to cross the frontier without that visa would either be stopped, or, if he attempted to proceed illegally, shot on his way to the border.

Claud duly applied for his visa. He had, he pointed out, a perfect right to it as a war correspondent and an editor interested in foreign affairs. The British government, also anxious to show enthusiasm for the non-intervention policy, thought otherwise. His visa was refused. The matter was immediately taken up by way of Questions in the House of Commons. There Lord Cranborne, then Under Secretary of State for Foreign Affairs, sought to justify the Foreign Office's refusal of the visa. The man in question he said, had actually taken up arms in the service of a foreign power. Technically, I believe, service with the Republican Militia had been more heinous than service with the International Brigade. He therefore could not be regarded as an ordinary newspaper-man. In fact to admit him to Spain, the government seemed to suppose, would be a breach of the non-intervention agreement. The government, Lord Cranborne announced, absolutely refused permission for this man to enter Spain ever again.

The man in question listened to this statement from a seat in the Gallery of the House of Commons. At the end of Question Time he left the House and took a bus to Victoria Station on the first leg of a journey to the Spanish frontier. His underground contacts in Paris told him that there were two ways of getting illegally across the frontier. One was relatively safe but arduous. It involved climbing quite a chunk of the Pyrenees. The other was physically speaking easy going. It involved only creeping across a fairly wide area of perfectly flat land. The difficulty was that this particular piece of land was under special surveillance by the French frontier guards. They were known to be bored and trigger-happy. They were liable to shoot at anything they saw moving on that patch.

After some thought Claud said: "I would rather do almost anything than try to climb even a small mountain, let alone a bit of the Pyrenees." He took the flat route and arrived successfully on the other side of the border. A couple of days after the London newspapers had reported the Foreign Office refusal of the visa and Lord Cranborne's statement in the House of Commons there appeared in *The Week* Claud's first despatch from Madrid.

Some months later there was a supposedly crucial meeting of the League of Nations at Geneva. The Spaniards were going to put their case against non-intervention and against the visible intervention of the Italian and German governments. Del Vayo and others insisted that it was important for Claud to accompany the delegation and report on the proceedings. It happened that Negley Farson was among the foreign correspondents present at that Geneva meeting. He in turn was a friend of the Canadian delegate.

They arranged a small comedy. The Canadian delegate gave a luncheon party in his flat. Among those invited were Lord Cranborne and Claud. The host managed to slur the formal introductions. Lord Cranborne did not catch the name of his fellow guest. He did however learn that his neighbour at the lunch table had been recently in Spain. He asked questions about the situation. Claud, as may be imagined, answered at considerable length. Discreetly, he left the party early. After he had gone Lord Cranborne enquired from the host who that man was. This stranger, said Lord Cranborne, had told him in half an hour more facts about the realities of the situation in Spain than he had been able to gather from experts at the Foreign Office over a matter of months. With all the pleasure of a man who has brought his play to a nice dénouement the Canadian delegate informed Lord Cranborne that "That was Mr. Cockburn. You remember what trouble you took to prevent him going to Spain."

Despite all this pother *The Week*'s coverage of the Spanish War seems somehow unsatisfactory. For this there were some obvious technical reasons. Owing to Claud's departure the paper had been left with no regular editor at all. And *The Week* had become so individual a product that it was extraordinarily difficult for anyone else to take over. But there were other reasons for a performance which now seems rather disappointing. These other reasons involved some knotty, not to say profound, questions of journalism in time of conflict. For instance at this distance it can be seen that *The Week*'s reports about the situation in Spain were both accurate in detail and grossly misleading in terms of the situation as a whole. They were accurate enough when they dealt with the Italian and then the German intervention. But they were misleading in their optimism. The reader had the impression that however hard things might be, however grim the outlook might seem, victory for the Republicans was, must be, ultimately round the next corner but one, or if not one, but two, or but three.

When the Republicans finally ran out of more corners to turn, Claud, naturally enough, was the object of some fairly bitter criticism by very disappointed people. They felt they had been led up the garden.

Claud was both distressed and unrepentant.

"There seem to be," he said, "two pieces of this problem. That's to say the extent to which I myself totally believed what I said, and the extent to which I was, more or less consciously, trying to get other people to believe it. But I don't think there's really such a clear line of division."

He went on to talk of a time when the Republicans were besieging the Alcazar. He told of a discussion which had taken place on the ramparts overlooking the Alcazar, between himself, an American journalist deeply sympathetic with the Republicans and Michael Koltzov, Foreign Editor of *Pravda*, one of Claud's closest friends. (Koltzov at that time was an intimate of Stalin, discussing the Spanish situation with him once or twice daily on the telephone from Madrid. Koltzov was shot two years later by Stalin in a Moscow purge.)

Koltzov, who up till then had been on good terms with the American, now actually spat in a gesture of disgust when he saw the man get out of his car and make towards them.

Claud asked, "Why?"

Koltzov started to talk volubly. Then the American reached them and put out his hand in greeting. Koltzov, looking like a stocky kind of small bird, with an enormous head, put his hands behind his back, and spat again. Now it was the American's turn to ask, "Why, Michael, what's the matter?"

Koltzov looked across at the besieged citadel of Toledo. "The matter," he said, "is that I have just had telephoned to me from Moscow the transcript of your latest report on the situation here—here in Toledo."

"Well? Do you disagree with it? Doesn't it give the facts?"

"What facts?"

"Listen, Michael, you know as well as I do that our side's in one hell of a mess. What's the good of pretending our militia here aren't demoralized and bewildered? Who's going to believe me if I tell the old story once again? Week or two ago I really believed we were going to take that Alcazar soon. Maybe by some act of desperate courage—and like I wrote in that piece, I've seen some of those acts here. But now it's time to be a bit more realistic. The men are demoralized. They think, and how right they are, there's been an incredible muddle somewhere at the top. They even believe, and you know it, that some of the people back there on top in Madrid are actually conniving with the other side. If I've heard that 'we are betrayed' stuff once in the last week, I've heard it twenty times. There aren't going to be any more acts of desperate courage. And you'll have to admit that most of the desperate courage right now is being shown by the other side. Those are the facts."

Koltzov said, "Yes. Those are the facts. How extraordinarily observant and truthful you are."

"Isn't it better in the long run to let the readers have the facts?"

Koltzov burst out in a passion. Although, he said, the thing made no kind of military sense, the Alcazar had been raised to the status of a symbol. More so in the outer world than in Spain itself. This, he admitted, was partly the fault of the Republicans' own clumsy propaganda. Because they had been grossly overconfident about the situation at Toledo, they had deliberately exaggerated the importance of the Alcazar. They had built it up as a symbol, because they believed that this would make their victory there more impressive.

"All childish nonsense," he said. "But the point is, now we're all stuck with this damned symbol. Millions of people all over the world think that what goes on here in Toledo is the key to the whole Spanish situation. They take it as a working model.

"If an enemy journalist, or spy, comes to this side and later writes that our people are demoralized, and implies that the heroes are over there in Alcazar, it doesn't matter. Nobody in London or New York or Paris who might have been usefully sympathetic to us, would be influenced in the least. But you, with your reputation . . . You really can spread alarm and despondency. And that's what you've done. You've done more harm than thirty British M.P.'s working for Franco. And then you expect me to shake hands with you."

The American said stubbornly that facts were facts, and the readers had a right to them.

"If you were a little more frank," Koltzov said, "you'd say that what you're really interested in is your damned reputation as a journalist. You're afraid if you don't put out this stuff, and it comes through someone else, you'll be thought a bad reporter, can't see the facts under his nose. Probably in the pay of the Republicans. That's why you, as the French say, have lost an excellent opportunity to keep your mouth shut."

Certainly so far as my own acquaintances in London were concerned, what Koltzov said about the Alcazar as a symbol was true. At that time, almost all of them were Conservatives. Thinking back, I would guess that, in so far as they thought about the Spanish War at all, they were divided about fifty-fifty between well-wishers of the Republicans and well-wishers of Franco. But the supporters of Franco were, in general, of two more or less distinct sorts.

Some were people who, on any issue, could be guaranteed to range themselves on the Right. There is no need to detail the reasons for their attitude to the Spanish War. But there were also a good many whose reactions were less automatic. Having no very deep political feelings, they seemed to see the war in a peculiarly personal light. Many of them, I am speaking of those I knew, had friends in Spain. And these had always been, to say the least, critical of the Republican régime. My London acquaintances thought of these Spanish friends as being in present or future peril from the Left. They regarded the Republicans as being in the nature of a flood or other natural catastrophe which, if unchecked, would damage or engulf some charming people.

To this type of Conservative, the defenders of the Alcazar appealed not so much because they were of the Right, but because they presented a comfortingly simple drama of beleaguered gallantry. So far as British public opinion was concerned, the Republicans needed all the gallantry that could be mustered on their side. It would have been exceedingly unfortunate for their men at Toledo to be represented as in any way demoralized. In this sense, Koltzov was right. And Claud refused to be drawn into argument as to whether the public did or did not have the right to read the truth. Attempts to argue produced a row.

"Who gave them such a right?" he would ask furiously. "Perhaps when they have exerted themselves enough to alter the policy of their bloody government, and the Fascists are beaten in Spain, they will have such a right. This isn't an abstract question. It's a shooting war."

Years later, when *The Week* was attacking the British government for keeping the British public in the dark about events on the Western Front, he was reminded of his earlier attitude. All he would say was that one had to make up one's mind according to circumstances. Would the truth do good, or harm? Asked who was to decide that, he again became deliberately pig-headed. "You are saying," he declared, "you can't see the difference between right and wrong."

This sort of outburst naturally put a stop to the discussion.

15 King and "Week"

STRICTLY by hindsight, it would seem that the Royal Abdication of 1936 would have been just what *The Week*'s doctor might have ordered. The paper must have been, one takes for granted, among the first to go to work on, for example, the relations between the King and Mrs. Simpson.

The reality was more bizarre. It is true to say that *The Week*'s handling of the matter began frivolously. It seemed to regard the American newspapers' excitement over these developments (which they were reporting while the British press muffled itself) as a devious attempt to distract attention from the realities of the Spanish War. *The Week* became at times quite governessy. Its tone was that of some grave editor of *The Times* complaining that the gossip column was invading the news pages.

It is odd to reflect now that, at that date, it really was regarded as an exceedingly grave matter for a British publication to report on the love life of the Monarch. Nobody knew what the penalties might be. And, as I have noted earlier, the distributors of *Time* magazine in London were so uncertain and alarmed that they sat up for hours with scissors, cutting out the revealing or offensive references to the blazing affair.

During the whole of the earlier part of the development, Claud was away in Spain. *The Week* was in effect being edited by an extremely informal committee of "friends of *The Week*". Communication, let alone consultation, with the editor was difficult. There was, that is to say, a one-way communication. His despatches from Spain usually, though not invariably, arrived. These despatches were not always soothing. One of them was prefaced by a note to staff, saying, "Seek to use this fine assessment of situation before some *Schweinerei* committed by God or Hitler or some others I can see in the café across the street proves it utterly mistaken."

As for consultations, they were out of the question. They would have to have been conducted over one of a battery of telephones from an upper room in the Telefonica building in Madrid. Behind the correspondent at the telephone stood a censor. The understanding was that the correspondent was not to deviate at all from the text as already submitted. And from time to time the conversations were interrupted by the bursting of shells near, and sometimes actually on, the building. It was no occasion for discussing the nuances of a complex situation in London. And in any case, that situation itself would have appeared to the man talking from Madrid quite farcically trivial. It certainly never occurred to him to use, on such an account, the delicate and sometimes dangerous opportunities offered him by one faction in the censor's department, to talk freely with London.

It was therefore impossible for the people in Victoria Street, on their own responsibility, to take a line which might, they thought, have led directly to a noose of some kind for *The Week*.

The result was an uneasy compromise. It seems that some of those consulted thought that cautious references should be made to American press comment with the idea of letting *Week* subscribers read between the lines. In other words, they were in favour of an old tradition of censorship evasion: if you cannot print the facts direct, print them in the form of denials. The readers will catch on. But there were others who genuinely thought that the American press comment, the news leaked to American correspondents, was part of a plot, and ought to be exposed as such.

This second argument was more important; more significant in relation to British attitudes. It explains a good deal of what now seems nearly incomprehensible political behaviour at the time of the Abdication.

Put quite simply the position was this: the Baldwin government had become in the eyes of the Left the central villain of the whole horrible drama of British politics in the Thirties. Groucho Marx used to sing, "Whatever it is, I'm against it." Whatever the Baldwin government was for, the Left was against. That part of it was easy. Then things became more difficult. Does it follow that whatever the Baldwin government is against, we are for?

Thoughtful Labour men and Liberals found in the matter of the King v. Baldwin clash a grievous dilemma. Claud returning briefly from the relative simplicities of Spanish conflict could see no genuine dilemma at all. He was unable to see why any such dilemma should be supposed to exist.

He saw Edward VIII as having somehow become a stumbling block in the path of Stanley Baldwin and his colleagues. Baldwin and colleagues, in his view, were the men who had repeatedly sought to sell out British interests in favour of their class interests. They were the men who had whole-heartedly accepted the Nazi occupation of the Rhineland. They were in closest alliance with the profiteers and racketeers of the armament industries. They were currently engaged in a policy designed to deprive the Spanish Republicans of arms against the Fascist revolt. Just who and what Edward VIII might be, or do, was irrelevant. Anyone who could in any way impede Baldwin and friends was to be supported.

People said: "But *The Week* itself has hinted that the King is influenced by the Nazis, admires Hitler."

"That is neither here nor there. Or rather, it is there, but not here. What in God's name does it matter what the little man did then? What does it matter what he even thinks? And how can it matter what woman he has or whom he marries? The mere suggestion that this is important is ludicrous. It in itself is adequate proof that this whole brouhaha is a plot by the government."

The repeated question "How can this man's sex life possibly matter to anyone?" was, in turn, in itself adequate proof that the editor's alien eye had still failed to adjust itself properly to British perspectives.

It thus came about that, for technical reasons while the editor was in Spain, but still more for political reasons, *The Week* quite failed, during the time when the affair was moving slowly towards its climax, to deal with it in a manner to which its readers had become accustomed.

Despite all this, *The Week* did, in fact "scoop" everyone.

In its issue of 14 October 1936, it reported plans afoot for "a social bomb to be exploded under the King. The ideal method envisaged by those planting the bomb would be for a reference to be made from the pulpit to 'the very different standards of conduct set to his subjects by the late King'."

Apart from being an undeniable scoop, *The Week*'s story is of interest on another level. It has been repeatedly stated since that the sermon preached by the Bishop of Bradford, indicating moral and/or religious disapproval of the King—the sermon which triggered off the public campaign against the King's marriage—was some kind of accident. The innocent Bishop, it has been said over and over again, had no idea of triggering off anything. He was just talking in a routinely Christian sort of way.

This seems the version likely to go down to history, as history. But Dr. Blunt's sermon was preached on 1 December. And *The Week*'s preview of it had appeared in mid-October.

In its issue of 9 December, *The Week* examined this coincidence.

After recalling its own prophecy, it noted that the Bishop of Bradford had just fulfilled it. It added that "the *Yorkshire Post*, owned and controlled by the Becketts, Mrs. Anthony Eden's family, wrote an editorial upon the text of the Bishop's words, and circulated it before publication to other provincial papers, and telephoned its contents to some London journals. Thus officially commenced the crisis."

The Week noted that the Bishop had "somewhat vehemently denied" that at the time he preached that notable sermon he had ever so much as heard of Mrs. Simpson.

It is possible that Dr. Blunt was in fact unaware of those fevered whisperings which were so exciting the more alert members of the Church, or, that if he had heard the whispers, he was incapable of appreciating their meaning. But this need not rule out the possibility that he was the chosen, though unconscious, instrument of persons bent on producing the crisis at this particular moment. Secondly, it by no means follows that because the *Yorkshire Post* is largely influenced by Mr. Eden, it was influenced on this particular occasion. Bradford is one of the centres of its circulation, and therefore a remark by the Bishop is of local interest.

However that may be, there can be no doubt that from the beginning of October there has flowed from official and semi-official sources a series of stories and rumours, a number of them patently untrue and all of them highly discrediting to the King. There can be no doubt that these stories were spread by, among others, persons occupying positions of trust under the Crown, and that their intensity and virulence most materially increased after the King's visit to South Wales.

This was the visit during which the King had toured the distressed areas of South Wales and made a promise to the miners. As Malcolm Muggeridge records, "The King was deeply moved by the welcome he received from the distressed inhabitants of these distressed areas, and by the melancholy circumstances of their lives. His sympathetic smile was appreciated, as was his reluctance to keep to the itinerary which had been arranged; and it was noted with satisfaction that he refused to keep himself wholly in the keeping of his Ministers in attendance . . . Several times the police cordon was broken: hymns were passionately sung, and miners' lamps joyously waved in the darkness. 'I am going to help you,' the King said, and in the message of thanks for the welcome he had received, repeated it—'Something will be done for you'."

Proceeding with its analysis of the crisis, *The Week* recounted that "the main complaints against the King, excluding the purely scandalous and unfounded attacks, can be divided under two mutually contradictory heads. In the one case it is said that he is entirely neglectful of his duties. It is suggested, for example, that he never gives the Cabinet notice of his movements, so that State Business is impeded. . . . Against this it is also suggested that the King is continually interfering in State affairs and is opposing the Cabinet not only over the Industrial Areas but also over Foreign Policy. This being so, there is at least a presumption that the crisis was engineered at this particular time with the object not only of removing Mrs. Simpson, but of also controlling, or alternatively removing the King."

Since the King abdicated only a couple of days after that was written, it might seem that *The Week* was belated in its analysis. This was true. The reason has been put on record by the editor. I will not retail here the whole of that true, though stranger than fictional, story. Very briefly summarized, what it amounted to was this:

Lord Louis Mountbatten, the King's principal adviser, and a patriotic opponent of Nazi influences in Britain, had repeatedly drawn the King's attention to *The Week*. The King started reading it. But, he enquired, how could he take the opinion of such a publication as valid, in contradiction to the opinion of most of his Cabinet? Claud was then asked to supply Fort Belvedere with an account of himself. A sort of elongated *Who's Who* entry. He did so. The King, it appears, remained interested in the strange little sheet.

As the crisis developed, it occurred to Lord Louis that *The Week* might just possibly be the last (however unwelcome) weapon available. Through John Strachey, Claud was approached with the question whether he would be prepared to issue a special edition of *The Week* giving the King's point of view? He was warned that the material would be highly dangerous: it would certainly include allegations which several members of the Cabinet could regard as libellous, possibly criminally libellous. It was further noted that, since this knife fight, there was a probability that the government, using its own resources at Scotland Yard, which were superior to those of the King, would make an indirect, but immediate attack. *The Week* would be seized or closed down on some pretext allegedly not related to the crisis. It could, for instance, be re-asserted that the editor, by fighting in the ranks of the Spanish Republican Militia, had become a traitor to his country. (This, I think, was technically true.)

Although, as I say, the King's supporters among the chiefs of the police were inferior to those of the government, they were not negligible. And as I have mentioned in quite another connexion, Claud, too, had contacts there. He was in consequence able to verify, or at least get a rough idea of, the attitude which the government was likely to take in the event of his paper making unwanted disclosures.

All preparations were made for the issue of a special edition. The material was to be sent late at night by despatch rider from Fort Belvedere to Victoria Street. *The Week*, for its part, had mobilized friends with motor cycles and motor cars, to take that special edition to a few hundred crucial subscribers. It was taken for granted that the rest of the special edition would be seized in the post.

A friend, essential to the enterprise, but doubtful as to its purpose, said to Claud: "So we're King's men now, are we?"

Claud said, "King's men, my foot. If the King has got around to supporting us against Baldwin, I wish him all the best of British luck." This frivolous observation only deepened the friend's depression. Claud, under this accusation of royalism, sought to reassure the friend as to the respectability of his ideas. He told him, for the first time, that he personally had taken part in an attempt to intervene in the Christmas Day broadcast of the old King George V.

He and others had dug up the cable connecting Sandringham with the B.B.C. A gramophone record was to be plugged in while the King was speaking. But at the last moment unforeseen technical difficulties arose. The party barely escaped arrest.

Long afterwards I asked Claud why he had thought the story of this fiasco a suitable one to tell his friend as they waited, on another misty evening in December, for the despatch rider from Fort Belvedere.

Claud replied, "I didn't want him to think that I was some sort of romantic. A King's man for the fun of the thing. I wanted to make him see that one is in favour of the King when his policy is, for the time being, correct. Otherwise not."

"Correct?"

"Correct according to my own views." Not for the first time in encounters with Claud, I was reminded of the well-known, peculiarly Scottish, epitaph:

> Here lie I, Martin Elginbrod:
> Have mercy on my soul, Lord God,
> As I would do, were I Lord God
> And ye were Martin Elginbrod.

That second December was a fiasco, too. Some time after midnight the despatch did arrive. The helpers of all kinds sprang to their posts. The men with motor cars and motor bicycles prepared themselves. But the message from Fort Belvedere was not the expected disclosure of Baldwin's dark doings. It was a sheet of paper with the words: "The situation has developed too fast."

16 Gift from God

LORD (then C. P.) Snow wrote, many years after *The Week* ceased publication, a book called *The Conscience of the Rich*. Several reviewers immediately identified the villain as the editor of *The Week*. Several other people wrote to Claud urging him to take libel action against Snow. Claud replied, reasonably enough, that since he was against the Libel Laws, it would be monstrous to invoke them on his own behalf.

Claud laughed happily as he read the supposedly offending document. But though he had no intention of action for libel, he was bothered by what did seem to him a quite serious aspect of the situation. At that time Snow purported to be a serious observer of the British social and political scene during the 1930s. And the nub, so to speak, of Snow's book seemed to Claud to be a travesty of that situation as it really was.

In the book, the villain is editor of a news-sheet called *The Note*. The news-sheet is a delicately attuned instrument of the Communist party. And this, in turn, is an instrument, apparently marvellously efficient, of the Comintern. How does this editor go about his business? Among other activities, he, as any reader of old-time spy stories knows, uses beautiful girls to further his evil purposes. They are dedicated beings, prepared to go anywhere and betray anyone for the Cause.

This pardonable fictional distortion certainly helps the plot along. It could also be misleading to anyone who took the novelist's work as being in any sense a social document, portrait of a decade, and so on.

The Week had its share of good-looking girls. Naturally the good-looking ones were preferred to the ill-favoured. But as news-gatherers none of them so far as I know, was notably effective.

Typical enough was the case of the Gift from God. Even had he known of this case, and others similar, the novelist would have had to forget them. They would have upset too many of the concepts on which his production was based. Claud christened her the Gift from God for several reasons. She was strikingly good-looking and also vivacious. Her rich and smart clothing, Claud declared, was a delight to the eye. She appeared quite suddenly in *The Week* office, filling the air with scent. She said that she wanted to work. And she wanted to work for nothing. She had more money than she knew what to do with. She just loved, she said, *The Week*.

The editor, of course, engaged her on the spot. And of course it was soon pointed out to him that there could be only one explanation of this phenomenon. She must, quite obviously, be a spy.

"Likely enough. What of it?"

"But you can't have a spy working right here in the office."

"We don't mind. So long as she works unpaid. Like that, the Special Branch or the Foreign Office Intelligence or whoever it is, will be actually helping to pay for the production of *The Week*. Splendid idea."

"But she'll report on you all."

"First of all, there is nothing to report. The telephone and mail are tapped already. And no serious person would come to this office who could not afford to have his name noted down in a little book. And then of course if she is a genuine spy, she could be fed false reports about matters arising. And then don't forget that Lenin said . . ."

It seems that a spy was discovered in the inner group of Bolsheviks. The spy was also a member of the Duma. Lenin was opposed to his expulsion. His clinching argument on that occasion was that the man could actively be used to publicly advocate policies which it was too dangerous for the Bolsheviks to advocate themselves. If this man were asked to make a really dangerous speech in the Duma he would first consult the Political Police. And the police would advise him to go ahead. Otherwise the Bolsheviks would consider him a weakling: perhaps not wholehearted in the cause. They would lose faith in him. They would cease to admit him to their innermost councils. And he would thus lose his value to the police.

The Gift from God was not, I am sure, ever a spy. And she worked hard on merely humdrum tasks around the office. Her only weakness was a liking for smart wedding receptions. One or other of her friends seemed to get married every week.

After the reception she would come into the office, tottering slightly, aglow with champagne. At such times she was not quite capable of ordinary work.

"But she does," Claud would say, "brighten the atmosphere. The mere sight of her makes one feel gay."

On top of that, I think he had the idea that some day somehow she must after all acquire some useful information. Perhaps he had been influenced by some book like that of C. P. Snow. There were plenty such already. And one day it really looked as though something of the kind were going to happen.

Claud was in pursuit of a story involving an enormous triangular Anglo-American-Dutch armament deal. Hints of it had been floating about the City and in Brussels for weeks. Everything seemed to turn on the more or less mysterious goings-on of a big American wheeler-dealer named Overbury. Overbury was mysterious not just about what he was doing, but about where he was doing it. Nobody seemed even to know from one week to the next which country he was in. After one champagne-drenched reception the Gift from God shimmered into the office babbling with gay talk about the party she had just left. The wedding turned out to have involved the daughter of an American magnate. The name of this man rang a small bell in Claud's mind. He remembered having seen it or heard it in a list of people associated with Overbury. He asked the Gift from God, not very hopefully, whether a Mr. Overbury had also been among those present.

She said yes, indeed he had. Claud was astounded. His latest information had been to the effect that Overbury was in Amsterdam. He asked tentatively whether the Gift from God had any speech with Overbury. She bubbled some more. Yes, indeed, she said.

"Actually he fell for me in quite a big way. He had had quite a few drinks. He had got to the stage magnates so often reach, when they want to tell you all about their business."

Claud asked, "Is that what he did with you?"

"He certainly did."

"That must have been interesting. What did he have to say?"

"Well I wasn't really listening. It was something to do with steel. Not very riveting I thought. Anyway people who go booming on and on like that tend to send me to sleep. I got away from him as soon as I could without hurting his feelings."

Claud said afterwards that if only C. P. Snow had understood that that was the sort of thing that really happened he would have understood a great deal more about the political situation in the Thirties in general and such matters as the relations between *The Week* and the Comintern in particular. He remarked that some people saw a chain of command in what was, more often than not, a lot of old rope tied together with granny knots.

The Gift also proved useful in fending off various unsuitable people who without any qualifications at all thought they would be just the right types to work for *The Week*. Some of these were certainly inept. Some of them possibly really were spies. And one or two would probably have been useful. But at such times as the Gift was alone in charge of the office all without exception were turned away. The reason she gave for this course of action was clear-cut. She said she had noticed that everyone who came to work for *The Week* sooner or later went off his head. She explained this with a beautiful smile, but without bothering to add "with the exception of those present".

It was true that there had been a rather large incidence of insanity among *The Week*'s employees and collaborators. As already mentioned, the efficient man from Vancouver, meeting Claud at the entrance to the Army and Navy Stores one morning had fallen on his knees there and loudly addressed him as his "Brother in the Sun". After several such episodes he had to be taken struggling to a mental home. Several similar aberrations occurred. A sort of climax was reached when Ben, the original financial founder, began to behave oddly.

One glorious summer afternoon he hired three Daimler cars. From an expensive florist he bought masses of flowers, which he arranged around him on the back seat of the foremost car. He then instructed the driver to proceed slowly round and round Hyde Park, the other two vehicles following in procession. At the end of an hour or so, it being cocktail time, he halted the *cortège* at the Dorchester Hotel. He had by this time removed his shirt. He went into the cocktail bar and sat there naked to the waist with his jacket draped over his shoulders. His appearance was so noble, and his manner so arrogantly confident that the staff, instead of throwing him out, assumed he must be some foreign dignitary taking part in one of the innumerable international conferences held in London. After an hour or so he left the hotel by a side entrance and strolled nonchalantly through the streets.

Claud's first knowledge of this happening was the arrival in *The Week* office of the three bewildered and exasperated drivers. It appeared that Ben had given the address of *The Week* as that to which the bill was to be sent. The drivers were just checking up. Also they had not been tipped. Equally bewildered, Claud squared the tips and said he would investigate.

Some time later, reflecting on various remarks made by the drivers, it crossed his mind that the man who had disappeared so strangely into the Dorchester might be Ben.

This suspicion seemed to be confirmed very late that evening. Claud was sitting with Philip Jordan in Philip's mews studio in Knightsbridge. A girl, a mutual friend, rang up to say that Ben was at that moment hammering on the door of her flat in Bayswater. He was shouting loudly in French. Sometimes he seemed to be declaring his love, sometimes to be threatening rape.

The girl begged Philip and Claud to come quickly and take him away before the door fell in. By the time they got there Ben had been joined outside the door by a taxi-driver. The taxi-driver explained that he had been driving Ben round and round London for an hour. He had waited peacefully downstairs for twenty minutes and had now come up to see about his fare. With the taxi-driver's help, Ben was manhandled back into the taxi and finally into Philip's studio. There Ben paced about muttering in a threatening manner. Once he lifted up a moderate-sized sofa and being a man of immense strength threw it across the room at the other two, declaring his hatred and contempt for them.

Remembering that Ben was fond of reading French aloud, Claud managed to draw his attention to a lengthy new novel just arrived from Paris. He begged Ben to read it aloud. This he started to do. He not only started but continued for nearly three hours. Claud and Philip took it in turn to try to creep upstairs to the telephone which was in the gallery of the studio. But at the slightest move the reader stopped abruptly, glared and prepared for further violence. It seemed better to listen to the whole of the rest of that book than provoke a brawl in which everyone, including the unfortunate victim of the brainstorm, was going to get badly mauled. It was dawn before Ben, apparently hypnotized by his own voice, suddenly dropped off to sleep. Only then was it possible to summon the aid of a friendly psychiatrist, for it was obvious that unless the matter could be put in the hands of such a man there was the danger of Ben being bundled off in a strait jacket and possibly certified.

When the Gift referred to this episode, Claud was naturally distressed.

"Do you really think," he asked, "that working here sent my poor friend mad?"

"Well," she said, "it must be quite a strain to be always looking at things through spectacles which are quite different from other people's spectacles."

"Are you trying to say 'distorting lenses'?"

"Not necessarily distorting. Just different. Brain-twistingly different, if you see what I mean."

IV

17 *Cliveden Set*

IF the unfortunate Ben had managed to hold out a little longer,
he would possibly have found the brain-twisting differences
slightly diminished. For 1936 had been a turning point of a
sort for *The Week* itself. It would, of course, be ridiculous to
pretend that the paper had directly affected in any notable
degree the thinking of the British public at large. But it is true
that, within the small but influential circle it reached, a
change of attitude was to be seen.

There may not have been a great many more people who
positively agreed with the views of *The Week*, though there
were some such converts in unexpected areas of Whitehall,
Westminster and the City. But there was certainly a significant
increase in the number of those who had begun to take *The
Week* seriously. Too many of its predictions and assessments
had proved correct. Too many of those who had flatly denied
its reports had woken up with red faces a month or more later.
Certainly it had quite often been wrong. But these mistakes
usually took the form of announcing that something was going
to happen much sooner than turned out to be the case. Claud
frequently proclaimed as an axiom that when you are absolutely
sure that something is going to happen within a month, you
should remind yourself that in reality it is almost certainly
going to take three months. But he broke his own rule about as
often as he observed it.

I doubt, however, whether the change of attitude towards
The Week really depended on people totting up its score of
correct predictions, like racing fans marking the performance
of a tipster. The more important fact was that an increasing
number of people had come to the bitter conclusion that *The
Week* was, perhaps, after all right about the realities of the
period; right about the key in which international politics were
being played. In particular, *The Week*'s picture of Berlin as the
centre of a violent and blood-thirsty conspiracy no longer
seemed so improbable as once it had. To the bringing about of

this change, *The Week* by its reports, and the German government by its actions, had both contributed.

A further factor was the extent to which *The Week* was quoted weekly in the international press. It was said, loosely enough, that next to *The Times* it was the most quoted British publication in the world's press. I say "loosely" because obviously there is no way of telling whether that was true or not. Nobody was computing all the quotations in papers from New York to Paris to Bombay and points East. Quite possibly the claim was exaggerated. The important point was that it could be quite seriously made and believed. Claud himself was certainly very far from discouraging such a belief.

He remarked that "it may be true what they say about a prophet being without honour in his own country. But, at any rate in England, if he can once get a few honourable mentions in foreign parts, the locals are apt to adopt a more respectful attitude. I have often thought I might have done well to have changed my name to Schermolinsky or Germinal or something in the first place."

Asked, years later, why nobody else seemed to be able or willing to imitate *The Week*, he said "because to employ *The Week* formula you need to be a good deal more committed, more starry-eyed and reckless than most people want to be."

Despite some increase in respectful attention, the years between the turning point of 1936 and the actual outbreak of war in the West, certainly required the full employment of the formula. There were, for instance, many well-wishers who more or less openly deplored the degree of *The Week*'s commitment. By this they usually meant that Claud should modify his "pro-Communist line". It would broaden the appeal. He replied that he had joined with the Communists because he thought they were in the main right, and saw no reason to alter his own opinions just because the Communists happened to hold the same ones.

As for the broader appeal, he argued that what the phrase really meant was that soothing syrup should be administered along with the bitter medicine. But then there was no lack of administrators of soothing syrup. The stuff was in ample, not to say nauseatingly, abundant supply. If *The Week* set out to broaden its appeal, he said, it would end up in the position of an old German Liberal friend of his, who, shortly before Hitler came to power, remarked: "And so, my young friend, we Liberals dash into battle under banners inscribed with our inspiring slogan 'On the one hand, on the other hand.' "

And what did people mean, he wanted to know, when they called him starry-eyed? It was, he declared, an accusation of non-cynicism. And to this he pleaded guilty. "There's that saying of Wilde's," he said, "about a cynic knowing the price of everything and the value of nothing. It always suggests that somehow they are doing well on the prices. But if you look at our cynics you find they're selling out for peanuts. Better to be a starry-eyed idealist."

It seemed to him to be pre-eminently a time for recklessness. Just because *The Week* was acquiring some sort of new status, friends urged that it be more "responsible". Claud much appreciated their good intentions, but he thought privately that being responsible was another term for not taking chances, for cowardice, in fact. There were, he opined, too many responsible people on the side of the Goods. They were the sort of people who would hardly open their mouths until they had interviewed three responsible witnesses and had the whole pro's and con's of the situation vetted by a sound solicitor. "In the meantime the Bads, who pretend to be responsible but aren't, have run circles round them."

When he thought of the Bads he thought, first and foremost, of Cliveden. Michael Astor has written that he is still not sure whether *The Week* "invented" the Cliveden Set or "discovered" it. As has been seen, quite early in 1936 Claud was in no doubt that this was no invention, but a genuine discovery. After about eighteen months of pointing and crying aloud on the part of *The Week*, the Cliveden Set suddenly became almost a cliché of the British and the international press. Literally not a week passed without some newspaper, in Britain, France or the United States, referring to it. Journalists from far parts of the world—there was one from Tokyo—turned up at *The Week* office with just one objective. They wanted directions as to how to get to see the Cliveden Set. Some of them even brought famous press photographers along with them. "It was as though," Claud said, "we had suddenly discovered Whipsnade. But a Whipsnade full of menacing, hitherto unknown serpents."

The photographers, at Claud's suggestion, used to lurk outside the Astors' London house on certain days to take pictures of the Cliveden Set, with Geoffrey Dawson and Lord Lothian swinging their umbrellas in unison, going to lunch.

It gradually became much more than a cliché. It became a symbol. And it was a symbol which fascinated people because it expressed a reality of which more and more people were becoming aware. In France everyone was familiar with the idea of "the 200 families who are ruining France". The 200 families were, broadly speaking, those powerful interlocking interests which were supposed to prefer, in the last resort, the risk of a France ruled by Germans of the Right to the probability of being ruled by Frenchmen of the Left. That supposition itself was for long derided by quite honest Frenchmen as a myth, an invention of Left propagandists. Then in 1940 it was seen to be about 80 per cent. true. The Cliveden Set was the corresponding British symbol or myth.

The members of the Cliveden Set naturally reacted furiously. Lady Astor publicly complained that she was in receipt of I forget how many thousand abusive letters weekly. All of them were motivated by *The Week*'s wicked invention of the Cliveden Set. She persuaded Bernard Shaw to write an article, of which the purport was to deny the existence of any such sinister Whipsnade.

Nothing could have better demonstrated the effectiveness of the tiny publication in Victoria Street. Claud himself was genuinely astonished. It was true that he had started the newssheet on the assumption that, however tiny, a sheet of the kind could somehow be manipulated so as to exert an enormous leverage. The results of his discovery of the Cliveden Set nevertheless appeared to him nearly incredible.

It seems extraordinary now that Claud cannot recall just how the discovery was originally made. But I suppose his own explanation of this irritating lapse of memory is understandable enough. When he first wrote of goings-on at Cliveden it was just another story. He saw it as important, but had no conception of the dimensions the whole affair was ultimately going to assume. And, of course, once the Cliveden Set was in the centre of the political picture, there were dozens of informants available. Some of them were liars, cashing in, or trying to, for political purposes of their own. Others were what Claud described as men of good will, with first-rate contacts, who now for the first time saw Cliveden as a menace. Most of them were Conservatives. And most of them were by this time prepared to go to almost any lengths to penetrate Cliveden and assist *The Week* to expose its policies.

The only clue Claud can recall as to where the information about Cliveden started to come from, is a conversation with Vladimir Poliakoff. This was not the original tip-off. *The Week* had already referred to Cliveden. But Poliakoff immediately showed considerable interest. He also supplied a good deal of further information. Claud had known Poliakoff for several years. At the beginning of their acquaintance, Poliakoff was the Diplomatic Correspondent of *The Times*. I am not sure exactly when he left *The Times*. But after doing so he worked with the *New York Times* as a very special type of foreign affairs expert, writing under the name of Augur. Rightly or wrongly his articles were treated as oracular, being quoted as the word from the horse's very mouth. And he was, in fact, exceedingly well-informed.

Russian by origin, he was violently anti-Communist. But he was still more violently anti-German. In the first half of the Thirties there was only one logical position for a man with those views to take up. He espoused the cause of Mussolini's Italy, which, before Hitler achieved overwhelming power, was also engaged in a simultaneous battle against Communism and against German hegemony in Europe. He was, in fact, constantly accused by his enemies of being an agent of the Italian government. Indeed he once brought a libel action against Claud and the *Daily Worker* on account of an article written by Claud suggesting that Poliakoff was the go-between or Third Man in a lurid secret intrigue between the Italian government and Neville Chamberlain. But the libel action did not impair the friendship between him and Claud.

There was another important figure on the London scene who held much the same views in relation to the Communists and to the German government as Poliakoff—Sir Robert (later Lord) Vansittart. Sir Robert was first head of the Foreign Office, then Chief Diplomatic Adviser to the British government. Broadly speaking, his policy was to appease Mussolini for the purpose of detaching him from Hitler. The policy, as everyone knows, failed utterly. But Sir Robert, at least for a time, believed that it might have succeeded had it not been for the intrigues of the pro-German party in London. They made it impossible to align Britain in a sufficiently credible and uncompromising front against Germany. It was only natural that Sir Robert, whatever his personal feelings about Poliakoff may have been, should have regarded him as a valuable ally. And there was no doubt that the combined resources of Sir Robert and the Italian embassy were capable of penetrating fairly deeply into the more or less secret machinations of the pro-Germans.

Poliakoff's conversational style was as devious and allusive as that of an old-time stage diplomat. But Claud recalls that in this first talk about Cliveden, Poliakoff drew, without seeming to, a pretty clear picture not only of what was going on at Cliveden, but also of the channels through which further relevant information about them might be obtained. It was indicated, though not said in so many words, that one of the indispensable things to do was to establish some line of communication with Sir Robert Vansittart. This was not going to be easy, because Sir Robert was nearly, if not quite, as hostile to the extreme Left as he was to the Nazis. However, after some false starts and rebuffs, a line was found. It was one of the means by which *The Week* was able to keep itself informed on the proceedings of the Cliveden Set and the "Cagoulords".

(This term coined by *The Week* became almost as familiar in France as the term Cliveden Set. It was based, of course, on the notorious Cagoulards, the hooded men, who for a time spearheaded Fascist conspiracy in France. The Cagoulords were Lords Halifax, Londonderry, Lothian and Astor.)

For two years the tussle with the Cliveden Set was a principal preoccupation of *The Week*. Although it could sometimes count on the undercover support of the Vansittart faction there could not be even the loosest kind of alliance. The reason was simple. *The Week*, despite some persuasive arguments from diplomatic and political strategists, at all times refused to be any less aggressive in hostility to Mussolini than to Hitler. It never believed that Mussolini could be bought off. And, as I have noted, it was apt to cause annoyance to the Italian government by exposing its essentially anti-British designs in the Mediterranean. Therefore a good many well-placed people in London who might have been prepared to play ball with *The Week* against the pro-Germans were hesitant and suspicious. They thought, to put it in a nutshell, that *The Week*, while obtaining information against the Clivedenites might, just in passing, pick up other information which it would presently use to take a nasty bite out of its pro-Italian informants.

The nervousness of all concerned was sharply increased by repeated evidence of the fact that *The Week* possessed astonishing sources of information within the Reich. Particularly explosive was a story published in *The Week* on 17 March 1937. For the story, whatever construction might be placed upon it, showed that *The Week* had an uncomfortably close-up view of German-Austrian-Italian relations at that particular moment.

It was headed "What they told General Krauss" and ran as follows:

"If, Sir, an invasion should be undertaken in the not too distant future, should we or should we not have to anticipate serious resistance by your armed forces?"

"On the contrary, your Excellency."

This, quoted in private verbal reports by both participants, was the climax of the secret conversation held at Obersalzburg, Bavaria, early last week between General Hermann Goering and the Austrian Infantry General Alfred Krauss "on special mission" to Germany.

According to General Goering, who shook with laughter as he recounted this part of the episode, the "patriotic" General Krauss actually clicked his heels and saluted as he offered his assurance of the readiness of the Austrian armed forces to join hands with the invaders of their country.

From a correspondent of *The Week*, whose name in a very different connexion is familiar to all observers of Nazi high politics, we have received a detailed account of the important confidential events attending the visit of General Krauss to Germany last week, ostensibly for the sole purpose of delivering a lecture on military subjects.

The Week pointed out that Alfred Krauss was one of the least widely known and yet perhaps the most influential of all the original theoreticians of Nazi foreign policy. His book, *The Importance of Austria or the Future of the German People*, published in Hamburg in 1923, expressed the general lines of Nazi foreign policy and the new German imperialism with more lucidity than did *Mein Kampf*.

There is, indeed, some ground for the belief that Krauss has to a large extent inspired the whole foreign-political thinking of Adolf Hitler, and is the real godfather of Nazi foreign-political theory.

He is at present head of the Union of Austrian Nationalist Officers, is one of the most powerful leaders of the Nazi-German attack on the present Austrian regime, and too powerful to be touched by the government despite its perfect awareness of this activity.

On arrival in Berlin, General Krauss was interviewed publicly at the microphone by a Nazi spokesman, and enabled to get off a broadcast to the effect that "we are all overcome with admiration of Hitler Germany and proud to think that Hitler is one of us, for your Hitler is our Hitler" etc. etc. etc. That, and the lecture, concluded the public doings.

General Krauss was then provided with a motor car, an aeroplane and an officer of the Reichswehr as his personal A.D.C.

In response to an urgent invitation he flew to Munich and motored thence to Obersalzburg, near Berchtesgaden, where he was received by Hitler himself.

The interview lasted four hours.

It was an historically important interview both for its role in the present phase of Mitteleuropa expansion, and for its unique illumination of the present German private official view of the Italo-German and Anglo-Italian situation.

There is of course no written record of the affair. The gist of it however was reported by Krauss to several people in Berlin and Vienna, and repeated in part by Hitler to Goering, and in the main confirmed in a subsequent interview between Krauss and Neurath, German Foreign Minister.

The German Chancellor opened with the customary statement on Germany's desire for peace, proceeding however immediately to the statement that Germany today is better equipped for war—relatively to other nations—than in 1914. He offered some figures showing the comparative training periods of different branches of the German armed forces, the comparative fire-capacity of German artillery and other units, etc. etc.

From this point on the interview became somewhat less obvious in character (this latter part is the part subsequently repeated to Krauss by Neurath).

Hitler emphasized the comparative ease wherewith Germany had brought pressure upon the Italian government in the Hapsburg affair, forcing Mussolini to order Gayda to write his famous article declaring the Hapsburgs to be a public nuisance.

Krauss in reply bluntly enquired whether the Chancellor was unaware that in fact he was being "double-crossed" by Mussolini and that the latter, while perfectly willing to assist Nazi ambitions elsewhere than in Austria, was in fact—according to information in Krauss's own possession—determined to use all means, including ultimately the Hapsburgs, to check German ambition in Austria. Krauss, in view of this information, declared himself unable to believe in the importance of the Gayda article, and desired to know whether the Chancellor in fact relied upon the "good faith" of Mussolini.

To this Hitler replied—according to Krauss and others—as follows (his words being translated by Neurath later into somewhat more diplomatic language):

We are under no illusions regarding Mussolini. We are not so foolish as ever to forget the double treachery of Italy during the world war, nor the part played in it by Mussolini himself. We know for instance that the British Foreign Office, War Office and Admiralty, all were thrown into foolish panic during the Abyssinian war by the supposed Italian air menace to the British fleet. Frightened by an aerial circus.

They scuttled, showed the white feather. But now they understand that they were wrong.

It must be recalled that this report was published at a moment when, particularly in Berlin and London, everyone was bring officially assured that the German government, having "adjusted" the situation in the Rhineland, had no further territorial demands to make. The soothing syrup was being poured fast and thick.

Nothing could have been more calculated to annoy the

syrup-pourers than publication of so frank an exchange of views between such personages.

It was significant that no notice of *The Week's* story was taken by the British press. Naturally there were many discreet enquiries from Fleet Street, and at least one Diplomatic Editor sought to comment on it, but was told that to do so would be "distinctly unhelpful".

There were, however, considerable repercussions on the Continent. In its issue of 21 April, *The Week* noted:

> The report of the secret conversations held at Obersalzburg, Bavaria, between the Austrian Infantry General Alfred Krauss and Herr Hitler and of those between the same officer and General Hermann Goering published by this news service (see *The Week* No. 204) and reprinted in Czechoslovak and French papers has, it appears, caused not a little anxiety in certain Austrian circles.
>
> As a result General Krauss's legal representative, Dr. Viktor Tschadesch, has issued to the press a statement denying that the trend of the conversation was as reported by us but *admitting that in fact the conversations did take place.*
>
> The same statement, published also in the *Prager Tagblatt*, further denies that "the situation in Austria, especially the Austrian military strength, was discussed in detail" but, by implication, admits that the situation in Austria was in fact discussed.
>
> Dealing with the conversations at length, the *Telegraf*, however protests somewhat overmuch. Speaking on behalf of the Austrian Military Front, it declares:
>
> "The Austrian army has always and at all times done its duty and those in the army, in the Austrian old-soldiers' movement, in the standing army, have a right to demand that no one besmirch and befoul the names of their sons who are already serving in the army. *The army therefore categorically refutes the challenge which General Krauss throws out . . . it seems that General Krauss has forgotten that he ever was a Kaiser's general.*"
>
> Thus, it appears, not only has the legal representative of General Krauss himself confirmed that the conversations did take place but that the Austrian Military Front regards it as quite possible that General Krauss did in fact say what, we repeat, he did say.

18 Hitler and Friends

THE late Robert Byron, high Tory and a devotee of *The Week*, listened, some time in the pre-Munich period, to the pro-German arguments of a minor Clivedenite. This was the son, naturalized as an Englishman, of an American who had made his money manufacturing, I think, lavatories. The son considered himself very much the English gentleman. He strongly favoured Hitler as, in the tired old phrase, a bulwark against bolshevism. After wearily hearing him out, Byron, his chin jutting over his high starched collar, said, "I suppose I should not be surprised to learn that you are prepared to sacrifice the interests of your adopted country in the supposed interests of your adopted class."

Claud, who was in the habit of referring to the Astors as "the ex-furriers from lower Broadway", was delighted with this remark, and gave it the widest possible currency. He in no way concealed the fact that to satirize and denigrate in every possible way people whom he regarded as simultaneously pompous, hypocritical and treacherous, gave him the keenest pleasure. The Clivedenites, for their part, were in a perpetual dilemma. On the one hand they felt the attacks upon them so damaging that they were forced, as has been seen, to defend themselves publicly from time to time. On the other hand they felt, with equal bitterness, that in so doing they were actually playing into the hands of *The Week* by giving it, so to speak, official recognition as a dangerous force. They were particularly embarrassed when the German Embassy, prodded by the preposterous Foreign Minister Ribbentrop, actually asked the Foreign Office to suppress *The Week*, as being disruptive of good Anglo-German relations. They knew only too well that it would not be long before the news of this démarche reached Victoria Street.

In fact the German Embassy's action was less totally imbecile than appears at first sight. In its issue of 31 August 1938 *The Week* remarked cryptically that "the newspapers of the future will indeed have some fun uncovering the details about the newspapers of the present, which the newspapers of the present *ex hypothesi* cannot print".

It will be recalled [*The Week* continued] that shortly after his trip to Germany (late in 1937) and before the invasion of Austria, Lord Halifax was very much to the fore in urging, and getting, a sort of autonomous censorship of the British press, under which it was considered "bad taste" and "not in the interests of international appeasement" to say anything unpleasant to Hitler. Even Mr. Low the cartoonist was, we understand, "approached" on the matter.

Then the Austrian invasion happened, and Lord Halifax as reported here at the time, sent for the Diplomatic Correspondents and told them that his "request" of a few days before was no longer valid, and that anyone could say anything he pleased about Hitler. So for a time they did.

In general, however, the censorship continued, and a well-known American paper was suppressed in Britain on account of an article judged to be "in the worst possible taste" and very offensive to der Fuehrer.

At the end of last week Lord Halifax had another shot at press control, and sent for proprietors, or representatives of proprietors, of the leading national dailies.

He had the rather tricky job of explaining to them that despite all the good work put in by the Bureau at No. 10, pouring out the happiness stuff, as a matter of fact the situation turned out to be more grave than somewhat, and would Lord B.'s leader-writers please try to come down out of their August moon and look at one or two of the facts. Results, the British press being what it is, were instantaneous and with a sickening thud readers of the *Daily Express* learned not that there will be no war but only that "the *Daily Express* believes there will be no war", a situation rightly judged to be full of menace. . . . The episode provided a somewhat grim demonstration of the degree to which in fact the government is able to orchestrate the supposedly free and independent British daily press.

Because of Claud's obvious pleasure in the running battle against the Clivedenites, there were those who thought the tone of moral indignation in which it was sometimes conducted

must be synthetic. Personally I think it obtuse not to understand that both the pleasure and the indignation were equally
genuine. There is certainly no question that Claud saw the
propaganda battlefield of London as crucial in the struggle to
contain the forces of Nazism threatening Europe.

The story of the failure so to contain them all the way from
the spring of 1936 to the autumn of 1939 has been told over and
over again from innumerable viewpoints. *The Week*'s news of,
and comments upon, the events of that period total well over
500,000 words, rather more than 80 per cent. of them written
by the editor himself. (At that time he became practically a
commuter between London and Vienna, London and Prague,
London and Geneva.) It would obviously be ridiculous for me
even to attempt to reduce this bristling mass of week-by-week
reports to anything in the way of a connected narrative.
Indeed, since they were never meant to be read as such, the
mere idea involves a contradiction in terms.

The atmosphere of the period will, I think, be much more
accurately evoked by quoting here at some length from two
issues of *The Week*, separated by approximately nine months.
The first is from the issue of 17 November 1937, a little more
than three months before Hitler marched on Vienna. The
second is from the issue of 17 August 1938, a month before
Munich.

In the first, *The Week* reported:

> The facts behind the almost unprecedented uproar accompany-
> ing the visit of Lord Halifax to Berlin . . . are considerably more
> sensational than the uproar itself.
>
> Paris and Prague—not to mention London—already excited by
> the news of the trip, have been thrown into a frenzy of speculation
> by first the Saturday story ("Hitler's terms") in the *Evening
> Standard*, and then by the extraordinary efforts of the Foreign
> Office and the morning newspapers to convince everyone that the
> report which drew such violent response from Berlin was the
> merest hot air . . .
>
> The true facts and the true background of this extraordinary
> and somewhat sinister affair—which are in reality the facts and
> the background of the Halifax visit itself—are these:
>
> The so vigorously, even furiously denied *Evening Standard* report

that the principal purpose of the Halifax visit to Berlin was to discuss a proposed Anglo-German bargain whereby Germany would offer a ten-year "Colonial truce" to Britain in exchange for a free hand to attack countries in Eastern Europe was in all but one essential, correct.

The point that was not correct about it was the suggestion that the proposal had come from Hitler (a suggestion underlined by the posters—"Hitler's terms").

In point of fact the suggestion did not come from Berlin. It came from London.

The plan as a concrete proposal was first got into usable diplomatic shape at a party at the Astors' place at Cliveden on the weekend of October 23rd and 24th.

Subscribers to *The Week* are familiar with the pro-Nazi intrigues centring at Cliveden and in Printing House Square on the eve of the outbreak of the Spanish War. The expulsion of *The Times* correspondent from Berlin put a spoke, as Printing House Square admitted at the time, in the wheel of certain Germanophile plans supposed to have matured earlier in the autumn.

The intrigue however continued, with Lord Lothian, the Astors, Mr. Barrington-Ward of *The Times* and its editor, Mr. Geoffrey Dawson (née Robinson), at the heart of it.

Throughout the month of October, correspondence on the subject of the Nazi colonial claims was poured into the columns of *The Times*.

By the weekend of October 23rd, the queer Anglo-American gathering at Cliveden was able to estimate pretty well the data assembled by this prolonged kite-flying. On October 28th *The Times* published its startling editorial on "The Claim to Colonies" —concluding with a pathetic plea for secrecy in any negotiations that might be carried on.

More however had been decided at Cliveden than the tenor of an article to appear in *The Times*.

It had been decided that in view of the state of feeling existing within the Conservative party—let alone other parties—on the question of Hitler's colonial demands, an attempt should be made to satisfy the appetite of German imperialism by the offer of an alternative. The alternative was none other than the unfortunate states of Central Europe, wherein Hitler was to be offered a "free hand".

The proposal was directed in the first place against that majority wing of the Conservative party which still opposes the public dismemberment of the British Empire, as being a price too high to pay for "accommodating" Germany.

For it is scarcely to be supposed that in that little knot of expatriate Americans and "super-nationally" minded Englishmen which has for years exercised so powerful an influence on the course of "British" policy, there were any so naïve as genuinely to suppose that the idea of a "ten years" truce is really an effective device for saving the British colonies and mandates from German attack, or so ignorant as not to be aware that the "free hand" in Eastern Europe is viewed in Berlin logically enough, as a desirable if not absolutely essential securing of the back door of Germany in preparation for the great Tag when the German armed forces will move through the front door against Western Europe.

The Cliveden meeting and *The Times* editorial ended stage one of the intrigue.

The second, according to *The Week*, was the final acquisition of Cabinet approval and support for the purposes of the London-Berlin intrigue.

It appears that Sir Samuel Hoare, Lord Hailsham, Sir John Simon and Sir Kingsley Wood were hotly in favour from the outset. Mr. Neville Chamberlain—still pursuing his, or perhaps Sir Robert Vansittart's, remarkable plan of trying to find out by trial and heaven knows by error, just how many pieces of silver the Italian government needs to betray the Rome-Berlin axis—was at first hesitant and even hostile. Mr. Eden's opinion was taken for what it was worth—which, in the present state of the Cabinet and of Mr. Eden, is exactly nothing.

Then occurred the most remarkable and significant of all the developments in this remarkable affair.

The final decision to send Lord Halifax to Berlin, and Mr. Chamberlain's adherence to it, was based not on consideration of foreign politics at all, but of domestic politics.

Led by Sir Kingsley Wood, the advocates of the plan brought up batteries of facts and figures and reports from local bosses to show that it may very well turn out that the "optimum" time for the present government to go to the country in a general election will be some time within the next fifteen months.

They pointed to the rising cost of living and the probable fall in Conservative votes which it implies, and to the alternative possibility of a sharp slump in business activity, implying an even sharper slump in Conservative votes.

Their estimate of the situation totted up to a conviction that the government has to get busy accumulating election capital rather quicker than had been supposed a few months ago. What, they urged on the Prime Minister, could be bigger capital of this sort than the appearance of an "appeasement" with Germany? An illusion which need not, after all, be asked to last longer than the evening of the next national polling day.

It was this consideration—the realization of the need for a hurried getting together of election ammunition—which finally swung the Cabinet behind the Cliveden scheme.

Mr. Eden thereupon (i.e. on Monday November 8th) resigned. Since nobody except the members of the Cabinet heard about it, it remained, like so many of Mr. Eden's nervous gestures, "a political event without consequences". Nevertheless, he did resign, and the newspapers published the fact that he was reported to be "simply furious". Then he withdrew his resignation, and satisfied himself with the "concession" that Lord Halifax when he returns is to report to Mr. Eden as Foreign Secretary first, instead of reporting direct to the Cabinet.

The Germans were of course delighted with the way things were turning out. It is a well-understood axiom of Berlin foreign policy in this period that "periods of relaxed tension" must be interpolated between the periods of aggression, because whenever there is relaxed tension between London and Berlin there is similarly an increase in the power of anti-French elements in Britain and in consequence a loosening of the Anglo-French entente. This in turn provides the ideal preparation for the next coup. (The "friendliness" which preceded the fatal March 7th when the Reichswehr was sent into the Rhineland was a classic case in point.)

The report of August 1938 stated:

It is understood from Berlin that full reports on foreign reactions to the mobilization of Germany are not expected to be in the hands of the War Council for one week at least, and that no "irretrieveable" action will be undertaken until after that date.

Apart from the special reports of emissaries such as Captain

Wiedemann, the German government, parallel with the mobilization, is carrying out what amounts to a sort of "mass observation" of foreign reactions.

This extends from a minute analysis of speeches and newspaper comment throughout the threatened states, to exhaustive reports of private conversations by private German emissaries with all sorts of people judged important either because they are supposed to be politically and financially influential (like the Clivedenites), or people with positions of importance in the military machine (like certain army officers), or "typical" of "middle-class opinion" like certain Conservative politicians.

Upon the results of these reports—as the history of the last few days has shown—very much depends. It is indeed privately admitted in Berlin that "one of the essential 'imponderabilia' which are being tried out by the mobilization, is precisely the strength of foreign reactions to the threat which it represents."

The Week recalled that a few weeks before the invasion of the Rhineland in 1936, Berlin itself had permitted and encouraged rumours to circulate to the effect that an invasion was contemplated. (Lord Londonderry, on his own admission, was one of those on whom this suggestion had been "planted".)

A little later the whole thing was officially denied, and the same British newspapers which are today issuing "soothing" bulletins about the mobilization were "in a position to deny that any sensational action by the German government in the Rhineland zone is contemplated".

Immediately after that the invasion took place.

An identical technique—as recognizable as a signature—was employed in the Austrian case. First, rumours of an impending "coup"—to try out the reactions. Then denials. Then assurances by the British press that "Herr Hitler is anxious for peace and the independence of Austria appears to be assured." Then the invasion.

The length of each stage of the operation can of course be altered at will, and according to circumstances. The speed at which the final phase is reached depends of course upon the success or otherwise registered in the preceding phases—success in the Rhineland and Austrian affairs being nearly 100 per cent.

In the mobilization we are entering stage three—the stage at which "mass observation" of foreign reactions (and above all of British reactions) becomes essential and decisive.

It is always at this point, too, that the necessity for the pro-German elements—particularly in the newspapers—to explain that "nothing particular is going to happen" becomes most acute: as is observable in the current press campaign.

The technique being identical the phenomena which it produces naturally recur too—even down to details such as the release to the British press of "exclusive" pictures of Hitler smiling: a method which ill-informed British observers are too apt to dismiss as merely imbecile but which the propaganda experts know to be considerable in its lulling effect on mass opinion.

It is impossible to understand fully the implication of the latest German move without understanding the phases of this well-tried and in the main successful technique, and in which one of them we now are.

Stories flew about London over the weekend to the effect that "Mr. Chamberlain has had a change of heart" and is now opposing the Germans, that the Cliveden Set is so frightened it is inclined to wonder whether it might not be as well to let Czechoslovakia save Britain after all, etc. etc.

Checking up as far as possible on these rumours—coming often enough from authoritative sources—the following appears to be the situation.

The theory that Mr. Chamberlain has been shocked into a new political position by the mobilization of Germany seems to be really based on the gravity of the view taken of the situation by the government's military advisers. The same thing, by and large, is true of the supposed jolt received by the influential "unofficial" friends of Hitler in London.

While the press mainly presents the mobilization question as though the issues were: "Is this a bluff, or isn't it? Has Hitler already fixed a date for the attack, or hasn't he?" the military people see the position differently and more clearly.

The fact as they see it is that within a few days and in the full view of Europe the German government has secured for itself a military advantage which traditionally is equivalent to quite a number of divisions and heavy guns: the advantage that is to say of being "a jump ahead of the game" in mobilization.

In this case it is a very long jump indeed.

Everyone remembers how the Ministers of the late Nicholas II in 1914 secretly held up and refused to transmit to the Army the Tsar's order to suspend mobilization in response to a plea and a promise from the German Kaiser, because they thought, or alleged they thought, that the German promise might conceivably be a hoax, and that in that case they would lose as much as twelve hours of mobilization time, which in turn might, they thought, prove actually fatal.

Yet the extent of mobilization on that occasion was a fleabite compared to the totalitarian mobilization of Germany this week, and the character and complexity of mobilization necessary for "total war" in the modern manner increases rather than decreases the advantage to be gained by "advance" mobilization.

This is the hard fact which no amount of discussion of "whether Herr Hitler really wants war" etc., etc.—still less fooling about with words and pretending that if you call it manoeuvres it is all right—can alter or for long conceal.

This is the simple and shocking state of affairs which is being presented with some force by the military men to the government this week.

So far as *The Week* was able to discover, however, the deduction so freely drawn from the alarm, bordering on panic, in British government circles as a result of these events and the current presentation of them, was "mere whistling in the dark".

It has been deduced that in face of this situation the British government would surely proceed at long last to a rallying of the possible allies, an assurance of the fullest support to the immediately threatened states, and the construction of a barrier against the threatened war as strong—relatively to the present German striking power as the similar barrier was on May 21st.

This deduction is being supported by news from Berlin, assuring London and Paris that if such steps were taken the German government would be no more willing to run its head into a wall and break its neck than it was on the night of May 22nd when it called off the offensive against Czechoslovakia, or than the Japanese were when they faced a similar risk at Changkufeng.

It is necessary to report however that despite all this alert deducing among the "well-informed observers" we have been unable to find any basis (beyond some hearty wishful thinking) for the view that Mr. Chamberlain is about to do any such thing.

On the contrary, indications at the beginning of the week are that precisely because of the intensification of the German threat, there is likely to be an intensification of the government's attempt to secure concessions for the Germans all round.

It is freely reported in Prague—from sources which usually know what they are talking about—that Lord Runciman received in the latter half of last week instructions to intensify his efforts to convince the Nazis that if they will just stop shuffling their feet for a moment, the British government and its unofficial agent will redouble their pressure upon the Czechs and upon the French.

With equal authority it was reported in London that Hitler—via Captain Wiedemann—had already by Tuesday night had thrown out to him suggestions of "renewed hopes" of "trade concessions" and of "talks about an Air Pact", which means, of course, talks about the goal of German imperialism, a Four Power Pact.

A similar reaction, our spies report, is to be noted among the Clivedenites, of whom it has been said that their only wish now is that the Czechs would "hurry up and get it over with"—meaning, would hurry up and break their Republic into pieces which can be fed to Hitler to keep him quiet.

It is perfectly true that the "Cagoulords" are scared to death: but their reaction to that condition—chronic with them and indeed with a large number of British citizens at the present time —is very different from what those would wish who are still hopeful that the available means of preserving peace may be utilized, and the fatal concessions policy abandoned, before it is too late.

On the other side of this somewhat gloomy situation, it has to be reported that there has been this week, as a result of the facts of the mobilization of Germany, a feeble but still noticeable further hardening of opinion among those few members of the Cabinet and that considerable number of members of the Conservative party whose doubts regarding the Chamberlain policy have been growing and developing ever since the resignation of Mr. Eden.

To suggest or even hint that these people are capable of any swift, independent and effective action at this moment would be absurd. Nevertheless, it is important to note every advance of position, however slight, in that quarter, if only for the reason that it acts as a slight but occasionally important check on the influence of the pro-German and pro-Italian elements.

19 The Racketeers

CLAUD once remarked that one of the most useful things *The Week* could do would be to reprint week after week those lines of Rudyard Kipling which ask

> Who shall doubt the secret hid
> Under Cheops' pyramid
> Is that the contractor did
> Cheops out of several millions?
> Or that Joseph's sudden rise
> To Comptroller of Supplies
> Was a fraud of monstrous size
> Upon Pharoah's swart civilians?

In the light of current experience, it would seem that if there is one thing certain about war preparations, now called defence preparations, it is that the public is going to be looted of enormous sums of money in exchange for goods which turn out to be shoddy almost before they are fully tested.

In the late Thirties *The Week* showed itself almost as much preoccupied with the scandalous behaviour of armament contractors, and with other, more directly, political flaws in the "defence" mechanism as with diplomatic affairs. Characteristic was its report on the situation as of 3 November 1937. It was based on first-hand information from dedicated and furious military men. It was designed to indicate just how little attention was being paid to the real needs of national defence, as compared to the requirements of party politics.

> A storm [*The Week* reported] which will get worse before it gets better is blowing up around the personality, political position and political future of Sir Thomas Inskip (Minister of the Co-ordination of Defence in the Chamberlain government). The big wind is blowing from the direction of the Army, with a minor squall threatening over at the Foreign Office.
> Since there will be a lot of things happening in the next few weeks and months of which this situation will be the background, it is worth reporting now just what the background is.

(i) There is the gout situation. The betting is heavily against health putting Mr. Chamberlain out of office before this Parliament ends, there is just enough chance of that happening nevertheless to force bosses and intriguers to think about the succession, and the betting on whether or not Mr. Chamberlain's health and inclinations decide him to carry on as leader of the Conservative party longer than that is pretty even.

(ii) Backing Inskip as against the near-favourite Mr. W. S. Morrison, is a slightly incongruous though characteristic amalgam of the solid people who want stolidity and the Church vote, with the more rambunctious Conservative youth in the House who want a leader who can be led, and the Church vote (e.g. it seems, the Imperial Policy Group).

(iii) The storm against Inskip—not merely as a possible future chief of the Conservative party but much more immediately as Defence Minister—comes from a group of Generals, Technical Advisers, Staff men in all three branches of the Armed Forces, who have been very busy for a long time collecting glaring instances of the appalling inefficiency of the war-machine of the country as at present constituted, and want changes involving, among other things, the appointment of a military man as Supreme Director of the "Defence Forces"—a new sort of job difficult to reconcile with the British Constitution but claimed by the military "young Turks" as essential.

So far there are no indications that the persons in question have got very far in thinking towards the real issues involved in attempting to move the vast mountain of graft, profiteering, racketeering, nepotism and common stupidity which is at present swallowing up the rearmament money in a manner gratifying to the speculators, though horrifying to the patriotic, and which has in fact very little to do with the question of the particular personality who happens to be at the Defence Ministry, or even with some reorganization of the governmental end of the defence system within the terms of things as they are.

A feature of the Inskip situation which is comical or disquieting or both, the way you choose to look at it, is that the Foreign Office is at the moment engaged in trying to put him into a sort of "solitary confinement" so far as foreign newspapermen are concerned.

A short while back Sir Thomas gave an interview to a foreign journalist wherein he expressed himself with a freedom not fashionable in the present British Cabinet on the subject of the German and Italian aggressors.

The journalist for some inscrutable reason showed the interview to the Foreign Office, who instantly "urged" (or instructed) him not to send it for publication.

Investigating, the Foreign Office discovered to its horror that for the time being at least Sir Thomas is genuinely dismayed by the persecution of the Churches in Germany, and being a person apt to speak his mind, was judged by them to be a very dangerous person to speak to foreign journalists.

For foreign newspapers are not under such fatherly control from Whitehall as are the organs of the local press, and heaven knows what Heath Robinsonian bit of jiggery-pokery might not be jerked off its hook if Cabinet Ministers were allowed to go about annoying Dictators. The situation is getting so that even a Cabinet Minister is scarcely allowed to talk except to himself.

It is stated that Mr. Churchill, on overhearing a Cabinet Member ordering a Horse's Neck in a West End bar, remarked: "Extremes meet. In France they have the united front. Here we have the united behind."

Despite its constant lamentations over public apathy or public incredulity in relation to the facts, *The Week* did have a genuinely high regard for the public intelligence. Indeed the editor would constantly lecture people who thought otherwise. "Anyone," he would say, "who believes that the public is somehow different from and inferior to himself is an arrogant nincompoop. We are the public. The difference between us and what is called the 'man in the street' is only that in many cases he has most of his time filled dodging the buses on his way to an office or a plant where he is going to spend his whole day sweating away at some exhausting task more likely to make money for somebody else than for him. He is no stupider than we are. He just does not have the time to inform himself of anything much beyond what the newspapers tell him. Our business consists precisely in making the time to inform ourselves and him.

"But since the man in the street is really an intelligent person it is not impossible for even a tiny paper like ourselves to com-

municate with him one way or another. With a few we com-
municate direct. At other times the facts we publish get taken
up by the big newspapers. And we ought not to forget that very
often the hostile press is just as useful in this respect as that
section which is at least well-disposed enough to print information of importance when it is drawn to its attention, provided
it is not actually dangerous."

In its issue of 15 December 1937 (No. 243) *The Week*
announced that a "thunderstorm" was gathering around the
British Air Ministry.

Two affairs both packed with political dynamite are near a
possible explosion point. One is commercial and financial. The
other—and more immediate—is military and political. The
most drastic efforts are being made to suppress both of them—
and the weapon of the Official Secrets Act is as usual ready to
hand.

People who ought to know claim—but we have no definite proof
of this particular assertion beyond their word for it—that Mr.
Chamberlain's decision at the weekend with Lord Swinton [the
then Air Minister] is influenced by the fact that his old friend is
driving around on the edge of a volcano which might at any
moment blow him, together with a large fragment of Cabinet
prestige, sky high. . . .

It is denied by no one that there are in the Royal Air Force
some of the most skilled pilots, skilled in navigation no less than
in bombing and fighting, in the world.

Nor is it denied that the men available for the Air Force and
for training as bomber pilots are as good material as could be
found anywhere.

But it is stated—and this is the centre of the charge—that the
mass of the new pilots are being, as far as bomber flying goes,
grossly undertrained, that the tests are absurdly low for this sort of
work, that the result is the catastrophic situation just referred to,
and that the principal reason for all this is a competition in
political prestige going on between the War Office and the Air
Ministry in which the number of pilots announced as fully trained,
and the number of recruits gained, are scoring points.

Obviously the lower the tests then the quicker people pass them,
the greater the encouragement to recruiting of a certain type—

though it is forcibly stated by expert observers that the situation as at present operated is a political gamble with very serious forces, which must have a certain effect on the attractiveness of the service to the best type of recruit.

Everyone knows that at the War Office Mr. Hoare-Belisha has been able to enhance his political prestige no little because of the astute publicity given to the rising figures of army recruitment. Recruitment figures have become a sort of simpleton's barometer of supposed efficiency and hence a sure-fire source of political capital.

The inadequacy of the tests, though it must certainly affect all arms, is held to have its worst effects on the bombing fleet since the problem of navigation encountered by bombing pilots are likely to be worse than, and more complex than those of pilots in other machines.

The position is claimed to be so serious that an agitation—necessarily of a more or less underground character—is going on in and around the Air Force to get the tests tightened up.

But it is regarded as certain that this would immediately have a bad effect on recruiting, and it is stated that the agitation for better tests is being held up in Whitehall for this political reason, regardless of the deplorable effects on the fighting efficiency of the air fleet.

Gloomily *The Week* added that

In view of the enormous power of the system, and the personages on which and on whom the responsibility for this situation rests, it is still dubious whether in fact anything will be done to remedy it, until the next war does for them what the last war did for certain personages responsible for a well-known shortage of shells.

The doubt as to what if anything is going to be done is enhanced by the fact that for the political position of the government, a removal of the lid from the air rearmaments situation would be liable to produce a reek of a damaging and unsavoury character.

The last paragraph was intended to be read in the context of *The Week*'s numerous references to the racketeering that went on in the armament industry and to the unsatisfactory character of the connexions that existed between the industry and persons connected with the government or the departments concerned.

In this case, to the pleasure of *The Week*, it was the most hostile section of the press which did most to draw public attention to the idea that there was perhaps something nasty going on in the woodshed. It did this of course by way of angry denial that anything of the kind was happening.

On 12 January 1938, *The Week* was able to point out to its readers:

> In the, at long last, public shindy which has now developed around the Air Ministry, are already involved forces which extend the conflict into one wherein the whole composition and even the political direction of the British Cabinet are involved.

It then referred to its previous report on the subject, and continued:

> The local daily press with its customary discretion maintained a silence in which, as they say, you could hear a jaw drop.
>
> Then the *Aeroplane*—frankly pro-Nazi weekly—hurried to the defence of Lord Swinton with a column and a quarter of denunciation of *The Week*, and a series of pooh-poohs amounting practically to a howl. The *Aeroplane* came rashly to the conclusion that *The Week* report was baseless and silly.
>
> Soon after that Air Marshal William Mitchell, and a member of the Air Council, admitted the charges were true, and the thunderstorm broke forcibly into the daily newspapers.
>
> Meantime however somebody who had got a sniff of another bit of the story, informed the *Sunday Referee* (owned by the Ostrers) that Mr. Winston Churchill was to be invited to replace Lord Swinton at the Air Ministry, to which the *Aeroplane* with a revealing indiscretion, replied in words to the effect that the Ostrers are Jews and Mr. Churchill is "Germanophobe" so rousing cheers for Lord Swinton.
>
> Within a few days of Air Marshal Mitchell's admission, the *News Chronicle* loosed off a small portion of the dynamite at the commercial end of the scandal, and the row was on.

The Week predicted that for the next rounds in the fight two background factors were going to be of large importance. One was the real position of Winston Churchill. The other was the attitude of the German government and its friends in London.

The truth about the rumours of Mr. Churchill's appointment to succeed Lord Swinton is illuminating.

The main facts on which the *News Chronicle* based its last attack on Lord Swinton had as a matter of fact been available for publication in another newspaper considerably before they were finally published in the *News Chronicle*.

It was supposed in fact that they were going to appear elsewhere at almost any minute.

The reason they failed to appear was that it was understood that Mr. Churchill urged delay.

The government was informed both that these damaging exposures were on the verge of explosion and that—so it was stated—Mr. Churchill was doing his very best to prevent any undue unpleasantness.

This was assumed by the friends of Lord Swinton to be part of an attempt by Mr. Churchill to muscle his way into the Cabinet position of his desire for which he makes no particular secret.

It was calculated by many observers that what Mr. Churchill was prepared to do was to exert himself to see that there was not too much of a public outcry about past sins in the Air Ministry, on the condition that he was offered a position in which he could feel himself empowered to prevent such sins recurring in the future. In this way the government would avoid a nasty scandal, and would have Mr. Churchill to thank for it; and Mr. Churchill would have very conscientiously both prevented a damaging attack upon the national government, and promoted his own advance towards once again saving the country and winning the next war.

Since in matters of defence Mr. Churchill is still the biggest independent political gun outside the Cabinet, the belief that he can be prevented from loosing off too destructive a broadside by being taken into the Cabinet is likely to play a considerable role in the government's defensive measures when the House of Commons re-assembles.

Closely connected with this position is the fact that, as indiscreetly blurted out by the *Aeroplane*, friends of the German government in London regard Lord Swinton as one of their most reliable allies, after Sir Samuel Hoare, in the whole British Cabinet.

Lord Swinton's associations with Germany go back to long before the time when he was Lord Swinton: to the time even before he was Cunliffe-Lister, but was a Mr. Philip Lloyd-Greame.

His legal practice at that time brought him into very close touch with the German electrical industry. His services were much appreciated, and after the war, though already on his way to Cabinet rank, he was understood to be seriously considering offers to pick up work with German-Belgian electrical interests.

It is stated by those who know him that Lord Swinton appears not entirely to have shaken himself free from the memories and traditions of that period in the mid-twenties when it was assumed in Whitehall that the most immediate British enemy was likely to be France, and that therefore all plans for the Air Force were to be made with such an objective in view.

Be that as it may, Lord Swinton certainly had the backing of the pro-German elements in and outside the Cabinet, and it is at the moment an open question: (1) How high the German government and particularly General Goering rate the importance of retaining this friend in high places, and (2) Assuming that they rate it very high indeed, how far they will be able to persuade their British friends of the primal necessity of keeping him in office . . .

Despite the strength which this factor affords Lord Swinton's position, it remains on the cards that the influence of certain fairly powerful manufacturers who do not by any means at all like the Secretary of State for Air, or the treatment by the Air Ministry of the aviation industry, may prevail.

For it is a fact that in his relations with industry Lord Swinton has not in the past always been entirely happy.

He was, it will be recalled, Chairman of the Tin Producers' Association, that patriotic concern formed in the summer of 1929 as a result of the efforts of Mr. John Howeson and his associates. He remained in that position until the harsh call of duty caused him in 1931 to have to sell all his tin interests and assume the position of Secretary of State for the Colonies—a Department, of course, intimately concerned with the regulation of the tin business.

The subsequent appearance at the Old Bailey, conviction, and imprisonment of Mr. Howeson was a sad termination to projects

which in their time had shone so brightly; particularly as one of
Swinton's Cabinet friends—Sir Samuel Hoare, then Secretary of
State for India and now Home Secretary—had himself suffered
irritating publicity and possible loss when Lewis Lazarus & Sons
employed as the brokers of the Howeson Group failed, disclosing
his name as one of the speculators on their list.

20 *The voice of Stalin*

THIS is no place to re-hash the grisly story of Munich and the events leading up to it. Certainly no *Week* reader could have been astonished by the extent of the Western surrender to Hitler, or the completeness of the victory of the pro-German party in London.

It had, for instance, reported in detail on the circumstances of *The Times* leading article suggesting the dismemberment of Czechoslovakia.

> Most sinister and sensational of the unpublished facts about the affair is that the outline of the proposal launched in the notorious leading article was submitted to the German embassy in London and was—in general outline—approved by them before publication.

It had reported the disastrous effects upon a Cabinet in which opposition to Hitler was slowly hardening of a document, supposedly from secret sources in Russia, indicating that the Red Army and Air Force were virtually non-existent. The document, the editor learned in Prague, had in reality been manufactured in Warsaw. It had been shown to members of the Czech government, in an unsuccessful attempt to bring about a breach between Prague and Moscow.

It had reported on the backstairs manoeuvres of the Labour party and trade union leaders, notably Sir Walter Citrine, to abort a campaign designed to force the government into a policy of resistance to Hitler.

Reverting to the crucial matter of *The Times* leader, it had noted:

> The moment the thing was out and the row began, *The Times* people and their associates split three ways. Some, like murderers who feign imbecility in order to escape the death sentence, declared they just had not known it was loaded, whole thing a deplorable

accident, we didn't understand what effect it would have, not really responsible for our actions.

Others, like a man had up for being drunk and disorderly who excuses his conduct by explaining he is a martyr to dipsomania, pointed out that after all *The Times* is always saying this sort of thing, so why make a fuss. This view they actually got published under the signature of the "Diplomatic Correspondent", who in point of fact is not the Diplomatic Correspondent at all but a fill-in man.

Others, and this was regarded as the most dangerous sign, declared (a) There are elements in the British government who have certainly in the past given their approval to the general line of selling out everything to the Germans. [*The Week* had said earlier that these were known in the Foreign Office as the "Give them Bournemouth Group".] (b) That though they dare not make their appearance now, these accessories before the fact will be raising their voices again in the Cabinet before long.

"Warmonger," "paranoiac," "malignant liar," "Moscow hireling" were among the printable epithets which, to the great pleasure of the editor, came showering into *The Week* office by post, telephone and even by telegram from distant shires. Even well-wishers found a good deal of the material too horrifyingly sordid to be true. By now, after all the ashes have been raked over, about 75 per cent. of it is accepted as almost a commonplace of history. Only the explanations and the excuses vary.

There is, however, one episode of importance to which not much attention has been paid. It is of importance for one minor and one major reason. The minor reason is that it had a profound effect upon *The Week*'s assessment of events between Munich and the outbreak of World War II. The major one is that it poses a fascinating, though perhaps unanswerable, riddle about Russian policy during the same period.

The episode occurred in Prague on the eve of Munich. Claud has published it briefly. There have been denials that it could ever have occurred. But the denials were made only by people who, by hindsight, found it difficult to believe. Claud on the other hand was present.

Also present was his old friend Michael Koltzov. Once again, as in Spain, Koltzov was quite visibly and admittedly acting as the direct agent of Stalin. At least it was assumed by the Czech government and by the Soviet Minister that such was his position and function. Claud was sitting with Koltzov at the Soviet Legation when the Minister was summoned, at a moment of the highest tension, to see President Beneš. At that moment, everything turned, as it turned later in Poland, on the question whether the Czechs would, in the last resort, actually invite the Red Army and Air Force to come to their assistance, which of course meant inviting them onto Czech territory.

On his return from the President's office, the Minister stated that the President had asked him two questions. First, if the League of Nations called for organized resistance to Hitler, would the Soviet Union participate? The answer was Yes. Secondly, if the League failed to act, but the British and French governments called for organized resistance, would the Soviet Union participate? The answer was Yes, again. The Minister, according to his own statement, waited, and then suggested that there was surely a third question which the President would like to put. He meant of course the question whether, in the event that neither the League, nor Britain and France, took action, and the Czech government appealed to Moscow, the Soviet Union would still respond? The Minister was ready once again to give the answer Yes. But the question was not asked. Beneš sat silent. And from this the deduction seemed clear that no such request would be made.

The Legation was full of Red Air Force officers, milling around waiting for news. They were from the Soviet air squadrons which, by *sotto voce* permission of the Czech government, had already taken up position on the military airfield outside Prague.

The interview with Beneš had been depressing. Further conversations with other members of the government proved even more so. It seemed finally to be clear that no invitation was to be extended to the Soviet Union. Indeed it appeared that the presence of the air squadrons had itself become unwelcome, as a possible provocation to Hitler. Orders were given for them to return to their bases in the Ukraine.

Just when it seemed that everything was over, a new urgent call came from President Beneš. It requested the Minister to secure immediately from Moscow an exact, up-to-the-minute verification of earlier estimates of the speed at which a given quantity of Soviet air power could be put into action from Czech air bases.

Koltzov, who had listened in to the message, rushed out of the Minister's room, dancing in delight. He told Claud, "It's going to be all right after all. The fight's on." The Minister had promised President Beneš to secure the information from Moscow within the hour and rush with it to the Palace. He did so. But in the interval something had happened to change the situation once again. The Minister returned from his visit in total dejection. When he got to the Palace, he was not admitted to see the President who had summoned him so urgently. He was informed that the Czechoslovak government was no longer interested in the information it had requested.

Then it really was all over. No resistance was offered to anyone. There followed a curious conversation between Claud and Koltzov. Naturally they spent some time mulling over the disastrous events of the morning. Claud, who was catching a late plane to Geneva, said he had to get to the bank before it closed, as he had to change English money into Czech currency to pay his fare and a large hotel bill for the past ten days. Koltzov, who hated to have a congenial conversation interrupted, said there was no need to hurry. He had plenty of Czech currency in his pocket. He would change the English pounds. Let them stay on in the café and talk. He made the exchange. Then he said, "This, of course, may be the death of me."

"How so?"

Koltzov put his elbows on the café table and fell into a kind of daydream. He said, "Well, for instance . . ." and proceeded, still seeming to be acting out some kind of dream, to put on a one-man dramatic performance, with himself taking three parts. He was himself, in a Moscow dock. He was the Public Prosecutor. He was the Judge. In the part of the Public Prosecutor he addressed himself, in the dock, as "citizen" not "comrade".

"Do you deny, citizen Koltzov, that in Prague on the date in question you received British currency from the well-known British Intelligence Agent Cockburn? Do you deny that you insinuated that same agent into the Legation of the Soviet

Union? Do you deny that you discussed with him the military dispositions of the Soviet Union, including the operation of planes at the Prague military airfield?"

Koltzov was a good actor, and the scene was highly convincing.

"You see," said Koltzov, shaking himself out of the daydream or nightmare, "how it might all come to pass."

During the latter part of this conversation, Koltzov appointed Claud London Correspondent of *Pravda*. He also invited him to be his special guest at a Writers Congress in Moscow early in the following year. He pointed out that Claud had to his credit in Moscow some enormous sum in roubles. These were royalties from the Russian translation of his book on Spain. It had sold in hundreds of thousands. It was impossible under the Soviet exchange regulations to get the money out. But he could have a splendid time trying to spend part of it in the country and then buy with roubles a first class ticket home via Peking, Tokyo, San Francisco and New York.

These matters settled, they parted for Geneva and Moscow respectively.

A couple of months later, Koltzov was arrested and shot by the OGPU, charges unknown.

The episode has a political importance which is worth considering. It suggests that, on that day in Prague, decisions were taken, power-shifts occurred, which decided the future of Russian policy, and in consequence of events in Europe. Suppose, for example, that the Russian war party had won. Suppose that its leaders had not been shot by Stalin. This is not to play simply the "if game". Clearly there was such a possibility. The planes were there, the mouthpiece of Stalin was there. The only people who deny it are those who were not there themselves.

Those who have found the story incredible have only one ground for their disbelief. It is that, by hindsight, they disbelieve that even in 1938 the Russians could possibly have intended to become involved, themselves alone, in war on behalf of Czechoslovakia; that they could have thought of firing the pistol which Hitler constantly complained was aimed at the heart of Germany. They adduce Stalin's crucial warning speech in March 1939, stating that the Soviet Union had no intention of "pulling other people's chestnuts out of the fire for them."

But the point is that, however apparently improbable, those events did in fact occur. And at the time they did not seem to Claud particularly surprising. In the crisis of May 1938 the Soviet Union had taken what could be regarded as a perilously positive line of resistance to German aggression against Czechoslovakia, and it had been successful. In other words, there seemed to be grounds for the belief that the long-term Soviet policy of "total defensiveness" which I mentioned early in this book had been totally abandoned. And Koltzov was, after all, both Foreign Editor of *Pravda* and the mouthpiece and direct agent of Stalin. How could he be passionately and publicly urging in Prague unilateral action, regardless of what the West might do, if that was not the policy of the Kremlin?

The facts are as stated. The explanation is, naturally, open to anyone to guess at. The trouble is every explanation must appear to anyone looking at the matter with the cool eye of the later historian, absurdly melodramatic. That is often the case when people try to figure out what was happening at a moment when the stakes were as huge as they then were.

Yet it really is possible that at that moment the advocates of a "forward" policy really were on top in Moscow. That they existed is certain. And it is certain that Koltzov was one of them. So were a good many others who had experienced the Spanish War at first hand. Most of them were subsequently shot, too. Koltzov quite certainly took the view that at that moment, in the autumn of 1938, Hitler was not ready for war, and was gambling on the non-resistance of his victims. Rightly or wrongly, he and his friends certainly believed that if the Soviet Union, at the invitation of Czechoslovakia, were to announce its intention to fight, regardless of what the West might or might not do, Hitler would almost certainly back down. The "almost" of course was a gigantic question mark. Suppose he did not after all back down? The belief of the "forward" party was that given the balance of military power as it then stood, and given that the Red Army and Air Force would be striking at Germany from Czechoslovak bases near the heart of the Reich, the Russians could win.

Naturally, in the light of the colossal Russian defeats of 1941, this opinion can appear absurd. So absurd, indeed, that people find it difficult to believe that it was ever held. Yet it really was held, and not by amateurs either. And I suppose it is at least arguable that there is no inherent contradiction between their view of the way things stood in September 1938, and the way things stood in the summer of 1941. It can be argued that in 1939, Stalin's return to the policy of "total defensiveness", expressed in the Soviet-German Pact, was justifiable. For by that time it was evident that the British and the French were leaning over backwards to avoid including the Soviet Union in any alignment against Germany. And from that, rightly or wrongly, the Kremlin not surprisingly deduced that the Western powers were still fondling their old, old notion of, at the last moment, seeing Hitler turn east rather than west.

It has always seemed to me that the really disastrous development of Stalin's policy came not in September 1939 but during 1940 and the early part of 1941. The evidence seems to show that "total defensiveness" had developed into a sort of mania or paranoia. From being a policy of defence it became a policy of total appeasement. And, towards the climax, the effort not to "provoke" Hitler degenerated into a readiness actually to eliminate Russia's defensive capacity on its western front for fear that serious defensive measures would be used by Hitler as an excuse for attack—as though Hitler was ever short of an excuse.

As I have said, the events of those crucial days in Prague, and Claud's long and intimate association with Koltzov, had a powerful effect upon *The Week*'s evaluation of Russian policy during 1939. I have always thought it strange that the news of Koltzov's execution, which affected him deeply, never alerted Claud to the possibility that a shift of power and policy had taken place in Moscow. Claud's explanation of this extraordinary failure in perception was simple. He knew that Koltzov was a man who had a reckless kind of arrogance in expressing his opinions. Above all, he had a reckless and savagely biting sense of humour. He never even tried to restrain his love of satire. And these qualities, as Claud had seen in Spain, made him a fresh crop of enemies almost every week. In Claud's opinion these qualities were in themselves quite enough to get a man shot in the climate of Moscow in

1939. It was not necessary to look for deeper reasons. And I must say that a good many people who knew both Koltzov and Moscow well, shared this opinion.

The result of all this was summed up by a friendly critic of *The Week*'s treatment of the diplomatic events of 1939. "*The Week*," he said, "has achieved the remarkable feat of being 70 per cent. right and 100 per cent. wrong."

Naturally *The Week* devoted major space to the negotiations which were supposed to be tending towards formation of an impregnable Grand Alliance against German aggression. Once again, its exposures of the vacillations and prevarications of the British government in its attempt somehow to build an alliance exclusive of the Soviet Union were widely regarded as showing exaggerated suspicions of British governmental motives. Once again, most of its allegations later proved only too well founded.

It was right, too, in drawing particular attention to the Stalin speech of March, as a warning to the West that they could not go on treating Moscow in that fashion indefinitely.

But when, as was so often darkly foreshadowed, the British government finally and catastrophically missed the bus, *The Week* entirely failed to appreciate the full consequences of what had happened, and the full import of the German-Soviet Pact. Absurdly, it estimated the Pact as essentially a German defeat. It supposed that the Germans had been forced by the fear of Russian power to go, as it said, "cap in hand to Moscow": And, even after the outbreak of war, it took more seriously than was justified the possibility that some joint action, led by the Russians, could still turn the clock back to something like the position of early 1939, and enforce peace.

It can, I suppose, be said that as things stood at that period of the "phoney war" that possibility appeared more practical than it looks in the light of subsequent events. Russian advocacy of such a policy was certainly in one sense sincere. It was not true, as was widely believed in Britain at the time, that the Russians were childishly delighted at the prospect of the "imperialist powers" tearing each other to pieces. On the contrary, as *The Week* well understood, they believed that if the war continued and developed, Hitler would win it. They calculated that he would first eliminate France, whereupon a peace party, composed of all the old pro-German elements, would come to power in Britain. They would make what terms they could with Hitler and then, sooner or later, Hitler would be free to turn against the Soviet Union. For that reason, any combination which could stop the war before it developed in that way, was most earnestly desired in Moscow.

As events showed, the Russian calculations were very far from absurd. And it was absurd for people in the West to swallow quite so easily as they did the vulgar theory of the Russophobes that Moscow's policy was a pure deception.

On the other hand, since the British government had shown itself opposed to co-operation with the Soviet Union to prevent the outbreak of war, it was considered naïve to suppose that it might somehow be induced to accept such co-operation after the outbreak.

But *The Week*'s much more serious error of judgement was to suppose that however sincerely the Russians might be in their desire to get the war ended then, they were going to run any serious risks to achieve that end. Total defensiveness was already merging into appeasement. And much of what *The Week* wrote on the subject both before and after the outbreak of war, reads like the utterances of a man who has forgotten to tear off a couple of leaves from the calendar.

21   Crack-up

LOOKING many years later through a certain copy of *The Week*, the editor paraphrased the well-known remark of Oscar Wilde: "Good Lord," he said, "what over-excitement I had when I wrote that."

The issue under review was that on 29 May 1940. Some degree of over-excitement is to be understood. It was written in the middle of the evacuation of the B.E.F. from Dunkirk. Under the heading "Awakening?", now absurd-seeming, *The Week* struck a note of grim hopefulness, which turned out to be in part wishful thinking.

> The events of the Western Front, and particularly the fate of the B.E.F., have produced a stirring, the beginnings of an awakening of public opinion—particularly working-class opinion—in Britain, which may turn out to have been after all the most vital event of the week.
>
> Reports from the most important sectors of the "Home Front" over the past weeks, have indicated that neither the exposure of the Norwegian fiasco (partially smothered in any case by the invasion of Holland and Belgium), nor the "incredible mistakes" in northern France, had done much more than ruffle the surface of opinion. [The phrase "incredible mistakes" was quoted from an official statement on the situation.]

The Week went on to refer to the disastrous General Gamelin, the supposed Commander-in-Chief of all forces in France, including the B.E.F.

The catastrophe of General Gamelin was seen as a typical consequence of the entire system under which the war was being run. *The Week* as usual, was eager to point out the noxious effects of official propaganda exemplified in the case of General Gamelin.

> The results of Gamelin's operations were especially shaking to those most inclined to swallow freely the official "dope" on the

war, and the products of various agencies of governmental propaganda in London and Paris.

A real effort had been made to build up Gamelin as the type of person in whom everyone should be glad to have confidence, and into whose hands millions of people should be proud and pleased to entrust their fate.

Typical was the contribution of the *Daily Herald*'s chief War Correspondent in France, who as recently as 27 December 1939 "nominated" General Gamelin as "the Man of the Year", stating:

"I have seen him at work. The French adore him. He is unassuming, not very tough. He makes no show, but he is surrounded by an aura of absolute military power—which with its allied qualities surpasses Napoleon's. From first to last he is a soldier. He grips at the imagination. Think of the extent to which civilization's future—your future—depends on his skill and judgment."

It was perhaps fortunate for those on high that the general public, thus addressed by the *Daily Herald*, did not take too seriously the advice given in the last sentence.

But in general it can be said that at least until the beginning of this week that section of the working public which felt, even obscurely, the implications of these grave events, was as the unsubmerged to the submerged sections of the iceberg. This week has loosed off depth charges of more profound and powerful effect. The same is true in France. And—though these reports may be coloured by official Allied wishful thinking—there are at least indications of the effects simultaneously produced in Germany as the endless hospital trains roll eastward with the German wounded.

The Week was always rather obviously straining to parallel its critical estimates of the situation in Britain with reports indicating that the Germans were none too happy either. Here there was an evident difficulty. Under war conditions most of its own channels of information from Germany were naturally blocked. And where they were not blocked, they were certainly clogged. This had the result of delaying information from Germany so long as to make it practically useless. This, in turn, meant that *The Week*, like other papers, was dependent on official intelligence channels. Of these it was by nature suspicious. And it considered, with some justification, that

British intelligence from Germany was wretchedly ill-organized.

At that time, anyone who publicly criticized the conduct of the war was naturally looked askance at by the authorities and by a vast majority of the public. In Claud's case the askance-looking was particularly sharp. On account of his Communist connexions he was suspected, again with some justification, of doing more than just criticizing the conduct of the war. It was thought that *The Week* was not doing only that. It was supposed that it was up to something more fundamental. It was suggesting that there was something wrong, so to speak, with the war itself. It seemed to be saying that given the existing social and economic set-up in Britain, France and Germany, the war at that stage was essentially a predatory struggle for power between two basically similar systems. To that extent, it seemed, this war could be equated with World War I. That war, too, had been represented as a war to make the world safe for democracy. And that, as the later facts of life had shown, had been an illusion. Examining this position of *The Week*, simple-minded critics, and not so simple-minded enemies, drew, or pretended to draw, the conclusion that *The Week* actually did not care who won the war. And from this it was an easy slide to the accusation that *The Week* really, for reasons which even the most simple-minded found inscrutable, somehow wanted the Nazis to win.

In the prevailing state of "over-excitement", partly genuine and partly synthetic, these emotions could easily be understood. But in fact a great many of *The Week*'s harshest criticisms, which at the time seemed so shocking, have by now been accepted almost as platitudes. In this connexion, it is worth quoting A. J. P. Taylor's *English History 1914–1945*. From the vantage point of 1966 he is describing the situation in the period before the German invasions of Norway and Western Europe:

"The government made nothing of the national mood. They remained a government of 'national pretence'. Chamberlain . . . and his fellows were at a loss to explain why they were at war, what they were fighting for. Their policy was in ruins. They had wanted to settle with Hitler on reasonable terms or, failing that, to shift the brunt of the fighting onto Soviet Russia. Now they were pledged to the defence of Poland—a pledge which they could not fulfil. Hitler offered peace when Poland had been conquered. The government, after some hesitation, turned down the offer formally in both houses of Parliament. But what now? Did the British government seek to overthrow Fascism throughout Europe? To destroy Germany as a great power? Or merely to substitute Goering, or some other Nazi, for Hitler as dictator of Germany? They did not know, and the British people were more or less told that they should not ask such questions. It was hardly surprisiug that in return the bulk of people came to feel that the war was little concern of theirs.

"The government were incapable of enlisting popular support. What was more, they did not want it. A war, based on popular enthusiasm, seemed to raise the ghost of the Left Wing Popular Front. It would be the Spanish Civil War all over again. Maybe not the burning of churches, or the raping of nuns. But the unions and shop stewards would have to be brought into partnership; the social order would be threatened; something like socialism would reign. Better far that ordinary citizens should carry their gas masks, read official instructions, and proceed quietly with their affairs. A poster appealing for National Savings was as characteristic of the Second World War at this period, as Kitchener's glowering face had been in the First. "YOUR Resolution will bring US victory." The men of the First World War had fought for King and country; the men of the Second were expected to conform to the requirements of the Higher Civil Service.

"Popular support seemed unnecessary. The war was running satisfactorily all by itself. There were no air raids. The R.A.F. made some ineffectual attacks on the German fleet and then contented itself with dropping propaganda leaflets. Kingsley Wood, Secretary for Air, met a proposal to set fire to German forests with the agonised cry: 'Are you aware that it is private property? Why, you'll be asking me to bomb Essen next.'"

In the circumstances, the passage in *The Week* of 29 May, which Claud later found "over-excited", is understandable. It amounts, I suppose, to a somewhat arrogant *apologia pro vita sua* on the part of *The Week*. It was rare indeed for *The Week* to express emotion. Looked at coolly from this distance, the *apologia* seems emotional almost to the edge of hysteria. In this sense, too, it is revealing.

It is perhaps necessary [*The Week* wrote] at this point—and especially for the benefit of newer subscribers—to recall that we have a certain title to report frankly upon the situation, its implications and necessities.

For years, despite cries of "sensation-monger" from some, and howls for our suppression from others, this News Service uniquely reported upon and exposed the character of the Nazi-Fascist menace to the world.

It was precisely the editor of this service who first reported on the existence of the Fascist "Fifth Column" in Britain and France; who, in fact, was the first ever to apply the phrase used by General Mola in his advance on Madrid in October 1936, to the general situation in Europe.

This was the first organ ever to report on the character of the German-Italian intervention in Spain—and was heartily denounced as a liar by several of those at present occupying places of power and authority in this country.

With the big press and the Labour leaders mouthing the praises of "non-intervention", we reported that "non-intervention" in Spain was a direct step to European war.

At a moment when—for instance—*The Times*, the *Daily Herald* and *New Statesman* were calmly proposing the dismemberment of Czechoslovakia, this News Service was reporting upon the real results of that action: and was denounced in print as the "Fat Boy of Europe" trying to "make people's flesh creep".

Our exposures of the work of the Fifth Column in Britain, of those in high places who were working for Hitler, of the policy of the Bank of England which was actually assisting the rearmament of Hitler, were the subject of threats of libel action, threats of suppression and loud jeers and sneers from those who declared this sort of thing to be "fantastic", "exaggerated", "sensational journalism", a "bee in the bonnet", etc.; for these people were as ignorant, stupid and disastrous then as they are ignorant, stupid and disastrous today.

At the time of the negotiations with the Soviet Government, we repeatedly reported on the necessity of securing that Pact which would have kept the peace; whereupon the various fools and villains, many of whom are still howling for our suppression, denounced us as probably "agents of Moscow", in receipt of "Red gold", etc. etc., and hurried on to explain to their deluded readers that the Polish Army was really superior to the Red Army, so that the Polish pledge made the Moscow Pact unnecessary . . .

At this moment, when not a few people, but everyone, can see that the people of this country are in the gravest danger, the Big press and the government propagandists continue the work of befuddlement and befoolment which they have carried on throughout these long years of the retreat of the people before the power of the ruling classes.

One day the people were told the Anglo-Italian Pact and the desertion of Spain would save them—just leave it to Chamberlain; Munich was to save them; the Polish Army would do it; Gamelin and Daladier would do it; Mr. X, Mr. Y, General Z, old Uncle Sam Roosevelt and all. In a mixture of frivolity and frantic searching for some symbol or other to attract the popular support, King Leopold (of the Belgians who had just surrendered) was built up into a sort of schoolboy's hero—a model for all of us—a moment later a bewildered public hears the very people who had been pointing to Leopold as the type and model denouncing him as a "Quisling" . . .

At this dangerous moment when the hearts of millions are troubled and angry for the fate of the men now said to be the victims of "incredible mistakes" and "unprecedented" treachery, the real Fifth Columnists and those in authority should be anxiously furbishing up the machinery of repression in fear of the very public which they proclaim as standing united behind them. They are very well aware that the picture they paint of the British people as a people of sheep willingly and blindly entrusting their fate to those "on high" is a false picture.

They will certainly seek to intensify the dictatorship and the repression. And yet it will be a dangerous one for the country: for the salvation of the country really lies, not in suppressing, but in releasing the forces and the powers of the people; it lies in the ability of the people to take a grip upon their own fate with confidence in their own power to deal with their enemies wherever they may be.

The tremendous achievements of the men on the front have heightened the self-confidence of the people. It was not they who made the "incredible mistakes" and then asked the working class for its "blood, toil, tears and sweat" in order to clean up the results of these mistakes.

There is a stirring among the people. Certain realizations are becoming more widespread. And, as we said, this may prove to have been, after all, the most profoundly important development of the week—the beginning of the awakening of the people in Britain.

It does seem, Claud commented later, that "our ball bearings were a good deal overheated."

In a sense it is true that the "awakening" predicted by *The Week* was already taking place under its eyes. But *The Week* did not share the general belief that the resignation of Neville Chamberlain and the coming to power of Winston Churchill had basically changed the situation. Its suspicions of those "on high" were by this time too deeply engrained. And so the result of its belief in the necessity for profound, fundamental change, blinded it, at least partially, to the reality of the changes which were actually taking place. Despite Churchill, and in face of a great part of the available evidence, *The Week* still darkly mistrusted the powers above. In my view, this was among its gravest errors of judgment. That fact that it is easier to see this by hindsight than at the time, does not make it untrue. *The Week*, in fact, was suffering from a kind of hardening of the arteries. Or, to change the medical metaphor, its reactions to reality had slowed down.

The editor had always declared privately that in his view the outbreak of war had quite possibly, for technical reasons— the needs of war censorship, the lack of informational channels —really make it impossible for such a paper to function effectively. He had not foreseen other "undesirable side-effects". Nor, in the intelligible excitement of lone wolfishness, did he notice these side-effects. In other words, he was unaware that *The Week* was in some respects displaying the same faults which it had so often denounced in others. It was living in the past. It was inclined to confuse slogans with realities. Its former alertness to real shifts of power and direction became notably diminished.

One of the last issues of *The Week* in January 1941 was devoted to a long report on dissensions and anti-governmental activities within Germany. Just before publication, *The Week* discovered to its surprise that the group of sources over whose information it had been working for some time, was also informing the *London Financial News*. This was in one sense reassuring. The *Financial News* was a highly responsible newspaper. *The Week* was relieved of the oppressive burden of the thought that it was compelled to rely entirely on its own judgement of such reports.

Analysing the financial policy of the German government on the labour front, *The Week* reported that:

> The German government—like the British government—has of course been making the most strenuous efforts to prevent the rise of working-class earnings ("in the national interest") partly by an actual restriction of the possibilities of consumption, partly by direct attack on earnings.
>
> Particularly of course it was desired that at a time when heavy overtime was being demanded in the factories for war purposes, these earnings should be somehow seized, neutralized or controlled by the State.
>
> In Britain this objective is being partially achieved as from this current week by the beginning of income tax "deduction at source" —that is to say, taken direct out of the factory worker's pay packet.
>
> The present deductions are based on the period April–October last year, which was one of very high overtime earnings in the great factory push of the summer and early autumn.
>
> It is true that in the large majority of cases, nothing like that amount of overtime earnings are now being made but the deductions based on the higher figures of the summer are having to be paid now. Indications from the industrial areas, particularly the war factories where the heaviest overtime was worked in the summer, are that this is already a burning issue.
>
> At the outset of the war, the German government and the great armaments employers—notably Krupp—were successful (partly as the result of the general national emergency propaganda) in getting basic overtime rates reduced and at the same time in promulgating and partially enforcing a decree by which *all* overtime earnings were to be made available to the State—apparently in the form of forced loans (somewhat on the Keynesian compulsory savings plan).
>
> Agitation in the factories against this proceeding was widespread. As in Britain, it was conducted "on the spot", that is to

say by the oppositional factory organizations corresponding very roughly, so far as their function and general aims are concerned, to the British shop stewards.

The Week believed it inevitable that this should be so in both countries—in Britain because the leadership of the official trade union organization was eagerly supporting the government, in Germany because the official organization, already a step further on than the British organization, was the governmental Labour Front.

The result of this agitation [continued *The Week*] was that despite the most desperate efforts, threats and appeals to the German workers "in the national interest", etc. etc., along lines now familiar in all the warring countries, the factory opposition became so strong that the system of all overtime earnings being handed over to the State had to be dropped.

The government and the big employers, however, maintained overtime rates at the lower rates introduced after the war and—in an attempt to get roundabout what they had failed to get direct—introduced heavy taxation of overtime earnings.

Again this was met with a new wave of agitation in the factories and again the strength and determination of the working-class resistance to threats and blandishment was such that the government was compelled not merely to restore the basic overtime rates existing before the outbreak of war, but also to abolish *in toto* all taxation of overtime and earnings.

It can readily be understood how heavy a blow this represented to the German war economy—for there, too, as in Britain, economists, business leaders and government representatives have loudly declared against the perils inherent in a rise of wages and of possible purchasing power for the working class during war time.

The immediate result has been to force the German government to seek to intensify its efforts to cut down working-class consumption of goods by other means—by tightening up the ration system, by continually increasing shortage of all sorts of consumption goods, removing some from the market altogether so that the working class has as little as possible to buy with its increased earnings.

This, on the other hand, has immediate social and political repercussions in Germany, sharpening the hostility to the government, not only in the factories, but also among the whole population, particularly the working-class housewives.

It would of course be absurd to deduct from this sharpening of the situation in Germany, that there is any considerable body of opinion—particularly working-class opinion—within Germany which in the slightest degree favours a victory of the war aims of the Anglo-American bloc . . . In other words it is not true that the organizers of this working-class resistance to the German government and its methods in any sense constitute a British "Fifth Column" within Germany—any more than British shop stewards, the Communists, and the other working-class resistance, constitute a German "Fifth Column" in Britain.

It is of course true that from the viewpoint of the government propagandists on both sides, it is desirable and even necessary to accuse such people of "Fifth Columnism": it would be a mistake to take this sort of propaganda seriously.

Both the British and German governments, in their attempt to prevent a rise in working-class wages, or in any way to defend their own policies, are forced, naturally enough, to accuse the leadership of those who resist of "Fifth Columnism"—just as in the last war the engineers on the Clyde and the German navy mutineers at Hamburg . . . were accused of being "agents of the enemy" by their respective governments.

This is all very well and probably useful for a time as propaganda —though it tends to wear a little thin in both countries as both Dr. Ley of the German Labour Front and Mr. Bevin (who talks sometimes of "orders from Moscow" and sometimes of "orders from Berlin") have recently found.

It is important to stress this point in relation to the German situation because reports of resistance in Germany are very commonly misunderstood, simply by reason of a failure to understand just this.

For although there are many people in Britain who find it quite reasonable to expect British working people to put up with any amount of "sacrifice" rather than "have Hitler over here", there are many who do not grasp the complementary fact that there are also large numbers of people in Germany who think any sacrifice by the working people reasonable, rather than "have Churchill over here"—or Vansittart for that matter, or the various allies of the British government, such as the Polish generals and landowners, who have already announced their intention of dis-membering Germany.

The fact is—and it is an important one—that of the govern-mental supporters alike in Britain and Germany who shout Fifth Columnist against the working-class opposition, some are fools and some are crooks, and all are highly and dangerously deceptive regarding the real situation developing within both countries.

For so far as these leading and often key workers in Germany— who have been able to affect so seriously the German war machine —are concerned, it is not a question of doing all this, running all these risks, for the sake of seeing Germany once again subjected to the control or dictation of the Anglo-American bloc—probably on terms even more onerous than those which existed in the days of the Weimar Republic.

By hindsight a great deal of this stuff seems considerably, if not wildly, unbalanced. The facts concerning the wage policy of the German government are correct. And no doubt it was important and encouraging to draw attention to them. The unbalance occurs in *The Week*'s estimate of German working-class resistance to them. As usual, and for reasons I have mentioned before, *The Week* was over-optimistic in its view of German working-class reactions. Even as late as 1941, it could not rid itself of the conception of a working class in perpetual smouldering revolt against the powers above. There was one difference between the attitude of *The Week* in this respect and that of other British publications. *The Week* had reported German movements of resistance in the early days when those movements really amounted to something—though seldom to as much as the paper supposed. At that time, other British papers, for all sorts of motives, had subscribed to the view of the Hitler regime as more or less monolithic.

They believed, rightly or wrongly, that such movements were led, or would at least very soon be controlled, by Communists. It was not a prospect to rouse the enthusiasm of British editors. Also, to take such movements seriously involved certain consequences. They could be openly encouraged and secretly supported. But this in turn was sure to lead to some kind of direct clash between the British and German govern-ments and this was the one eventuality to be avoided at almost any cost. The same motives were almost equally powerful in determining the attitudes of the British Labour leaders. Anti-communism and various degrees of pacifism made them exceedingly hesitant to support such movements in Germany. And since they could, or would, not support them, the natural thing to do was to pretend that they were not there at all.

By 1941, the press, the government and Labour leaders outside the government were eager to believe in the existence of effective anti-governmental activities in Germany. But by then such beliefs were, for the most part, illusory. *The Week* reached the same position by a different road. But its beliefs were no less illusory for that.

A very superficial and naïve observer could have supposed that the British government would have welcomed the type of report from Germany quoted above. Naturally, there was no such welcome. Sticking out like a sore thumb was the fact that *The Week* kept equating German situations with British situations. To draw parallels, however economically exact, between the wage policies of say Mr. Bevin and Dr. Ley was shocking and unseemly. For the suspicious or hostile critic could easily proceed to draw unpleasant conclusions. If that sort of equation was being made then *The Week* was "really" saying that there was no difference between the British and German régimes. That, by extension, could be held to mean that it did not care who won the war. And by a leap of fantasy, the reasoner could come eventually to the conviction that somehow *The Week* wanted the Germans to win.

The issue of January date was the penultimate issue of *The Week*. In fact it was the ultimate issue of the unbroken series from the end of March 1933 actually to reach subscribers. A further issue was written. If it had ever reached the subscribers it would possibly have surprised them quite a lot. For it was devoted to events in the United States, Ireland and Chile. Rather absurdly, as things turned out, the editor had allowed himself to be persuaded by friends in high places that a couple of innocuous issues of the paper would save it. In reality, the decision to suppress it had already been taken a considerable time before. The issue of 15 January was seized by the police before it could appear and the paper banned.

The *Daily Worker* was banned the same day. Claud has

recounted elsewhere the comical circumstances of the actual ban. The police called first at the offices of the *Daily Worker*. Having served there the official notice of the ban and seeing the editor of *The Week* prominent among those present in the *Daily Worker* office, the leader of the police squad told him that *The Week* was banned.

It stayed banned until some months after the German invasion of Russia. Then, to the disgust of many of the Labour leaders, the Labour party at its Annual Conference voted by a large majority in favour of lifting the ban on both the *Daily Worker* and *The Week*. Naturally this decision was the result of months of campaigning up and down the country. Innumerable speeches had been made, innumerable pamphlets written. Claud detested public speaking. In fact he did his best to duck his share of it by claiming that every speech of his resulted in a mass defection of supporters. Even so he did make well over a hundred speeches at points all the way from Portsmouth to Inverness.

During this "free press' campaign he probably wrote more words weekly than he had previously written for *The Week* and the *Daily Worker* combined. He admitted afterwards that in the excitement of the campaign he had hardly given a thought to what was to happen as and when the stated objectives were achieved. And when they were achieved, he realized with some dismay that in fact, under the totally changed conditions of wartime, there really was no true function for *The Week*.

Comically enough, the Communists, for reasons of their own, also gave it to be understood that they would be very happy if *The Week* did not resume publication. Their reason was simple. They felt that the "free press" campaign on behalf of the two publications had, in most people's minds, established the idea that *The Week* was in some way an organ of the Communist party. Therefore the Communist party would be held responsible for its reports and opinions.

But the reality was that *The Week* was not an organ of the Communist party, and the Communists had no control over it at all, financial or otherwise. The only link was the person of the editor. It was not a situation which the Communists found entirely reassuring. Everything seemed to point to the desirability of *The Week* failing to resume publication.

On the other hand, Claud reasoned, it is really absurd, not to
say fraudulent, to stump the country roaring for freedom, get
several hundred thousand people roaring with you, and then,
on freedom being regained, give the thing a sniff and a shrug
and say you find you don't care to have it after all. Reluctantly,
The Week re-appeared.

As Claud had foreseen, under the conditions of total war
there was really nothing useful or interesting for *The Week* to
do. Claud's own interest in the paper dwindled. He thought he
would be much better employed as a war correspondent.
He made efforts to this end. But the government still thought it
perilous to allow Communist sympathizers near the battlefields.
He did succeed in getting to Algiers for a couple of months,
and later, just before the end of the war in the West, to San
Francisco for the foundation meeting of the United Nations. I
had for some time been assisting with the editorship, and
during these and other periods of Claud's absence, I edited
the paper.

In Claud's opinion, *The Week* was due to expire anyway. He
declared that it was impossible that what was dead right for
the 1930s could possibly be right for the 1940s, war or no war.
What in fact brought about its demise was a decision to have
it printed. It seemed an attractive idea and was in fact lethal.
The costs were high. And the printer, who seems unfortunately
to have shared Claud's scepticism as to the paper's future,
refused more than the barest minimum of credit. For a while,
Claud continued to try to shore up the trembling financial
structure with loans from friends. Then he realized he was only
asking people to throw good money after bad, and, without
notice to anyone, closed the paper. Later, a great many people
said with sincere regret that if only Claud had announced in
the paper that it was in these grievous financial straits, they
would have been delighted to rush to its assistance, lend money,
organize relief funds and so on. Claud said he knew they
would. He knew also that they would be wasting their time
and money. That was why he had closed down without notice.

The post-ban *Week* had moved to a small office building in
Bloomsbury. There were half a dozen other tenants of the
building. At that time it was, for some reason, impossible to
get your telephone cut off until such time as the post office

chose to do it for you. When *The Week* quit, the post office omitted to cut the telephone off. The telephone rang and rang. The other tenants, behind those flimsy Bloomsbury walls, kept complaining. There was no one to answer it, and nothing to be done. *The Week*'s telephone had to go on ringing and ringing in that abandoned office just as it had from morning to night year after year when someone *was* there, eager to answer it.

As I came near the end of this book, I asked Claud whether he did not think there ought to be something in the way of a general summing up, or assessment, of *The Week*'s achievement. What did that achievement amount to? What effect did it have on its day and age?

Claud said: "If you care to write another 100,000 words or so, then go ahead and assess. But if not, not. Either you have to weigh it all up at enormous length, or just leave it to the reader to draw his own conclusions."

I think he is right. But there is one sort of assessment which it is possible to make without writing any 100,000 words.

During the past few years I have been in Dublin, London, New York and Washington. And there have, of course, been innumerable visitors to our house in Youghal, Ireland. It is perhaps not surprising that a large number of our visitors should turn out to have been, all those years ago, readers of *The Week*, though neither Claud nor I were aware of it until they told us.

But what really has astonished me is the quite extraordinary number of hitherto total strangers in, say, London or New York, who in the course of conversation, or simply on hearing my name, suddenly turn out to have been, as a distinguished middle-aged prelate in London put it, "weaned and brought up on *The Week*". They include many sorts and conditions of men. I know of at least a dozen who state with pride and pleasure that they started reading *The Week* at their preparatory schools.

Claud does not care for questions such as "Was it all worthwhile?" His reply is either metaphysics or stage Irish. "If I hadn't known it was going to be worthwhile, I wouldn't have done it in the first place, would I?"

Certainly it seems to me that a sustained effort to tell the truth, or what one passionately believes to be the truth, must always be worthwhile.

Index

Other titles from Comedia